Bluebonnet
TRAIL
Cookbook

Additional copies may be obtained at the cost of $ 17.95, plus $3.00 postage and handling, each book. Texas residents add 7.75% sales tax, each book.
Send to:
Bluebonnet Trail Cookbook
P. O. Box 62532
San Angelo, Texas 76906

ISBN Number 0-9647290-0-8
LCCN: 95-94609

First Printing   5,000   December, 1995

Printed in the USA by
WIMMER
The Wimmer Companies, Inc.
Memphis

Table of Contents

Introduction

Family recipes passed down from generation to generation are as much a part of the family as any precious keepsake, memento or photo album. Special, because they are made with the most important ingredient…LOVE. And sometimes when they're cooking, the aroma triggers a cherished moment in time or a special memory.

Madeline Daddiego
Mohair Council of America
New York, New York

The ***Bluebonnet Trail Cookbook*** is a tribute to all who have made this part of Texas a feast for the eyes of all who receive it. This includes the men and women of agriculture, the families who prepare and serve meals at odd hours, the friends, the shearers, the workers who descend on the ranches and farms; and the many meals handed out the back door. We have included the favorite recipes of those who are part of a program of which we are all very proud. We hope we have captured the memories and traditions that are a part of our heritage.

Enjoy

your own BLUEBONNET TRAIL by planting
the enclosed Bluebonnet seeds.

Mimi Wardlaw Allison is the wife of Robert Allison, a West Texas rancher in Terrell County. They are the parents of three fine children, McNeil, Clay and Anita. In raising two "hollow legged" boys, there has always had to be lots to eat around the house; Anita was sure to learn to cook. Because of the joy of fellowship that sharing meals with friends and family brings, cooking is a privilege that she has long enjoyed. After growing up on the family ranch in Val Verde County, Mimi has stayed actively involved in the ranching industry with her own and now Robert's family.

Nancy Rink Johnson is the daughter of a San Angelo pioneer bootmaker. Nancy is married to Jerry Johnson, a longtime rancher, from Sonora. They have five children, Brett and Brad Johnson, Miles, Matt, and Preccia Miller, and Laura, Miles' wife. Nancy has always had a love for cooking and has the ability to prepare a meal without knowing if there will be seven or seventeen around the table. Nancy and Jerry operate Photo Ranch, a professional photography studio, where Nancy specializes in wedding photography and has won an international wedding photo contest.

Preccia Miller attributes much of her love for cooking to many people. Her mother because she always allowed her the freedom to create anything her heart desired. Her grandmother for always reminding her that the way to a man's heart is through his stomach. Her Aunt Eva because of her elegance in presenting and preparing meals to perfection, and her second dad, Jerry, for encouraging her and eating anything she cooked. Preccia grew up on ranches in Sutton and Crockett counties and graduated from Sonora High School and Stephens College in Columbia, Missouri. She currently lives in Dallas where she is employed by Sonora Mohair and Company which manufactures mohair fabric, yarn, and garments.

Being a fifth generation product from both parents, **Anita Allison** is a true tribute to the West Texas ranching heritage. Growing up on the family ranch with two older brothers and all their friends to cook for, she learned the art of cooking at an early age. Anita graduated from Texas A&M University in 1993 with a degree in Agricultural Development. Currently, she resides in San Angelo where her "Good Friend Group" has been highly influential. She proudly acknowledges each of them.

The **Bluebonnet Trail Cookbook** would like to thank the following individuals for all of their support, help, and encouragement during this project:

Jerry Johnson of Photo Ranch for the photography.
Nancy Jones for the art work.
Russell Rogers for the Cowboy Poetry
McNeil Allison
Robert Allison
Brett Carpenter
Brett Johnson
Asa Jones
Mary Ellen McEntire
Laura Thorp
Lori Woehl
Mindy & Molly Woehl
Cinco de Mayo

And all our many contributors who made this cookbook possible.

This book is a collection of recipes, memories, and stories from friends and families of West Texas. We do not claim that all of these recipes are original, but that they are the favorites of the contributors. We thank each contributor for the many wonderful recipes and the fond memories that came from the heart. Unfortunately, all of the recipes submitted could not be used due to similarity and duplication. We apologize if your recipe was not included.

Texas Bluebonnets

On March 5, 1901, the bluebonnet was declared the state flower of Texas. The royal beauty and enchanting fragrance of the Texas bluebonnet has turned many a cowboy's dream and inspired the legislator's eloquence.

The Texas bluebonnet variety, Lupinus Texensis, is said to be a great home lover. Some claim that it never crosses the border. Even though the bluebonnet can grow as far north as the Canadian border and west to the Pacific coast, the coloring is not nearly so brilliant as in Texas.

Texas' own first lady, Lady Bird Johnson, wife of Lyndon B. Johnson, the thirty-sixth president of the United States, is the undisputed queen of wild flowers in America. Through her dedication and attention on the bluebonnet trails, she has used her leadership to transform the American landscape and to preserve its natural beauty as a national treasure.

When seeking out the beautiful bluebonnet, here are some tips for you to keep in mind:

- Make sure you are not romping around amid the flowers on private property.

- There are laws against impeding traffic, so use common sense if you want to slow down to enjoy a view. Doing 30 mph on Interstates 10, 20, or 30 is not common sense.

- Obey signs that prohibit parking along the roadways. When you do park, get all the way off the road and off improved shoulders. But don't drive into the flowers.

- Signal before entering or leaving the roadway.

- It's best to park on the side of the road that the flowers are on, so you don't have to cross the lanes of traffic to get to them.

- Watch out for snakes and fire ants!

- Above all, take a camera to capture the royal beauty of the bluebonnet to share with all your family and friends.

Pedernales River Chili

4 pounds chili meat
1 large onion, chopped
2 cloves garlic
1 teaspoon ground oregano
1 teaspoon comino seed
6 teaspoons chili powder
1½ cups canned whole tomatoes
2-6 generous dashes liquid hot sauce
salt to taste
2 cups hot water

Place meat, onion, and garlic in large, heavy fry pan or Dutch oven. Cook until light-colored. Add oregano, comino seed, chili powder, tomatoes, hot pepper sauce, salt and hot water. Bring to boil, lower heat and simmer about 1 hour. Skim off fat during cooking.

Chili meat is coarsely ground round steak or well-trimmed chuck. If specially ground, ask butcher to use ¾-inch plate for coarse grind.

Mrs. Lyndon B. Johnson
First Lady 1963-1969

LBJ Ranch Deer Meat Sausage

½ deer
½ hog
25 ounces salt
20 ounces black pepper
8 ounces red pepper
2 ounces sage

Mix together for 200 pounds of sausage.

Mrs. Lyndon B. Johnson
First Lady 1963-1969

This is a favorite recipe at the LBJ Ranch. The finished product is recommended for late Sunday morning breakfast with scrambled eggs, hominy grits, hot biscuits and boiling hot coffee. Or, it can be served for a late-afternoon snack in hot biscuits.

Spinach Parmesan

3 pounds of spinach
6 tablespoons Parmesan cheese
6 tablespoons minced onion
6 tablespoons heavy cream
5 tablespoons melted butter
½ cup cracker crumbs

Cook the cleaned spinach until tender. Drain thoroughly. Chop coarsely and add the cheese, onion, cream and 4 tablespoons of the butter. Arrange in a shallow baking dish and sprinkle with the crumbs mixed with the remaining butter. Bake for 10 to 15 minutes.

Mrs. Lyndon B. Johnson
First Lady 1963-1969

Brandied Fruit

dried apricots
golden raisins
pineapple chunks
canned peaches
whole cranberries

Drain well pineapple chunks, peaches, and cranberries. Layer fruit ending with cranberries. Dust with brown sugar. Dab with sweet butter. Pour dry sherry over all. Bake in 350° oven for twenty minutes.

Mrs. Lyndon B. Johnson
First Lady 1963-1969

No measurements were given with this recipe. It's up to the cook!

Double Divinity

2 cups sugar
⅔ cup water
½ cup light corn syrup
2 eggs whites, slightly beaten
1 teaspoon vanilla
dash of salt

Combine ½ cup of sugar and ⅓ cup of water and cook until small amount of syrup forms soft ball in cold water (240°). Cook remaining 1½ cups of sugar, ⅓ cup of water and corn syrup until it forms a hard ball in cold water (254°). Cool first syrup slightly. Add slowly to egg whites, beating constantly about 1 to 2 minutes, or until mixture loses its glass; add second syrup in same way. Add vanilla and turn into greased pan. Cut in squares when cold. Yields approximately 40 pieces.

This candy is softer and creamier than regular divinity.

Mrs. Lyndon B. Johnson
First Lady 1963-1969

Baked Beans

2 16-ounce cans small baked beans
6 tablespoons catsup
1 tablespoon Worcestershire sauce
3 tablespoons dark brown sugar, packed
1 teaspoon dry mustard
3 tablespoons grated onion

Bake partially covered in a 2½ quart casserole at 325° for 1½ hours.

Barbara Bush
First Lady 1989-1993

Barbecued Chicken

1 3-pound fryer, quartered
1 large garlic clove, crushed
1 teaspoon salt
½ teaspoon freshly ground pepper
1 tablespoon oil
3 tablespoons lemon juice

Put ingredients in a heavy ziplock bag. Shake to coat well. Refrigerate for 24 hours if possible, turning the bag several times. When coals are ready, place chicken on the grill, skin side up, basting with the marinade. Cook until well browned before turning. If baking in oven, bake at 400°, skin side down first. About 20 minutes before chicken is done, begin using your favorite bottled barbecue sauce or the following homemade version.

Barbecue Sauce
¼ cup cider vinegar
2¼ cups water
¾ cup sugar
1 stick butter or margarine
⅓ cup yellow mustard
2 onions, coarsely chopped
½ teaspoon each salt and pepper
½ cup Worcestershire sauce
2½ cups catsup
6-8 tablespoons lemon juice
cayenne pepper to taste

Combine the first seven ingredients and bring to a boil, cook on low 20 minutes or until onion is tender. Add the remaining four ingredients and simmer slowly for 45 minutes. Taste for seasoning. This sauce freezes well.

Barbara Bush
First Lady 1989-1993

11

Red, White & Blue Cobbler

A quick method of making this dish is to use 1 can each of blueberry and cherry pie filling. Place the blueberry pie filling in bottom of 8x8 glass baking pan. Spread evenly and then place the cherry pie filling on top, smoothing to edges of pan. Place in 400° oven to heat while preparing topping. This dish is great served with vanilla ice cream.

Blueberry Filling
- ¼ cup sugar
- ½ tablespoon cornstarch
- ½ teaspoon lemon juice
- 2 cups fresh or frozen unsweetened blueberries

Mix sugar and cornstarch in a saucepan and add all other ingredients. Cook until thickened. Put into 8x8 Pyrex pan and keep hot in a 250° oven while making cherry filling.

Cherry Filling
- 1 can sour pie cherries
- ½ cup + 2 tablespoons sugar
- 1½ tablespoons cornstarch
- ⅛ teaspoon cinnamon
- ⅛ teaspoon almond extract

In a saucepan mix dry ingredients. Gradually stir in juice from canned cherries and cook until thickened, adding cherries and flavorings at the end. Smooth cherry filling over blueberry mixture. Keep warm while making topping.

Topping
- 1 cup flour
- 1 tablespoon sugar
- 1½ teaspoons baking powder
- ½ teaspoon salt
- 3 tablespoons shortening
- ½ cup milk

Mix dry ingredients and shortening until it is like fine crumbs. Stir in milk and drop by spoonfuls onto hot filling. Bake at 400° for 25 to 30 minutes or until brown.

Barbara Bush
First Lady 1989-1993

Zuni Stew

1¼ cups pinto beans, soaked overnight and drained
1 teaspoon salt
1 bay leaf
1 teaspoon dried oregano
1 pound tomatoes, fresh or canned
2 ancho chilies
1 pound mixed summer squash
4 ears corn (about 2 cups kernels)
1 teaspoon ground cumin
½ teaspoon ground coriander
2 tablespoons corn or vegetable oil
2 yellow onions, cut ¼ inch squares
2 cloves garlic, finely chopped
2 tablespoons red chili powder
8 ounces green beans, cut into 1-inch lengths
4 ounces Jack or Muenster cheese, grated
½ bunch cilantro leaves, roughly chopped
whole cilantro leaves for garnish

This stew is a great one dish meal if you have a garden or have just visited the Farmer's Market. You can serve it with cornbread or tortillas.

Cook the pre-soaked beans for about 1½ to 2 hours in plenty of water with the salt, bay leaf and oregano. Remove them from the heat when they are soft but not mushy, as they will continue to cook in the stew. Drain the beans, and save the broth. Peel, seed and chop the tomatoes; reserve the juice. Open the chili pods and remove the seeds and veins; then cut the chilies into narrow strips. Cut the squash into large pieces. Shave the kernels from the corn. Heat the oil in a large skillet, and sauté the onions over high heat for 1 to 2 minutes. Lower the heat, add the garlic, chili powder, cumin, and coriander and stir everything together. Add a little bean broth, so the chili doesn't scorch or burn. Cook until the onions begin to soften, about 4 minutes, then add the tomatoes and stew for 5 minutes. Stir in the squash, corn, green beans, and chili strips along with the cooked beans and enough broth to make a fairly wet stew. Cook slowly until the vegetables are done, about 15 or 20 minutes. Taste the stew and adjust the seasoning. Stir in the cheese and chopped cilantro, and garnish with whole leaves of cilantro.

Laura W. Bush
Office of the First Lady of the State of Texas 1995

Cocktail Sauce

2 cups catsup
2 cups chili sauce
¼ cup cider vinegar
¼ teaspoon Tabasco
½ cup prepared
  horseradish
¼ cup finely minced
  celery
¼ cup finely minced
  onion
2 teaspoons
  Worcestershire sauce

Mix together and refrigerate. Serve with seafood.

Tartar Sauce

2 cups mayonnaise
2 tablespoons chopped
  dill pickles
2 tablespoons finely
  chopped stuffed green
  olives
2 tablespoons grated
  onion
2 tablespoons finely
  chopped parsley
1 tablespoon capers
2 tablespoons lime juice
¼ tablespoon garlic salt

Combine ingredients and cover tightly in fridge. This keeps for weeks.

Fried Shrimp

2 eggs
1 cup milk
1 pound large shrimp (uncooked)
1 cup flour
½ teaspoon garlic salt
36 saltines, smashed with fingers (should be coarse)

Beat the eggs and add the milk. Clean the shrimp and split down the back to butterfly. Dip in the seasoned flour, then the egg and milk, then in the smashed saltines. Fry in deep fat until golden brown. Serve with a good cocktail or tartar sauce. Serves four.

Ann W. Richards
Governor of Texas 1991-1995

Jalapeño Cheese Cornbread

1½ cups cornbread mix
¾ cup milk
1 egg
½ green onion, chopped
½ cup creamed corn
¼ cup chopped jalapeño pepper
¾ cup grated cheese (Cheddar or Monterey Jack or both)
1 tablespoon sugar
2 tablespoons oil
bacon bits, chopped pimiento, garlic

Combine all ingredients and mix well. Pour into buttered baking dish and bake at 425° for about 25 minutes or until done.

Ann W. Richards
Governor of Texas 1991-1995

Gazpacho

1 large onion
1 large cucumber, peeled and cored
1 large green pepper
3 cans Rotel
1 can tomatoes
1 quart tomato juice
1 can beef consommé
4 teaspoons olive oil
2 small cans frozen lemon juice
Tabasco sauce
salt and pepper
dash of red pepper

Grind the onion, cucumber, green pepper, Rotel, and tomatoes using a blender or finely chop. Place in a large pan or bowl with the remaining ingredients. Serve cold.

William P. Clements, Jr.
Governor of Texas 1987-1991 and 1979-1983

Crayfish Stoufee

1 pound crayfish
1 stick oleo
½ tablespoon flour
1 onion, chopped fine
1 bell pepper, chopped fine
2 pods garlic, chopped fine
green onion tops, chopped fine
parsley, chopped fine
salt, red & black pepper to taste

Melt the oleo in skillet; add flour and stir until blended; add onions, and garlic and cook until tender. Add crayfish and cook about 15 minutes, stirring occasionally. Add seasoning, bell pepper, green onions, and parsley. Cook over low heat until seasonings blended. Serve over white or wild rice.

William P. Clements, Jr.
Governor of Texas 1987-1991 and 1979-1983

While Dolph was Governor, I found that it was very helpful to serve guests assembling for lunch either cold soup or fruit juice or this vegetable frappe. It was especially liked by the gentlemen guests. -Janey Briscoe

We served many business luncheons at the Governor's Mansion and found that men preferred medium rare rolled roasts or sirloin strips. The roasts were prepared simply, merely seasoned with salt and pepper. Occasionally dried cayenne pepper was inserted into the meat as an additional seasoning and a surprise. The steaks were always char-broiled to medium rare. This spinach ring is a perfect accompaniment! -Janey Briscoe

Tomato Juice Frappe

1 large can tomato juice
1 bay leaf
1 teaspoon Worcestershire sauce
few drops of Tabasco
juice of ½ lemon

Simmer the above in a one quart saucepan. Do not allow to boil, but merely simmer so that the bay leaf flavor is extracted and other spices are well blended. Then place in a large container to freeze. Take out later in the day or the next day and allow to thaw only enough to whip or stir vigorously. Distribute in wine glasses or sherbet glasses. Place in freezer to be kept firm but not re-frozen.

Dolph Briscoe
Governor of Texas 1973-1979

Spinach Ring

2½ cups chopped cooked spinach
1 cup milk
3 tablespoons butter
3 tablespoons flour
⅓ teaspoon nutmeg
1 teaspoon grated onion
2 tablespoons lemon juice
2 eggs, well beaten
1 teaspoon salt

Mix together and pour into a well buttered quart ring mold. Place in pan of hot water and bake at 375° until firm. Unmold on hot round tray or plate. Can be made and served in individual molds.

Dolph Briscoe
Governor of Texas 1973-1979

16

Caramel Soufflé

2 pounds granulated sugar
12 egg whites
butter for coating pan

Place 1½ cups of sugar in a skillet. Heat over medium heat until a brown syrup, pour into a 3 quart casserole or bundt pan that has been completely coated with butter. Cool thoroughly, then coat the entire pan and the cooled syrup with butter. Beat egg whites until stiff. Add one pound of sugar gradually to the egg whites, beating constantly. Put the remaining sugar in the skillet and brown to a syrup. Add a little water and cook until syrup forms a thread. Pour into the egg whites and beat at medium speed on mixer. Increase to high speed and beat for 12 minutes. Pour into the buttered container and bake at 300° in a pan of hot water for about one hour or until firm but light. Turn out on a serving tray at once.

Dolph Briscoe
Governor of Texas 1973-1979

If you wish to prepare the soufflé early in the day, leave in pan and return to 350° oven for about 20 minutes. It must be warm or hot to come out of the pan. This dessert was well liked and often requested. - Janey Briscoe

Picoso

18 serrano peppers
2 cloves garlic
1 teaspoon vegetable oil
dash of salt
1 teaspoon fresh lemon juice
3 cans whole tomatoes

Boil peppers in water until they have lost their bright green color and are drab olive green. Peel the garlic and the peppers. Put garlic, peppers, oil, salt and lemon juice in a blender. Blend until these are completely pureed. Turn blender off and on while adding tomatoes (without the juice). Pour in large container, it makes about a quart. Keeps well in the refrigerator.

Dolph Briscoe
Governor of Texas 1973-1979

Many people have requested my Picoso recipe. We keep fresh home fried tostadas for a wonderful snack. This recipe has been in our family for years. It is used with eggs and some salads as a dressing. There are a million things you can use it with! - Janey Briscoe

Salads for business luncheons at the Governor's Mansion were usually quarter heads of lettuce with this delicious dressing. It is particularly good with the addition of tomato wedges. Make sure all elements of the salad are thoroughly chilled. -Janey Briscoe

Horseradish Dressing

1 cup sour cream
½ cup mayonnaise
1 teaspoon lemon juice
¼ teaspoon dry mustard
1 tablespoon prepared horseradish
¼ teaspoon onion juice
2 teaspoons chopped chives

Mix thoroughly and chill.

Dolph Briscoe
Governor of Texas 1973-1979

Mrs. Thigpen's Cucumbers in Sour Cream

3 cucumbers
1 cup sour cream
1 teaspoon vinegar
Texas A&M University 1015 onions

Wash, peel and thinly slice cucumbers. Place cucumbers in bowl and lightly salt. Drain any salty liquid from cucumbers. Place salted cucumbers in ice cold water until crisp. Mix the sour cream with vinegar. Pour this mixture over the cucumbers. Add the onions, sliced, and lightly toss into cucumbers. Refrigerate.

Rick Perry
Commissioner of Agriculture of Texas

"Home on the Range"

"Home on the Range" was written by David Guion, born in Ballinger, Texas in 1892. David was 13 years old when he composed the song.

Bob Lee and John D. Sutherland's Cabrito

Slaughter and skin a 2- or 3-month-old goat. (Or buy one already prepared for cooking.)

Season with salt, black pepper, garlic salt, and onion (quartered).

Wrap carcass in foil. Bake in 300° oven for 15 minutes to the pound. Or, better still, dig a pit and build a fire at the side. As the fire turns to coals, place coals in pits. For a grown goat, double your cooking time.

Use barbecue sauce on the side.

Liz Carpenter
press secretary to Lady Bird Johnson

Sister Alice's Buttermilk Candy

- **2 cups sugar**
- **1 cup buttermilk**
- **1 teaspoon baking soda**
- **1 tablespoon white corn syrup**
- **½ stick butter**
- **1 teaspoon vanilla**
- **2 cups pecans**

Cook all but vanilla and nuts in three-quart or larger saucepan to the soft ball stage (240°). Add vanilla and pecans, and beat until mixture becomes opaque and starts thickening. Rapidly drop spoonfuls onto wax paper.

Liz Carpenter
press secretary to Lady Bird Johnson

Bluebonnet Trail Scholarship Winner 1995

We would like to congratulate Julie Childress on being our Scholarship winner. Julie is attending Texas A&M University where she is pursuing a degree in Agricultural Development. She is the daughter of Mr. and Mrs. Pleas Childress of Ozona, Texas.

This recipe is a combined effort by Julie, Pleas, Sandra and Sadie Davidson, our 4-H nutrition leader. It took several tries to find one tasty and easy to fix. Our families love the taste, but if you want more "just lamb flavor", you can use the marinade for a shorter time and leave out the orange extract. It won 1st in the Crocket County 4-H Food Show.

Lamb a L'Orange

2 pounds American lamb - boneless loin or leg

Marinade
½ cup "Lite" soy sauce
¼ cup cooking sherry
2 tablespoons ketchup
½ teaspoon orange extract
½ teaspoon black pepper
¼-½ teaspoon garlic powder
4 tablespoons olive oil

Garnish
2 oranges
mint
parsley
paprika

In a non-metal bowl, combine all the ingredients for the marinade sauce and blend well by hand. Trim all the excess fat from the lamb and then slice ¼ to ½ inch thick pieces, across grain. Place pieces of lamb in bowl with marinade for at least two hours or overnight if desired. Remove lamb from marinade and coat with olive oil. Place lamb in skillet and sauté over medium heat for approximately 2 to 3 minutes on each side or until desired degree of doneness. Place meat slices on plate and heat the remaining marinade in skillet for approximately 1 to 2 minutes. Baste meat with heated marinade. Arrange the lamb, sprinkle with paprika, and garnish with fresh mint or parsley and orange slices. Serves eight 3-ounce servings.

Julie Childress
Ozona

Cowboy's Dream

Now a cowboy's life ain't all fun and games,
It's not just saddlin' your horse and ridin' the range,
Or givin' ol' pet cows funny little names,
No,
For those of you who might misconstrue,
Sit a bit and lets talk a thing or two,
About a cowboy's game,
An' this ol' lonesome name,
Ya' see a cowboy's life is gettin' more complex,
An' for some of you it might perplex,
The conditions we live in are dubious at best,
But we ain't much different then all the rest,
We just try to make a livin' an' care for ours too,
Why we worry about things just like most folks do,
Things like feedbills, fences, anthrax an' such,
Cancer eye, drought, an' low stock prices ya' can't touch,
High leases, repairs, and now quarterly tax,
Mus'nt forget the coyote that don't relax,
On them new born critters that come in the spring,
And an occasional screw-worm tha'd make a tough man turn green,
But a cowboy's life ain't a bad one at all,
And were not just a Neanderthal,
When it comes to figures an' makin' things work,
You might look at him an' think he's gone berserk,
With his wild concoctions and off-handed perk,
But it's a good means of livin' and we're thankful of that,
An' wouldn't trade burlap for a fancy door mat.
Now I hope I've opened a few eyes with this tale,
An' not made anyone's dreams gone pail,
'Cause in this day an' time a cowboy's game's kind'a frail,
So stick with your dreams and work hard as you can,
Blood, sweat an' tears is the only plan,
And remember at night to thank the Lord for his guidin' hand.

Russell Rogers

APPETIZERS & BEVERAGES

Todd's Texas Calf Fries

Todd is a good Texas A&M buddy of Clay and Anita. Clay's hint to Todd is that calf fries should always have cayenne pepper in them.

To clean: When possible, always freeze calf fries before cleaning completely.

To prepare: thaw fries in hot water, separate when partially thawed and completely remove outside skin layer or membrane. This is much easier when fries are not completely thawed. Fries will have the same texture as a peeled peach.

To cook: Cut fries into chunks about the size of a half dollar and sprinkle with black pepper according to taste.

2 cups milk
2 eggs
seasonings: salt, pepper, Tabasco sauce
flour
cornmeal

In a bowl, mix milk with eggs; add 5 shakes of Tabasco sauce, pinch each of salt and pepper. In separate bowl mix equal portions of flour and cornmeal. Dip calf fries in milk and eggs mixture then into the flour mixture. Fry in at least ½-inch of oil or deep fry. Cook fries until they float to the top of the oil. Drain well over newspaper or old issues of your Livestock Weekly.

For sauce, mix Worcestershire sauce with ketchup and picante sauce, or use Aus Jus sauce.

For Yankee Calf Fries, follow the above directions except leave out Tabasco sauce and mix approximately 2 cups of crushed crackers with 1 cup of cornmeal for batter.

The best oil to use in deep frying is peanut oil if available and affordable.

Todd Firkens
Canyon

"Johnson's Draw" Jalapeño Quail

8 quail
1½ cups softened butter or margarine
1 lime
salt and pepper to taste
2 mild jalapeño peppers
8 thick slices bacon

Rinse and dry quail. Rub with softened butter; sprinkle with salt and pepper, squeeze on lime juice. Slice the jalapeño peppers into 4 strips per pepper and remove seeds. Insert strip of jalapeño in each quail cavity and wrap the bird with thick slices of bacon. Broil, turning, until tender and a crisp brown, about 35 minutes.

Better yet cook over an open mesquite fire.

Brett Carpenter
San Angelo

This spicy appetizer disappears about as fast as a covey!

Venison Strips or Bits

2-3 pounds venison back strap, cut into small ½x1½ inch strips
½ cup flour
2-3 teaspoons salt
1 teaspoon pepper
cooking oil

Place the flour, salt and pepper (I use more salt and pepper than I would ordinarily use) in a plastic bag, shake to mix seasoning. Place portions of the meat in the bag, shake to coat strips. Fry in about ½-inch cooking oil or deep fry in the Fry Daddy for about 3 to 5 minutes. Taste for seasoning and doneness.

Donald likes to soak the meat in buttermilk before flouring but it is not necessary.

Molly Allison
San Angelo

Jalapeño Gravy

¼ cup pan drippings or butter or oil
¼ cup all purpose flour
2-2½ cups warm milk
½ teaspoon salt
⅛ teaspoon pepper
1 teaspoon fine chopped jalapeños

On very low heat, blend oil and flour well. Add warm milk. Stir and simmer until thick. Serve over chicken fried steak or anything you enjoy cream gravy with.

Joan Motl Tucker
San Angelo

This is finger food that doesn't get into the serving dish—disappears as fast as can be cooked. Great appetizer at a party. And always the first taste after the hunt. My father, Asa Jones, says that the secret to good venison is the way the meat is dressed in the field. A carefully gutted and cleaned carcass keeps the meat from having a strong taste.

This is a fool proof recipe that is quick and easy! They freeze well and are excellent for last minute or unexpected guests!

Turkey Balls

1 cup finely ground smoked turkey
1 8-ounce package cream cheese
3 tablespoons mayonnaise
garlic to taste (fresh or powdered)
½ cup finely chopped pecans
2 tablespoons chopped parsley

Mix turkey, cream cheese, mayonnaise, and garlic; shape into balls. Combine pecans and parsley and roll balls until covered. Chill and serve with crackers.

Wendy Wardlaw
Del Rio

Mama Lisa's Famous Italian Stuffed Mushrooms

1 package of medium mushrooms
¾ cup plain breadcrumbs
2 tablespoons olive oil
¼ teaspoon salt
1 tablespoon grated Parmesan cheese
1 teaspoon dried parsley flakes

Wash mushrooms and drain completely; remove stems and chop in small pieces. In a bowl, add chopped stems, breadcrumbs, olive oil, salt, cheese and parsley. Mix well. Take small amounts of mixture and place inside mushroom caps. Place on lightly oiled baking dish and place in oven for 20 minutes. Optional: Remove from oven and place under broiler for 3 minutes for crisp tops. Place on platter and garnish with lemon wedges.

Please use only olive oil for this recipe. This is one flavor that cannot be substituted.

Madeline Daddiego
Mohair Council of America
New York Office

Goat Cheese Nachos

¼ pound goat cheese, crumbled (Texas goat cheese or feta, not chèvre)
2 tablespoons soft cream cheese
1 tablespoon sour cream
1 tablespoon chopped parsley
pickled jalapeño slices
salt & pepper to taste
fried corn tortilla chips

Mix together cheeses, sour cream and parsley. Season with salt and pepper. Put small spoonful of mixture on each chip. Top with jalapeño slice. Bake at 275° about 5 minutes or until cheese melts.

Brad Johnson
Chicago, Illinois

Beef Cocktail Dip

5 slices bacon
2 pounds lean ground beef
2 chopped onions
1 minced clove garlic
2 diced tomatoes
½ cup chopped pimento
½ cup toasted almonds
1 6-ounce can tomato paste
2 diced jalapeños
½ cup raisins
½ teaspoon ground cumin
½ teaspoon oregano
¼ cup brown sugar
salt & pepper to taste

Fry bacon, drain, crumble and set aside. In ¼ cup bacon drippings, brown beef, onions and garlic and cook until done. Stir in the remaining ingredients and cook 15 to 20 minutes longer over low heat. Turn into chafing dish and serve hot with corn chips or tortilla chips. Also very good served with small flour tortillas.

Mimi Allison

Back in the early 1970's my sister-in-law, Elaine Wardlaw, from Del Rio and I worked very hard to copy a chili dip recipe from the San Felipe Country Club. We feel like we came up with something much better than what we were aiming for. This recipe has been served at many a Fling Ding party since then. Also, my son, McNeil Allison, won a blue ribbon in 4-H using this recipe.

Hot Sausage Dip

1 pound hot sausage
1 pound lean ground beef
1 onion
2 pounds Velveeta cheese
1 can Rotel
1 can cream of mushroom soup

Sauté onion and add crumbled sausage and beef. Brown well and drain. Mix the cheese, tomatoes and soup. Heat until cheese melts. Add meat to cheese mixture. Blend and serve.

Valda Livingston
Marfa

Broccoli Dip

½ cup chopped onion
½ cup chopped celery
½ cup chopped mushrooms
3 tablespoons butter
1 package frozen, chopped broccoli
1 6-ounce package garlic cheese
1 can condensed mushroom soup
1 squeeze of lemon juice
dash of Tabasco sauce
dash of Worcestershire sauce

Sauté onions, celery, and mushrooms in butter. Add broccoli. Mix in cheese and mushroom soup. Cook over low heat until cheese melts. Squeeze lemon, dash of Tabasco and Worcestershire sauces. Serve in chafing dish with tostadas, toast, or crackers.

You may prepare this ahead of time and refrigerate. Heat slowly before serving.

Phyllis Rhodes
Kerrville

Frijole Dip

2 pounds frijoles
1 ham hock
2 large onions, chopped
1 green pepper, chopped
3 cloves garlic, chopped
½ pound sharp cheese
1 tablespoon chili powder
2 tablespoons Worcestershire sauce
1 teaspoon Tabasco sauce

Wash, pick over and soak beans overnight in plenty of water to cook them in. Add ham hock or salt pork if desired. Add all ingredients but cheese and cook slowly for at least six hours - do not have much liquid. Put beans through a food mill or ricer. Return to fire and add salt and pepper to taste. Seasoning can be changed to suit the taste. Just before serving add the grated cheese - let melt and mix well. Serve very hot.

Mrs Norbourne Smith
Submitted by Mary Ellen McEntire
San Angelo

My next door neighbor in Del Rio, Mrs. Jimmy Roots, has given many fabulous parties, and a favorite on her bountiful table was a bean dip using a recipe given to her by her mother, Mrs. Norbourne Smith.

Black Bean Dip

1 can black beans
1 can Rotel
1 block cream cheese
1 squirt lemon juice
3 teaspoon salt
3 teaspoons pepper
garlic powder to taste

Drain Rotel and black beans. Place all ingredients in a saucepan. Cook over medium heat until cream cheese melts. Stir frequently. While cooking add lemon juice, salt, pepper, garlic powder. Serve hot or cold with tortilla or any chips.

Brandi Ware
Dallas

If you use less fat cream cheese, this dip will only have 1 to 2 fat grams. The black beans only have 1 gram of fat and the Rotel has none. Preccia Miller and I made this recipe up while walking through the store one afternoon.

Shrimp Dip

1 pint real mayonnaise
1 pint sour cream
1 tablespoon dried parsley
3 tablespoons dill weed
3 tablespoons onion flakes
1 teaspoon seasoning salt
2 small packages miniature cooked shrimp
½ can chopped water chestnuts

Combine all ingredients together and serve as a dip.

Barbara Jennings
Sonora

Bean Dip

3 cans black bean, drained
3 cans white corn, drained
2 jalapeños, chopped
¼ medium onion, chopped
1 red bell pepper, chopped
½ cup fresh cilantro
1 small bottle of Italian dressing - no oil

Mix all ingredients together using only about ¾ of the bottle of dressing. Chill and serve with tostadas.

Annabelle Allison
San Angelo

It's been said that a square nail, or a cup of Coca-Cola, or a tablespoon of brown sugar, or a teaspoon of ground ginger, or a tablespoon of castor oil added an hour before serving, may help avoid the social problem caused by beans. We've also tried soaking them in soda water.

Friendship Recipe

1. Take 4 parts genuine interest in the other fellow.
2. Strain to remove any bits of idle curiosity.
3. Add what tastes in common you have and pleasant conversation as it seems needed.
4. Stir at unexpected intervals with a kind act and cook rich and smooth.

This will keep indefinitely but, should not be stored away. Keep it handy and use daily.

Edwards County Merry Heart Club 1883-1995
Phyllis Sweeten Rhodes

Tortilla Wraps

3 8-ounce packages cream cheese, softened
1 carton sour cream
2 bunched green onions, chopped
5 jalapeños, chopped
juice from ½ lime
3 dashes garlic powder
2 packages flour tortillas

Mix everything in blender or food processor and spread on tortillas. Roll up like enchiladas and re-frigerate overnight. Slice in 1-inch pieces. Arrange on a dish with a bowl of salsa.

Buy the cheap flour tortillas - they are thinner.

Frankie Lee Harlow
San Antonio

This recipe is from YaYa Aldrete, Cris's wife, who is a fabulous cook as well as drop dead gorgeous!

In A RUSH Dip

This is so easy! It probably doesn't even qualify as a recipe but is very good if you are in a rush for something for a small crowd to munch on, and you can get to the store. Go to HEB and buy:

1 large carton pimiento cheese
1 large jar chopped pimientos
1 small jar picante sauce
1 large sack king size corn chips

Drain the pimentos, mix with the cheese and add as much picante sauce as you like. Serve with the corn chips.

Frankie Lee Harlow
Del Rio

I entered this recipe in my first 4-H Pecos County Food Show and won Second Place with it. Anytime we have a "get together" at the ranch we serve this dip. It is always a hit!

Hawaiian Spinach Dip

1½ cups mayonnaise
1 cup sour cream
1 package dehydrated vegetable soup mix
1 can chopped water chestnuts
1 box frozen chopped spinach, cooked and drained
4 chopped green onions
celery salt to taste

Mix all ingredients together and put in the center of a hollowed out Hawaiian bread. Serve with the Hawaiian bread. Makes ten ½ cup servings.

Chey-Anne Gage
Iraan

This is great served over cream cheese or served with ham. You can add peach or apricot preserves for a wonderful taste.

Jezebel Sauce

1 18-ounce jar pineapple preserves
1 18-ounce jar apple jelly
3 tablespoons dry mustard
½ cup plus 2 tablespoons horseradish
1 tablespoon coarsely ground pepper

Combine the ingredients together and refrigerate. Use the jelly jars to store the sauce.

Nancy Johnson

This makes a handy Christmas remembrance but must be refrigerated after mixing.

Easy Apricot-Jalapeño Spread

1 16-ounce jar of apricot or peach preserves
⅓ cup diced canned jalapeños
1 8-ounce package cream cheese, or more

Combine preserves and jalapeños with a little juice from jalapeño bottle at least one day before serving. Pour preserves over room temperature cream cheese and serve with soda crackers, party crackers or corn chips.

Jean Read
Ozona

Eloise's Cheese Roll

1 pound American cheese
3 ounces cream cheese
1 cup pecans, chopped fine
3-4 garlic cloves, minced
chili powder

Grate the American cheese, chop pecans with garlic cloves. Mix together well. Soften cream cheese and mix with your hands until well blended. Roll out on wax paper sprinkled with chili powder. Roll into 2 logs. Serve with crackers.

Eloise McKissack
Submitted by Carol Santry

My Mother gave this recipe to me many years ago. I make these every Christmas and give them to my friends.
Carol is a very dear friend and I have watched her make these rolls. She is blind and does all of her own cooking. Carol is a wonderful cook and has a wonderful sense of smell and taste; so, you know that if she says it's good, then it is! -Nancy

Jalapeño Cheese Spread

1 16-ounce box softened Velveeta cheese
3 ounces softened cream cheese
1 cup finely chopped pecans
1 4-ounce jar diced pimentos
1 4-ounce can chopped green chilies
¼ cup chopped jalapeño peppers
½ cup chopped green onions

Beat together the two cheeses. Add the remaining ingredients and mix well. Serve with Harvest Crackers.

Anita Allison
San Angelo

This is our absolute favorite dip that has become part of the holiday tradition. Clay can sit down and eat a bowl by himself. It is so good, don't wait until the holidays to make it!

I found the original recipe for this about 35 years ago in the Standard Times. When we moved, Dale thought it was trash and threw it away. I went to the newspaper and searched until I found it again. It has since been a traditional Christmas delicacy at our house that our children have taken with them now that they are grown and married.

Cheese straws and/or dough may be frozen. Pecans can be added, dough rolled up and sliced like refrigerator cookies. Dough may also be wrapped around stuffed olives or small bits of sausage and baked.

Aunt Martha's Cheese Straws

1 pound sharp Cheddar cheese
3½ cups sifted flour
¼ teaspoon salt
3 sticks butter or margarine
¼ teaspoon cayenne pepper

Grate cheese with fine grater; keep in refrigerator until ready to use. Sift flour, salt, and pepper together. Cut butter into the flour mixture. Be sure butter is good and cold. Mix flour and butter mixture with your hands until it is the consistency of coarse meal. Add grated cheese and mix with your hands until the dough is yellow all the way through. Roll out ¼ of the dough into a rectangle. Measure length of cheese straws to 2½ inches. Cut with pastry wheel; then cut width about ½ inch, or finger size. Place on ungreased cookie sheet and cook for 7 to 10 minutes at 375° until golden, not brown. Makes about 15 dozen.

Kay Wall Bates
San Angelo

Crab Mold

1 can fancy white crab meat
1 can mushroom soup
1 envelope Knox gelatin
3 tablespoons cold water
¾ cup mayonnaise
1 8-ounce package cream cheese (softened)
1 cup finely chopped celery
2 green onions, chopped (green ends included)

Drain crab meat and run cold water through it and drain again. Heat soup. Dissolve gelatin in water and add to warm soup. Add cream cheese, mayonnaise, celery, and onion. (I always use a little lemon juice, but it is not necessary.) Mix gently. Put in oiled mold and refrigerate overnight. Waverly crackers are best to serve with this.

Winifred Rose
Del Rio

Cheesed Olives

1 stick butter (or oleo)
1½ cups flour
2 cups grated sharp cheddar cheese
½ teaspoon salt
1 teaspoon paprika
1 medium jar small stuffed olives

Let ingredients sit at room temperature. Blend together to form stiff dough. Drain olives and dry with paper towel. Pinch off about 1 teaspoon of dough and roll around olive to form a covered ball. Freeze on cookie sheet. Store in plastic bags in the freezer. Bake at 450° for 12 to 15 minutes, while still frozen. Makes about 52.

Dorothy Cauthorn
Ozona

Virgil loves to make these while watching TV, AFTER I have made the dough and drained the olives. We have made thousands and everyone loves them!

Crab Triangles

6 English muffins
1 stick margarine at room temperature
1 jar Old English Cheese Spread
1 can crab meat, well drained
1½ tablespoons real mayonnaise
½ teaspoon garlic powder
½ teaspoon salt

Mix all together and spread on the English muffins. Cut each muffin in quarters. Freeze on a cookie sheet and then store in a plastic bag for future use. Broil 8 to 10 minutes until bubbly, watch carefully so not to brown.

Preccia Miller
Sonora

I won Second Place with this recipe in the Concho Cookery in 1987.

Cajun Canapés

2 cans refrigerator buttermilk biscuits
½ pound pork sausage, cooked and drained
1½ cups grated sharp cheddar cheese
¼ cup chopped green pepper
2 green onions, sliced
¼ cup mayonnaise
2 teaspoons lemon juice
½ teaspoon salt
½ teaspoon paprika
¼ teaspoon cayenne
¼ teaspoon garlic powder
¼ teaspoon thyme

Bake biscuits according to directions on can - turning over half way through. Cool. Scoop out the middle of the biscuit. Preheat oven to 400°. Mix remaining ingredients in a large bowl. Spoon 1 tablespoon of mixture on each biscuit half. Bake 5 to 8 minutes, until cheese melts. Serve warm.

You can put a slice of tomato on top, too.

Venetta Smith
Sonora

West Texas Boys Ranch

We can't talk about ranch heritage without talking about West Texas Boys Ranch. The ranch, which was begun in 1947, provides loving, caring families and homes for boys in need so they can become healthy, happy, self-sufficient citizens with strong Christian values. The people of West Texas are proud of West Texas Boys Ranch and strongly support it with their contributions and memorials. We all believe a gift to the ranch is a good investment in the lives of boys. West Texas Boys Ranch will guide these boys to become the young adults we will all be proud of. And that's a good return on your dollar!

Ruby's Red Punch

3 mashed bananas
1 pint mashed strawberries
2 packages cherry flavored drink mix
1 package orange flavored drink mix
3 cups sugar
1½ quarts water
9 tablespoons lemon juice
1 46-ounce can pineapple juice
1 quart 7-up

Mash bananas and strawberries; add fruit flavored drink mixes and sugar. Add water, lemon juice, and pineapple juice; stir until well mixed. Freeze until solid. Remove from freezer 4 hours before serving and thaw until slushy. Pour in 7-up. Serves 30 people.

Mama D (House Mother)
Delta Delta Delta - Texas A&M University
Submitted by Anita Allison

Coffee Punch

1 cup dry instant coffee
½ cup cocoa
1¼ cups sugar
1 cup boiling water
3 quarts milk
1 teaspoon vanilla
1 quart heavy cream, whipped
½ gallon vanilla ice cream
1 cup bourbon (optional)

Combine coffee, cocoa, sugar, and boiling water. Blend until smooth. Stir in milk, vanilla and bourbon. Fold in whipped cream and ice cream just before serving. Serves 40.

Preccia Miller

Mama D used to make this punch whenever we had a special party at the house. It is wonderful! Ruby was one of our fabulous cooks who made up the recipe. It has been served and loved at many bridal parties and teas!

Fling Ding Punch

1 12-ounce can frozen orange juice
1 12-ounce can frozen lemonade
1 46-ounce can pineapple juice
1 quart club soda
1 quart ginger ale
1 quart vodka

Mix in order given. Serves 40.

Barbara Jennings
Sonora

Fling Ding Dance

The Fling Ding is a uniquely Sonora, Texas entertainment. The Dance, held each year in a wool warehouse, was organized in the late '30's being disbanded for a short time in the early days of World War II. Since 1954 many big name bands such as Jimmy Dorsey, Glenn Miller, Bob Crosby, Ray Price, and many more have furnished music for over one thousand couples who attend. One highlight of this gala, "invitation only", event are the many parties given before and after, at which many of the recipes in this book are served.

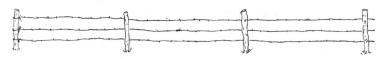

Nan's Punch

1 can frozen pineapple-orange-banana tropical punch
1 2-liter bottle ginger ale or Sprite

Mix these two ingredients and serve in a punch bowl with a pretty ice-fruit ring.

Nan Beckwith
Progreso

Party Punch

3 packages lemon-lime flavored drink mix
1 46-ounce can pineapple juice
1 large can frozen orange juice
2 large cans frozen limeade or lemonade
2½ cups sugar
3½ quarts water
2 tablespoons vanilla
2 tablespoons almond extract
1 3 liter bottles Sprite or 7-up

Dissolve sugar in one quart of the water in sauce-pan. Do not boil! Cool and add the remaining ingredients. Put in a 5 gallon cooler with a lot of ice. To use in a punch bowl, put in gallon jugs and pour into a punch bowl filled with ice. This can be made a day before the party.

Mary Jane Esser Morrison
The Esser Ranch at Kendalia "A Century Ranch"

One of my dearest friends, Cleo Pfeiffer, gave me this recipe. At hot summer outings it is always a hit!

Good Easy Punch

6 mashed bananas
1 large can frozen lemonade concentrate
1 large can frozen orange juice concentrate

Have the frozen concentrates slightly softened. Mix all ingredients well. Consistency will be like a frozen slush. Freeze in plastic container. To use as an individual drink, add 1 tablespoon to 12 ounces 7-up. As a punch for many, add 23 tablespoons to 1 quart 7-up, or the whole recipe to 3 liters 7-up. Float cherries and orange slices in punch poured over crushed ice.

Mrs. Richard Mayer
San Angelo

Mock Champagne

1 bottle white grape juice
1 bottle sparkling water

Mix equal parts of each ingredient to create Champagne!

Nan Beckwith
Progreso

This eggnog makes our holidays even more festive! My mother, Mrs. Howard Espy, used this recipe; thus, it has certainly become a tradition!

Eggnog

6 eggs
¾ cups sugar
1 pint cream, whipped
1 pint milk
1 cup bourbon

Separate eggs into two bowls. Add ½ cup sugar to yolks while beating. Add ¼ cup sugar to whites after very stiffly beaten. Add whiskey slowly to yolks while stirring. Fold in whites. Add milk and whipped cream. Sprinkle with nutmeg, of course! Enjoy!

Mary John Espy Phinizy
Gail

My Favorite Recipe

Preccia Miller

In 1987, my Senior year in High School, I entered this recipe in the San Angelo Standard Times, Concho Cookery Recipe Contest and much to my surprise I won first place in the vegetable category plus Best of Show. So I want to share this easy and Best Ever Cheese Soup recipe with you. I am noted for loving cheese! The first meal I have ever made had four pounds of cheese that my second dad, Jerry, grated for me. He asked me if I wanted to add more cheese to any of the recipes I had submitted for this cookbook.

Best Ever Cheese Soup

1 stick butter
2 grated carrots
3 chopped green onions
2 chopped celery stalks

Sauté the above on low heat, then add:

2 cans chicken broth
3 cans cream of potato soup
½ pound grated jalapeño cheese
½ pound grated Longhorn cheese
3 heaping tablespoons sour cream

Sauté the carrots, onions, and celery in the butter. Heat the broth, soup, and cheese, stirring frequently. Add sautéed vegetables to the soup mixture and heat thoroughly. Remove from heat. Add sour cream. Salt and pepper to taste.

"Let me tell you why you are here. You're here to be salt - seasoning that brings out the good flavors of this earth. If you lose your saltiness, how will people taste Godliness?"

Matthew 5:13

This is a very quick dish to prepare with a good combination of colors and flavors. To complete your meal, serve with corn bread and a salad on the side.

Santa Fe Soup

1½ **pounds ground beef**
1 **package dry ranch dressing mix**
1 **package dry taco seasoning mix**
2 **cans pinto beans**
1 **can kidney beans**
1 **can regular corn**
1 **can tomatoes**
1 **can Rotel tomatoes**

In a Dutch oven, brown the ground beef. Add the dressing and seasoning mixes. Add the canned ingredients, but do not drain them. Bring to a boil. May be served with any type of grated cheese sprinkled on top.

Sarah Wade
Sonora

I received this recipe from my friend, Cissy Simpton. Children and adults love it! Great for church suppers.

Taco Soup

2 **pounds lean ground meat**
1 **small onion, chopped**
1 **large can green chilies, chopped**
1 **teaspoon salt**
½ **teaspoon pepper**
1 **large package taco seasoning**
1 **package dry ranch style dressing**
1 **can hominy**
2 **cans ranch style beans**
3 **cans stewed tomatoes**

Brown meat and onion. Add remaining ingredients and bring to a boil. Simmer for 30 minutes. Serve in bowls and top with grated Cheddar cheese and sliced green onion tops.

Jeannie Lewis
Del Rio

YO Ranch Hotel Tortilla Soup

6-8 cans chicken broth
½ cup chopped onions
4-6 bell peppers
1-2 teaspoons salt
½ teaspoon black pepper
½-¾ teaspoon ground oregano
¼-½ teaspoon ground cumin
1-2 jars pimiento slices
4-6 yellow squash
4-6 zucchini squash
2-3 tablespoons fresh cilantro leaves
2-4 chicken breasts, skinned, boned, fat removed and cut into small slices
1-2 avocados
2-4 cups shredded Monterey Jack cheese
fried tortilla strips or corn chips

Seed and cut bell peppers into ½-inch wide strips. Slice squash and zucchini into ¼-inch rounds. In a large soup pot pour one can chicken broth and heat. Add onions, cilantro (very important ingredient), bell pepper strips, spices, and salt. Allow to boil for several minutes. Add rest of broth and bring to boil before adding pimientos. Add squash rounds, a cup or two at a time, allowing to return to a boil after each addition. (For faster boil, pot may be covered.) Cover and turn heat down and allow to simmer for an hour. Turn heat up and add chicken strips a few at a time. Allow chicken to cook for 35-45 minutes. Remove from heat and add chopped avocado. Place a couple of tablespoons cheese in individual soup bowls. Ladle soup over cheese and sprinkle generously with fried tortilla strips or corn chips.

This recipe can be adapted for lower fat content by using no-fat chicken broth, low or non fat cheese, and omitting avocados. Other parts of chicken may be used. Canned diced tomatoes may be added after chicken.

Sid Hoover
Ozona

Life for a stay-at-home, cookie baking Grandma changed dramatically when a cousin of mine introduced me to the Riverside and Landowners Protection Coalition rights years ago. One of the positive results of the battle for private property rights has been the opportunity to meet a multitude of other concerned country folks (and some city ones, too.) During that first year of meetings in Kerrville, my cousin, her mother, and I ate tortilla soup at the YO Ranch Hotel restaurant buffet. After a discussion of the ingredients we each remembered, YO Ranch Tortilla Soup is the result.

This recipe is a favorite and I sure am glad it was passed my way. The lime juice is the secret. It is great!

Tortilla Soup

2 tablespoons butter
2 tablespoons olive oil
1 large diced onion
2 ribs chopped celery
6 tablespoons lime juice
1 can chopped tomatoes
salt and pepper
3 15-ounce cans chicken broth
2 chicken breast halves
2 garlic cloves
½ teaspoon ground cumin
1 teaspoon chili powder
corn tortilla chips
Monterey Jack cheese

Heat butter, and olive oil; add onions and celery and cook until tender. Add chicken, chicken broth, and seasonings. Simmer 20 minutes. Add lime juice and tomatoes Add tortilla chips and cheese to each individual serving.

Jeri Duncan
San Angelo

Los Patios Cheese Soup

¼ cup butter or margarine
½ onion, chopped
3 stalks celery, chopped, and some leaves, minced
2 carrots, minced
2 10¾-ounce cans chicken broth
3 10¾-ounce cans potato soup
8 ounces yellow cheese, grated
parsley flakes and chives
black pepper to taste
3 tablespoons cooking sherry

Melt butter over low heat and sauté onions, celery and carrots. Add chicken broth, cover and simmer for 30 minutes. Add potato soup and bring to a boil. Then, add cheese, parsley, chives and pepper. Simmer 15 minutes. Add sherry and stir. Yields 10 cups.

Amanda Andrews
San Antonio

 *Soups*

Chicken Vegetable Soup

1 chicken
5 cups water
1 teaspoon salt
½ teaspoon pepper
1 chopped medium onion
2 cups chopped celery
2 cups diced carrots
2 cups diced potatoes
2-3 cups cooked rice
4 chicken bouillon cubes
1 pound Velveeta cheese

Cook chicken pieces in water with salt, pepper, onion and celery for 1 hour or until chicken falls off the bone. Remove chicken, skin and bones and return chopped chicken to broth. Add the carrots, potatoes, rice and bouillon cubes and cook over low heat 1½ hours. Cut up cheese and add to soup. Heat until melted and serve. Serves 8.

Kaye Alexander
San Angelo

Tomato Soup

1 large can tomatoes
1 stalk celery
1 small piece of onion
salt and pepper
½ teaspoon baking soda
⅓ stick butter
2 tablespoons flour
2 cups milk

Combine can of tomatoes, celery, onion, salt and pepper in saucepan. Cook slowly for about 15 minutes. Add baking soda and let stand for a few minutes. Melt the butter; add flour and mix well. Add milk and cook until slightly thickened. Put the tomato mixture through the blender and add to milk mixture. Salt and pepper to taste. Sprinkle with fresh parsley.

Clara Maudell Drake
Submitted by Mary Ellen McEntire
San Angelo

A very hearty soup. Be sure to have plenty on hand because seconds are always requested.

To loosen skins of tomatoes and peppers, toast them dry on a frying pan on the fire, or in the oven, then remove from heat and put in a tightly closed paper bag for 15 minutes. Then the skin comes off easily when taken out of the bag.

Red Bell Pepper Soup

1 tablespoon olive oil
4 tablespoons unsalted butter
6 roasted red bell peppers, halved, seeded, and thinly sliced
3 shallots, peeled and thinly sliced
1 pear, peeled, quartered, and thinly sliced
1 quart chicken stock
2 roasted yellow bell peppers, peeled, halved, seeded, and thinly sliced
dash of cayenne pepper
salt and freshly ground white pepper
¼ cup heavy cream

Heat the oil and butter in a large saucepan and sauté the sliced vegetables and pear over medium heat until tender, 5 to 10 minutes. Add the stock, roasted peppers, cayenne, and salt and pepper to taste. Bring to a boil and simmer, covered, for 30 minutes. Puree the soup in small batches (approximately 2 cups each) in a food processor or blender. Pour the soup into the pan, add the heavy cream, and reheat over low heat. Serve the soup hot, with a dollop of crème fraîche or sour cream and a sprinkle of chopped fresh parsley.

Preccia Miller
Dallas

Cheese Soup with Vegetables

1 pound chopped onions
1 stick butter or oleo
2 pounds frozen stir-fry vegetables
1 pound grated American cheese
1 quart chicken broth
1 quart half and half or milk
2 tablespoons cornstarch
1-2 cups chopped cooked chicken

Sauté onions in butter. Add vegetable and broth. Cook until tender. Blend in cream and cheese. Add cornstarch in water if needed for thickening.

I cook my chicken for broth with pepper and poultry seasoning and of course, salt. For a richer taste add 1 tablespoon of Knorr's chicken broth crystals.

Jean Reed (Mrs. Nat)
Ozona

This was originally a cheese broccoli soup reborn when the draws were running too high to go to town and the "broccoli" in the freezer turned out to be "stir-fry vegetables."

Chunky Cream of Potato Soup

16-24 peeled potatoes
4 stalks celery
1 small onion
4 carrots
1 teaspoon salt
9 pints half and half
2 sticks butter

Cut or cube the potatoes into a large kettle. Cut the celery into small pieces, and do the same with the onion, and add to the kettle. Peel the carrots and grate. Put them in the kettle. Sprinkle salt and add enough water to cover the vegetables. Cook over medium heat until the potatoes are soft and a fork goes through easily (30 to 45 minutes). Drain off the water and add the half and half, salt and pepper to taste, and the butter. Set the kettle back on the stove over low heat, and simmer (do not boil, milk will curdle) for a couple hours.

Miles Miller
San Antonio

This is my favorite soup, especially good when you are sick. I told Mom that I wanted my favorite soup recipe in "her" cookbook. This way I'll never lose my recipe because I'll always have her book.

The carrots are for color and a little sweetness. For extra good taste, crumble in a little crisp bacon.

Carrying a grudge is like a run in a stocking. It can only get worse. Forgiveness is the answer.

Cream of Artichoke Soup

1 finely chopped medium onion
2 tablespoons butter
2 tablespoons flour
2 cups chicken broth
2 14-ounce cans artichoke hearts
1¼ cups evaporated milk
¼ cup finely chopped parsley
½ teaspoon garlic powder
salt and pepper to taste

Rinse, drain, and chop the artichoke hearts. Sauté onion in butter add flour and cook 5 minutes, stirring constantly. Add chicken broth and artichokes. Cook on medium heat until mixture thickens stirring constantly. Add milk and heat well. Add parsley, salt, garlic, pepper to taste. Sprinkle more parsley on top before serving. Good served hot or cold.

Carol Giles
Hillingdon Ranch, Comfort

Soups

Catfish and Shrimp Soup

2 tablespoons olive oil
2 cups chopped onion
2 minced cloves garlic
1 28-ounce can tomatoes
3 tablespoons tomato paste
1 bay leaf
4 cups water
1 cup dry white wine
1 bottle clam juice
½ pound shelled medium shrimp
2 catfish fillets, cut in 1-inch cubes
½ teaspoon salt
¼ teaspoon pepper
parsley
lemon slices

In large soup pot, heat oil. Sauté onion and garlic until onions are transparent. Add tomatoes, tomato paste and bay leaf. Cover and simmer 25 minutes. Add water, wine and clam juice. Simmer uncovered 45 minutes. Add shrimp, catfish, salt and pepper. Cook 10 minutes, remove bay leaf and garnish with parsley and lemon slices. Makes 8 servings.

Sadie Puckitt
San Angelo

We have a catfish farm on our ranch in Water Valley and make this quite often.

I sometimes add chopped celery with the onions and Tabasco sauce to taste.

Spinach Salad Dressing

4 tablespoons cider
    vinegar
4 tablespoons mayonnaise
4 tablespoons Durkee's
    dressing
2 heaping tablespoons
    horseradish
dash of Tabasco
salt and pepper

Blend all ingredients. A
great change from the
standard spinach salad
dressing.

Francine Hardeman
Sonora

Lemon Salad Dressing

1-2 tablespoons fresh
    lemon juice
zest from the lemon
    (optional)
½ teaspoon salt
fresh ground pepper
1 minced shallot
    (optional)
fresh herbs (chives,
    parsley, basil,
    tarragon)
½-¾ cup oil

Mix all ingredients until
salt has dissolved. Mix in
oil. Will keep in
refrigerator for 2 weeks.

Clara Winters
Brady

Authentic Caesar Salad

1 teaspoon freshly cracked pepper
1 garlic clove
2 anchovy fillets (flat, not rolled)
1 coddled egg yolk
1 tablespoon lemon juice
1 teaspoon Dijon mustard
½ cup olive oil
1 teaspoon red wine vinegar
1 tablespoon Worcestershire sauce
dash Tabasco
½ head Romaine lettuce, sliced against grain
(not torn)
½ cup Parmesan cheese
1 cup croutons

Grind pepper into wooden bowl. Mince garlic with
pepper and anchovies to form a paste. Add yolk,
lemon juice and mustard. Mix until creamy smooth.
Slowly add oil in a fine stream, whisking constantly,
until emulsified. Add vinegar, Worcestershire and
Tabasco. Mix well. Add lettuce, Parmesan and croutons. Toss well.

Brad Johnson
Chicago

Avocado and Grapefruit Salad

Peel and slice the avocado. Peel the grapefruit, being sure to remove all pith and membranes separat-
ing the segments. Arrange the slices of avocado and
grapefruit segments over salad greens and serve
with small amount of French dressing poured over
the salad.

Mimi Allison

Salads

Summer Green Salad

4-5 cups assorted green leafy lettuce
1 cup sliced fresh strawberries
½ cup toasted walnuts
1 small red onion thinly sliced

Wash and dry the lettuces and/or spinach. Break into bite size pieces and mix with the other ingredients. Top with the Raspberry Vinaigrette.

Raspberry Vinaigrette
1 tablespoon raspberry preserves
1½ teaspoons salt
1½ teaspoons pepper
¼ teaspoon minced garlic
¾ cup raspberry vinegar
1½ cups canola oil

Combine all ingredients except oil in blender. Blend well. With machine running, slowly add oil until thoroughly blended. Makes 2½ cups.

Vicki Rees
San Angelo

Vegetable Salad au Gratin

1 medium size cauliflower
2 packages frozen cut green beans
1 teaspoon salt
½ cup water
1 8-ounce package sharp American cheese, shredded
½ cup mayonnaise or salad dressing
2 tablespoons sweet pickle relish
2 tablespoons bottled oil & vinegar dressing

Trim cauliflower and break into florets; mound in center of large frying pan. Break up beans and place around cauliflower; sprinkle with salt. Add water; cover and heat to boiling, simmer for 10 minutes or until vegetables are tender and water is absorbed. Sprinkle cheese over cauliflower. Mix mayonnaise, pickle relish and oil & vinegar dressing in a cup; spoon over beans.

Nell S. Walker
College Station

French Dressing
1 can tomato soup
⅔ cup vinegar (cider or wine)
⅔ cup oil
½ cup sugar
1 diced onion
1 diced green pepper

Combine ingredients in jar and shake until mixed.
Nell S. Walker
College Station

This dressing is good on all kinds of salad greens.

49

Cucumber Salad

1 3-ounce package lime jello
1 tablespoon vinegar
1 tablespoon grated onion
1 cup boiling water
1 cup grated, drained, unpeeled cucumber
1 tablespoon horseradish
1 cup mayonnaise

Dissolve jello in boiling water. Add remaining ingredients then place in a mold. Refrigerate several hours until set. Serve.

A food processor can be used for the cucumber but be sure to drain well.

Ruth Johnson Lott
Mineola

Tomato Soup Salad

2 envelopes plain gelatin
½ cup water
1 can tomato soup
6 ounces cream cheese
1 tablespoon lemon juice
1 cup salad dressing
½ cup minced celery
½ cup minced green pepper
¼ cup minced onion

Soften gelatin in water. Heat soup in double boiler. Add cheese and gelatin, stirring until dissolved. Beat with rotary beater. Cool. Fold in lemon juice, dressing, and vegetables. Pour into lightly oiled 1½ quart mold. Chill 4 to 5 hours. Makes 10 servings.

Peggy Dunbar
Rocksprings

My husband's mother, Mary Dunbar, (Mrs. Ned), was one of those wonderful cooks who just don't seem to be around now. I was allowed to "inherit" her recipe box. This salad, although a favorite of Allen's, is either loved or hated by all who taste it.

Salads

Ileene Levitan's Italian Slaw

1 large cabbage
1 large onion
¾ cup sugar

Shred cabbage and thinly slice onion. In a large serving container layer cabbage, onion and sugar making 4 layers. Cover with the sauce and refrigerate.

Sauce
1 cup apple cider vinegar
¾ cup canola salad oil
2 teaspoons sugar
1 teaspoon salt
1 teaspoon dry mustard
1 teaspoon celery seed

Gently boil all ingredients until sugar is melted. Pour over cabbage and cool overnight. This is a wonderful crisp slaw and will last a couple of weeks in the refrigerator.

Vicki Rees
San Angelo

Cabbage Salad

1 head finely chopped cabbage
4 large diced tomatoes
1 large diced onion
fresh jalapeño chopped peppers to taste
8 limes (juice)

Stir cabbage, tomatoes, onions and jalapeños together. Pour over all the juice of the limes. Let stand for an hour or so and sprinkle with salt and pepper to taste.

Great rolled up in corn tortillas!

Joe W. Friend
Submitted by Glenda McMullan
Iraan

Italian Dressing
1 bottle Italian Dressing
3 tablespoons sugar
3 tablespoons Parmesan
cheese
1 raw egg

Combine all ingredients together in blender.
Nancy Johnson
Sonora

This salad dressing is very much like the one they serve at the Olive Garden. It is wonderful!

My brother Joe and I grew up during the "screw worm" era, so we did a lot of horse-back riding to gather the "wormies". We doctored them first with Tecolie as they came out of the shearing pen, then later with "White King". What a great day when the screw-worm was eradicated!

Sprinkle a little lemon juice over apples and bananas diced for salad to prevent discoloration. Or you can use 7-up to prevent the discoloration.

"Jones House" Spinach Salad

fresh spinach, washed and stems removed
1 cup salad oil
⅓ cup apple cider vinegar
1½ teaspoons salt
3 tablespoons sugar
1 tablespoon Parmesan cheese
¼ teaspoon garlic salt

Prepare spinach. Mix remaining ingredients in blender or shake in a fruit jar. Pour over prepared spinach.

Can add to spinach: chopped green onions, red onion rings, mushrooms, eggs, bacon, and/or sesame seeds. Add anything of your choice. The dressing is the best part!

Lolabeth Jones
Sonora

Apricot Salad

1 3-ounce package apricot gelatin
1 cup boiling orange juice
1 cup cold buttermilk

Dissolve gelatin in hot orange juice. Cool slightly. Add buttermilk. Pour into small mold and chill to serve.

Eva M. Rink
San Angelo

Don't let anyone see you make this! They may not like buttermilk, but they will love this. I even use it for a light dessert.

Cranberry Gelatin Salad

1 13-ounce can crushed or tidbit pineapple
1 6-ounce package cherry gelatin
1 cup cold water
1 16-ounce can whole cranberry sauce
1 cup chopped celery
½ cup chopped pecans

Drain the pineapple, saving the juice. Combine juice with enough water to measure 1 cup. Pour into saucepan and bring to boil. Add gelatin and stir until dissolved. Stir in 1 cup cold water. Chill until thickened. Add cranberry sauce, pineapple, celery and pecans. Chill until firm. Makes 8 to 10 servings.

Ethel Miller (Mrs. J.B.)
Ozona

Pink Panther Salad

1 large tub of whipped topping
1 large can cherry pie filling
1½ cups of pecans
1½ cups coconut
1 small can pink lemonade
1 can sweetened condensed milk

Combine all ingredients in a large bowl. Refrigerate. Can either be served as a salad or dessert. Will keep in the refrigerator up to 10 days. Makes 20 servings.

Edith Word Decker of Marfa
Submitted by Ethel Miller

Buster's Vinegar and Honey

Take 1 tablespoon honey and 1 tablespoon apple cider vinegar with 8 ounces of water. This is a cure-all for a cold, arthritis, hay fever, and old age - and if it doesn't work, call him and he'll bring over his castor oil. Buster is one of the very few men I know, that goes longer and stronger each day - nothing seems to slow him down. At 83 young, he still rounds up sheep and goats on foot, hauls his own stock, and counts goats with rocks. We love you Buster! —
—Nancy

This is basically a fat free recipe - enjoy!

Cherry Jello Salad

1 large box cherry jello
2 cups water
1 8-ounce package fat free cream cheese
1 8-ounce package plain yogurt
1 can lite cherry pie filling
1 12-ounce can diet Sprite

Heat the jello and the water in the microwave for 1½ minutes; set aside. Mix together remaining ingredients. Add in the jello mixture. Chill. May garnish with fresh cherries or mint leaves. Yields 10 servings.

Mary Beth Ince
Mason

Wine Salad

This salad was a favorite of Jerry's dad, M.C. Puckett. A few weeks before Thanksgiving or Christmas he would show up with the wine and say "don't you think it is about time to make the salad"?

1 medium bag small marshmallows
1 large bottle maraschino cherries
1 cup wine
½ pint whipping cream
1 tablespoon sugar
1 small can crushed pineapple, drained
2 cups chopped pecans

Cut maraschino cherries in half, reserve juice. Combine marshmallows, cherries, cherry juice, and wine in a large bowl, cover and set overnight. Stir 1 or 2 times. The next day whip the whipping cream with sugar until stiff. Fold together with wine mixture and remaining ingredients. Put in long Pyrex dish, cover with foil and put in the freezer. Serve frozen. Keeps several weeks.

I use Wild Cherry-Mogen-David wine, but I'm sure most any would be good.

Jane Puckett
Fort Stockton

Pretzel Salad

Crust
  2 cups broken pretzels
  1 cup melted margarine

Combine pretzels and margarine. Press evenly in bottom of 13x9x2 inch baking pan. Bake at 350° for 15 minutes. Let stand until cool.

Filling
  1 8-ounce package cream cheese, softened
  1 cup sugar
  1 9-ounce carton frozen whipped topping, thawed
  1 16-ounce can crushed pineapple, drained
  1 cup pineapple juice reserved
  1 cup water
  1 16-ounce package strawberry gelatin
  2 10-ounce packages frozen strawberries, partially thawed

Combine cream cheese and sugar, beating until smooth; fold in whipped topping. Spread creamed mixture on pretzel crust. Combine pineapple juice and water in saucepan, bring to a boil. Add gelatin, stirring until dissolved. Add strawberries and pineapple to gelatin mixture. Cool until partially thickened, then spoon evenly on cream layer; chill. Yields 16 to 20 servings.

Ethel Miller(Mrs. J.B.)

Ozona

I have so many fond memories in the kitchen with Ethel. She and I would do a lot of talking doing dishes (something I really miss.) She would always say, "Do unto others as you would have others do unto you." She is probably one of the best Christian women I know, and has set a wonderful example for her family. Thank you Ethel for being that example, especially for my children, Miles, Matt, and Preccia. This is something I hope I can hand down to my grandchildren. - Nancy

I served this one night at a Rib Supper at our Round House where the Allisons and the Johnsons were guests. Everyone at the supper wanted the recipe.

Poppy Seed Dressing
1½ cups sugar
2 teaspoons dry mustard
2 teaspoons salt
⅔ cup apple cider vinegar
2 cups oil
3 tablespoons poppy seeds

Stir thoroughly first 5 ingredients. Add oil and beat until thick; add poppy seeds.

Make half a recipe when you only need a small amount.

Nancy Johnson
Sonora

Poppy seed dressing is good with cantaloupe balls and fruit or excellent with the following combination: finely shredded red cabbage, thinly sliced avocado, and halves of fresh grapes.

Sauerkraut Salad

¾ cup sugar
½ cup vinegar
1 can drained sauerkraut
½ cup chopped celery
½ cup chopped onion
½ cup chopped green pepper
2 tablespoons pimento
1 teaspoon dill seed
¼ cup salad oil

Mix sugar and vinegar and bring to a boil. Pour the mixture over the other ingredients and place in covered container (wide-mouth jar, covered dish, etc.) and allow to sit for at least 24 hours. MMMM-good!

Martha Lee Meador
Eldorado

Pecan Rice Salad

1 7 to 8-ounce package wild pecan long grain rice
4 ounces feta cheese, crumbled
½ cup sliced green pepper
½ cup sliced yellow pepper
½ cup chopped green onions (tops included)
¼ cup pine nuts, toasted
1 2-ounce jar diced pimientos, drained
¼ cup olive oil
2 tablespoons tarragon white wine vinegar

Cook rice according to package directions. Cool slightly. Add next six ingredients. Combine oil and vinegar, salt and pepper to taste, and add to rice mixture. Cover and chill. Makes 8 servings.

Francine Hardeman
Sonora

Potato Salad

5 pounds potatoes, cooked
6 hard boiled eggs, crushed
1 teaspoon chili powder
2 teaspoons onion salt
juice of 2 lemons
1 can pimientos
1 cup dill or salt pickle
1 teaspoon black pepper
mayonnaise
salt to taste

Add salt last of all. Use enough mayonnaise to moisten.

This salad is better if left standing several hours or overnight in ice box before serving.

Mildred Zesch
Brady

Gerda Kothmann gave me this recipe. St. Paul Lutheran Church served this salad to the Hereford Association when they met in Mason.

Potato Salad for 50

12½ pounds potatoes
9 hard cooked eggs
1 cup onion, diced
2 cups pickles, chopped
salt and pepper
1 pint mayonnaise
3 tablespoons of mustard (optional)

Cook and dice potatoes. Chop eggs, onion, pickles and add in. Salt and pepper to taste. Mix in mayonnaise. Refrigerate.

The pickles you use may be sweet, dill, or sour.

Mrs. Jack Brown
Del Rio

Clipper Club

Originally formed as a bridge club in 1940, the Clipper Club has become a favorite social event of the Loma Alta neighborhood. Now it's roping for the young and old, games for the kids, good barbeque, and dancing under the stars. This is still a wonderful opportunity to take a break from busy ranch work and have a good visit with your neighbor.

57

Vermicelli Salad

1 10-ounce package twisted vermicelli, broken once
3 tablespoons lemon juice
3 tablespoons salad oil or French dressing
½ cup chopped celery
½ cup chopped bell pepper
½ cup green onion
½ chopped pimento - if no red bell pepper
½ cup chopped ripe olives

Boil vermicelli until done. Drain and rinse. When cool enough to handle with hands, make 3 mounds in a bowl. Sprinkle generously with Accent and add lemon juice and salad oil. Mix and cover tightly, refrigerate overnight. Next day add other ingredients. Salt, pepper and add mayonnaise. Blend; mix and let stand several hours or overnight.

The flavors seem to penetrate with time and get better.

Hope Huffman
San Angelo

Chicken Salad with Sundried Cherries

1 large, whole cooked chicken breast
¼ cup sundried cherries
2 teaspoons tarragon
2 tablespoons chopped pecans, toasted
salt and coarsely ground black pepper to taste
½ cup mayonnaise
¼ cup sour cream

Chop and shred chicken. In large bowl, mix chicken, cherries, tarragon, pecans, salt and pepper. In separate bowl, mix mayonnaise and sour cream; fold mixture into chicken. Mix well.

Brad Johnson
Chicago, Illinois

Shrimp Mousse

1 can tomato soup (undiluted)
1 package gelatin
½ cup warm water
2 3-ounce packages cream cheese, softened
1 cup real mayonnaise
1½ cups finely chopped celery
1½ cups chopped green onion
¼ teaspoon ground basil
dash cayenne pepper
1 pound cleaned and deveined chopped cooked shrimp

Bring soup to boil, dissolve gelatin in ½ cup warm water and add to soup. Then add softened cream cheese and blend until smooth. Fold in rest of ingredients. Pour into a mold sprayed with non-stick cooking spray and gel overnight.

Boil shrimp using seafood seasoning or shrimp boil for added flavor.

Joan Shackelford
Brenham

Chicken Salad

½ cup butter
2 cups mayonnaise
¼ cup fresh minced parsley
½ teaspoon curry powder
¼ teaspoon minced garlic
pinch marjoram
salt & white pepper to taste
4 cups cooked chicken breast
1 cup green seedless grapes
1 cup red seedless grapes
½ cup toasted slivered almonds

In small saucepan melt butter; cool to room temperature. Gently stir butter into mayonnaise, adding herbs and seasonings. Pour mixture over bite size pieces of chicken, grape halves, and almonds. Toss gently and chill until ready to serve. Can be made a day ahead.

Savannah Mayfield
San Angelo

Men, most of the time, do not care for chicken salad. My husband loved this recipe!

My husband's grandmother, Maude Rudasill used to serve this salad when she was hostess for a ladies luncheon.

Tuna Salad

1 tablespoon gelatin
½ cup cold water
2 6-ounce cans tuna, flaked
⅓ cup lemon juice
1 cup chopped celery
¼ cup chopped green peppers
1 cup salad dressing

Dissolve the gelatin in the water and add to above ingredients; pour into Pyrex dish and refrigerate until set.

Dressing
⅔ cup chopped cucumber
¼ cup chopped green pepper
¼ cup chopped radishes
3 tablespoons chopped green onions
salt to taste

Combine all ingredients and put on top of salad before serving.

Darlene Epperson
Rocksprings

A rancher's wife was late getting to hotel coffee shop one morning. Seeing her husband alone at the counter, she hugged him from behind and said, "I bet you are surprised to see me." The man, a total stranger, turned and said, "Lady, I sure am."

A Rancher's Reality

Well I was raised in central Texas on a small ranchin' place,
where my ancestors settled there was nary a trace,
of civilization like you see today,
but things have changed for the best they say.
The best I might contest,
for it is hard to see,
as I look around at the city folks a closin' in on me and my way of life,
a man is hard pressed to find a wife to put up with this livin' as hard as it is,
Ah they see the romance in the old west report,
the nostalgia and grace of a lost time an' place where folks travel no more.
So unless you're a big feller and own quite a spread,
with money from oil it is easy to buy bread,
but the small rancher finds it hard to even make grub
or get a hot bath in a cast iron tub,
and women are hard found that would get down on there knees and scrub the floors
as your grandmother did to please,
her hard workin' man who would pour his soul into the life of this land,
for the things that he loved and he'd ask nothin' from the good Lord above,
'cept a rain now and then,
to fill the tank above the pens.
But things aren't all that bad ya see,
there ain't many fellers left like me,
now I went to school so's not to be a fool above civilization,
growth and population booms.
See their pushin' and shuvin' and demanding more room,
w'y their trying to put farming out on the moon,
but for a while now they haven't much choice for if they won't eat beef we'll feed
'em soy,
beans that is a legume by chance,
w'y that old beef cow's kinda lost her romance,
in the hearts of some city folks who thinks meats bad for your health,
that animal's a treated like she's got wealth,
royalty I say,
why some folks think that a-way I don't know,
but if you read the bible in Genesis where God made heaven and earth,
he put the beast upon this land,
not to run it with an upper hand,
but to nourish the one that he called man.
So for the time bein' we'll raise artichokes,
'cause if they still plan on strivin' and getting ahead,
us dry land ranchers better work hard 'fore we go to bed,
for it's left up to us to feed this old world with little thanks
and sometimes even a cuss from our citified pears,
but we take it in stride and work through the day,
a sellin' our good for very little pay,
now I have few complaints as I lay down at night and listen to the coyote yappin' in
the clear moon light,
I thank God for this way of life,
and I wouldn't trade it for any strife,
it's peaceful and gracious like he meant it to be,
and I thank him for loanin' it to the likes of me.

Russell Rogers

This is Robert's special dish and we love it when he fixes it. Guests know they are special when they get Robert's German pancakes for breakfast. We are too!

Camp Toast
bread slices
1 tablespoon butter
1 tablespoon honey

Melt butter and honey together in iron skillet. Toast bread in skillet on each side.

Very good cooked on campfires, but equally as good prepared on the kitchen stove.

James Lee Leonard
Del Rio

German Pancakes

5 eggs
¾ cup milk
¾ cup flour
½ teaspoon salt
1 tablespoon sugar
clarified butter
softened butter
powdered sugar
lemons

Blend the first 5 ingredients together and let set in refrigerator overnight. The next morning gently stir with a spoon. Do not use an electric beater. Heat about 2 tablespoons of clarified butter in either a glass baking dish or well seasoned cast iron skillet; use something with high sides. Pour about ¾ cup batter into prepared dish and bake at 450° for 12 to 15 minutes. Immediately after baking, spread with softened butter, sprinkle with powdered sugar and squeeze half a lemon over pancake. Roll pancake up and sprinkle with more powdered sugar.

We like to eat it out of the dish so it stays hot. You can mix them up the morning you want them, but I have found out they cook much better if I mix them up the night before.

Robert Allison
San Angelo

Breakfast time was family time when the kids were at home. Yes, we all had to get up a little earlier, but it was worth it. The family together; eating, praying and bible reading. What fond memories.

Baked French Toast

4 large lightly beaten eggs
⅔ cup milk
3 tablespoons sugar
¼ teaspoon vanilla
6 1-inch thick slices of Texas Toast bread
½ stick butter

In a large flat dish combine the eggs, milk, sugar, and vanilla. Let the bread soak in the mixture in one layer for 2 minutes, turn and let soak until all the custard is absorbed. In a large flat baking dish melt butter in a preheated 400° oven. Add the bread in one layer. Bake for 15 minutes, turn the bread and bake for 10 minutes more. Serve with maple syrup or honey, dust with powered sugar and garnish with fresh fruit.

These freeze well. Keep some made up for a snack or company.

Joan Motl Tucker
San Angelo

Mrs. L.C. Brite's Pancakes

1¼ cups flour
½ teaspoon baking soda
½ teaspoon salt
1 teaspoon baking powder
1 teaspoon sugar
1 egg
1¼ cups buttermilk
2 tablespoons soft shortening

Sift together the dry ingredients into a mixing bowl. Stir in the next 3 ingredients. Cook on griddle and enjoy with plenty of syrup and butter.

Jane Brite White
Marfa

Pancakes

3 separated eggs
½ cup cottage cheese
½ cup plain yogurt
¼ cup skim milk
½ cup flour
¼ teaspoon baking powder
¼ teaspoon baking soda
¼ teaspoon salt

Mix dry ingredients, then add all others, folding in the beaten egg whites. Cook on slightly greased (vegetable oil spray) griddle.

Annette Lasater
San Angelo

I was born and raised in Sonora. At the present, I am associate editor for *Restaurants and Institutions Magazine*, a magazine for chefs and restaurant owners.

Gingerbread Pancakes

3 eggs
¼ cup plus 2 tablespoons light brown sugar
¾ cup buttermilk
¾ cup decaffeinated coffee, prepared
¾ cup water
3 teaspoons ground cinnamon
3 teaspoons ground nutmeg
3 teaspoons ground ginger
1½ teaspoons ground cloves
3 cups all-purpose flour
3 tablespoons margarine, melted
1½ tablespoons baking powder
3 teaspoons baking soda

In large bowl, combine flour and other dry ingredients. In separate bowl, combine wet ingredients except margarine. Add wet to dry; mix with wooden spoon until thoroughly wet but still very lumpy. Add margarine; mix briefly until blended. Batter should still be lumpy. Cook on 375° griddle until surface is covered with bubbles and edges look dry, turn gently, barely lifting off the griddle, and continue cooking about 2 minutes, or until a peak at their undersides reveals a golden brown.

Brad Johnson
Chicago, Illinois

Buttermilk Waffles

2 eggs
2 cups buttermilk
2 cups flour
½ cup vegetable oil
1 teaspoon baking soda
3 teaspoons baking powder
½ teaspoon salt

Preheat waffle iron. Beat the eggs and buttermilk in a bowl. Add the rest of the ingredients and beat until the batter is smooth. Bake in the hot waffle iron until steaming ceases. Usually about 4 to 5 minutes.

I mix mine up in the food processor. Batter will keep in fridge about 2 days.

Mimi Allison

Breakfast Pizza

1 pound pork sausage
1 8-ounce package refrigerated crescent rolls
1 cup frozen hash browns
1 cup grated cheddar cheese
6 beaten eggs

Cook and drain the pork sausage. Set aside. Separate dough and arrange on ungreased 12-inch pizza pan. Press seams together to form crust. Bake 2 to 3 minutes in 350° oven until dough begins to rise. Remove; layer pizza crust first with hash browns, eggs, sausage, and top with cheese. Bake at 350° for 20 to 25 minutes or until done.

Use 2 to 3 medium potatoes, baked and chopped for hash browns.

Serve with fruit and juice to top off your breakfast pizza!

Lori Woehl
Midland

We like to eat our waffles with applesauce and powdered sugar instead of syrup. However, McNeil eats his with applesauce, powdered sugar, and syrup. In the spring when the strawberries are in, we eat the waffles with strawberries and whipped cream. This has to be the very best breakfast of all. I like to fool myself that it is all right to indulge at breakfast.

This is a great breakfast for hard working cowboys and cowgirls to fill up on before going out to round-up goats and sheep during shearing.

Country Breakfast

I love to prepare the ingredients ahead of time. They are especially good fixed on an open camp fire, in an iron skillet, in the mountains.

potatoes
bacon
onions
eggs
canned green chilies
grated cheddar cheese

Cook and chop several potatoes. Fry several slices of bacon and crumble. Chop several onions and sauté in small amount of bacon grease. Add potatoes and heat through. Stir occasionally. Salt and pepper. Add several beaten eggs and one can chopped green chilies and pour over all. You can stir in the egg and green chili mixture or just let them sit on top. Cover and cook on low until eggs are done. Add grated cheese over the top, sprinkle bacon on top of cheese. Cover and let cook until cheese melts.

Kaye Pfluger
San Angelo

Sunshine Morning Cake

*I*rma entered her original recipe "Sunshine Morning Cake" in the Joske's Great American Housewares Fair Bake-off contest, in 1980 and was the winner in the cake division. Daddy gave it the name.

2 packages dry yeast
¼ cup warm water
2 sticks oleo
½ cup milk
2 tablespoons sugar
¼ teaspoon salt
3 beaten egg yolks
2½ cups all purpose flour

Dissolve oleo, milk, sugar and salt in saucepan on low heat. Cool to lukewarm. Add beaten egg yolks and yeast mixture to butter mixture. Mix well and stir in flour. Cover and refrigerate dough at least 4 hours.

Divide dough in half; store other half in refrigerator while working with first half. Roll first half dough very thin into an 18 or 19 inch square on a

Continued on next page

Sunshine Morning Cake (continued)

lightly floured surface. Spread ½ cinnamon-pecan filling on dough with spatula and roll up jelly roll fashion. Place in a well greased ten inch tube pan. Repeat process with remaining dough and filling. Place on top of first ring in tube pan having ends of the two rolls on opposite sides of the pan. Using a sharp knife cut through both rolls in several places, cutting to the bottom of the pan. Bake at 325° for 45 to 50 minutes. Cool slightly and remove from pan. Glaze top and let drizzle down sides.

Cinnamon-Pecan Filling
  3 tablespoons sugar
  1 tablespoon ground cinnamon
  ¼ cup milk
  3 tablespoons honey
  1½ cups finely ground pecans
  3 egg whites
  1 tablespoon cold water
  1 cup sugar

Combine sugar and cinnamon in saucepan; stir in milk and honey. Cook over low heat just until hot. Cool slightly and add pecans. Combine egg whites and water; beat until frothy. Gradually add one cup sugar, and continue beating until peaks form. Stir in pecan mixture.

Glaze
  2 tablespoons squeeze margarine or butter
  1 cup powdered sugar
  1 tablespoon milk
  ½ teaspoon vanilla

Combine all ingredients, stirring until smooth. Glaze cake.

Irma Woodard
Alamo Ranch, Kimble County
Submitted by daughter Paula Locke
Kerrville

Breakfast Casserole

3 split English Muffins
2 tablespoons soft butter
1 pound bulk sausage
1 4-ounce can chopped green chilies
3 cups grated cheddar cheese
1 cup sour cream
12 beaten eggs

Spread the cut side of each muffin with butter and place face down in a lightly greased 13x9 inch baking pan. Cook sausage in a skillet until browned, stirring to crumble; drain the grease. Sprinkle the sausage, green chilies and grated cheese over the muffins. Combine the sour cream and beaten eggs and pour over the sausage and muffins. Cover and refrigerate overnight. Remove from refrigerator and let stand 20 to 30 minutes. Bake uncovered at 350° for 40 to 45 minutes. Serves 8 to 10.

I have also made this with yogurt or light sour cream instead of the sour cream. Also you can substitute bread for the muffins.

Mimi Allison

A wonderful company breakfast when you don't want to be in the kitchen. We also serve it for Christmas morning breakfast with fresh fruit. I learned this one from my sister, Nan Beckwith, from Progreso.

Green Chilies and Eggs

10 eggs
½ cup flour
1 teaspoon baking powder
1 pint small curd cottage cheese or sour cream
1 pound Monterey Jack cheese
½ pound sharp cheddar cheese
½ cup margarine
2 small 7-ounce cans chopped green chilies

Beat eggs and add remaining ingredients. Bake at 350° for 25 to 30 minutes. Serves 5 to 6.

Linda Sue Gage
Iraan

The cowboys at our house request these eggs for breakfast when we're shearing.

Add water to omelets, milk makes eggs tough.

One Rise Cinnamon Rolls

Topping
  1 cup heavy whipping cream
  1 cup brown sugar
  1 cup chopped nuts to your desire

Let cream set to room temperature. DO NOT WHIP. DO NOT SUBSTITUTE. Mix brown sugar and cream in ungreased 9x13 inch pan. Let stand while preparing filling and dough mixture.

Filling
  ½ cup granulated sugar
  2 teaspoons cinnamon
  ½ cup soft butter

Mix the sugar and cinnamon. Spread the butter over the rolled out dough(following) and then sprinkle with the sugar cinnamon mixture.

Rolls
  3-3½ cups flour
  1 package yeast
  ¼ cup sugar
  1 teaspoon salt
  1 cup hot tap water
  2 tablespoons soft butter
  1 egg

In large bowl blend 1½ cups flour and next six ingredients. Beat 3 minutes at medium speed. Stir in remaining 1½ to 2 cups flour. Knead on floured surface for one minute. Roll dough into 7x15 inch rectangle. Spread filling over dough. Starting at long side, roll tightly, seal edges. Cut into 16 to 20 rolls. Place rolls on cream mixture. Cover and let rise until doubled 35 to 45 minutes. Bake rolls in preheated oven at 400° for 20 to 25 minutes. Cool 10 to 15 minutes before turning out on tray!

Glenda McMullan
Iraan

We've been blessed to meeting lots of people in our rodeo travels. This recipe is from the kitchen of Billie Kaye Harms (Mrs. Dennis Harms), Livingston, Montana. Hers is also a ranching family.

Sweet Rolls

I fixed these Sweet Rolls for the Sonora School System for 33 years. Since my retirement, it has been a privilege to fix my Sweet Rolls for many parties. Now I can share this recipe with everyone.

Melt together:
 1 pound butter
 3 cups sugar
 ¼ cup cinnamon

Mix together:
 3 cups warm water
 ½ cup sugar
 1 tablespoon salt - yes salt
 ⅓ cup oil
 3 tablespoons yeast

Let stand 5 minutes to soften. Stir in enough flour to make mixture into softball. Cover and let rise 30 to 45 minutes. Turn dough out on floured bread board. Roll dough out ½-inch thick. Spread with ½ melted butter and sugar mixture. Starting on the right side, roll dough into a large roll. Cut into slices ½-inch thick, place in deep pan and spread with remaining butter and sugar mixture. Let rolls rise 30 minutes. Bake in oven at 325° 25 minutes or until done.

The more the Sweet Rolls are made, the better they are. They need a lot of T.L.C.

Pauline Skains
Sonora

Vinegar Rolls

4 cups water
1 cup sugar
¼ cup apple cider vinegar
1 stick butter
2 teaspoons vanilla
3 cups biscuit mix
1 cup milk
2 tablespoons melted butter

In a saucepan put the water, sugar, vinegar, and butter. Bring to a boil and add vanilla. In a bowl mix the biscuit mix, milk, and butter; mix well and roll out ¼-inch thickness, sprinkle with ¼ cup sugar and 1 tablespoon cinnamon. Roll up and cut 1-inch thick pinwheels. Line a 13x9 inch Pyrex pan with pinwheels; pour hot vinegar, water mixture over them. Bake at 350° for 20 to 25 minutes or until pinwheels are browned.

Lynette Barnes
Rio Frio

Whole Wheat Bread

1 cup lukewarm water
2 packages dry yeast
1 egg, slightly beaten
½ cup sugar
2 teaspoons salt
2 cups white flour
1½ cups whole wheat flour

Mix together in a large pan or bowl. Let rise until double - about 1 hour. Put on lightly floured board and roll out with rolling pin. Cut with biscuit cutter. Melt ½ cup butter. Butter a bundt pan and save remaining butter to dip each biscuit in. Put side by side in bundt pan. Let rise again until double in size. Bake 350° for 30 minutes.

Vallree Draper
Sonora

This recipe has been adapted by me, but the original was used by my grandmother during the depression at her cafe in Leakey, Texas.

Health Bread

2 cups milk
1 cup cooking oil
3 yeast cakes
1 cup lukewarm water
4 eggs, beaten
4 teaspoons salt
½ cup sugar
½ cup molasses
1 cup water
5 cups whole wheat flour
7½ cups white flour
¼ cup wheat germ
1 cup uncooked oatmeal

Mix milk and oil together, dissolve yeast with lukewarm water. Mix egg, salt, sugar, molasses, and water together and add milk and the dissolved yeast. Knead the flour, wheat germ, and oatmeal together with other ingredients. Place in greased bowl. Add several teaspoons corn oil. Turn dough until covered with oil. Cover with damp cloth. Let rise until double. Knead again on floured board. Shape into 6 loaves. Put into greased pans. Let rise again. Bake at 375° for 45 minutes or until done.

This is very healthy!

Annette Lasater
San Angelo

I chanced to hear two old timers talking about Black Jack Ketchum robbing the train at Barnhart. First man said he was right because he was at Big Lake at the time and it was the talk of the neighborhood. Second man changed the story some and argued, "I know I'm right because I was holding the horses."

Breads

Light Crust Ice Box Rolls

2 cakes yeast - rapid rise is good
2 cups lukewarm water
½ cup sugar
½ cup shortening
2 teaspoons salt
1 egg
6 cups flour or bread flour

Dissolve the yeast in the lukewarm water. I add a little of the ½ cup sugar to this mixture. Cream the sugar, shortening, salt and egg together. Alternate flour and liquid until all flour has been added. Knead until smooth (I use a dough hook in my mix master for about 10 minutes.) Put in a greased bowl and cover with warm damp cloth and let rise until double. Punch down and shape into rolls in a greased pan. Let rise about 45 minutes to 1 hour in draft-free place. Bake in hot oven at 400° for 10 to 12 minutes.

This dough will keep up to a week in ice box. I also use this dough for cinnamon rolls. Let rise first time and roll out jelly roll style. Make a mixture of brown sugar, butter and cinnamon and spread on dough; roll up and cut for cinnamon rolls. Let rise and bake at 400° and ice with powdered sugar icing.

Peggy Wilson
Mertzon

I don't think there is anyone that does not like homemade bread. During shearing, lamb marking and calf marking time, I usually have these made up for sandwiches. I have a ham cooked and make sandwiches with miracle whip or mustard on the rolls with a ham slice between. Delicious!

73

My Mom baked these rolls and loaves of bread every Thursday. We had the rolls with butter and jam for our dinner on bread baking day.

This is a recipe that has been in my mother's family, Johnnie Dell Powell, for many years. When Joe and I married at a young age, she gave this to me and I have used it ever since. I haven't found another that works better for me. This recipe is a big hit with the grandchildren. They can also help roll it out - or knead it, and it still turns out perfectly.

Bran Ice Box Rolls

6 cups flour
2 packages yeast
¾ cup lukewarm water
1½ cups boiling water
1 teaspoon salt
1 cup bran cereal
¾ cup sugar
1 cup shortening
2 eggs

Dissolve yeast in lukewarm water. Pour boiling water over the bran, sugar, and shortening; mix. Add beaten eggs, yeast, salt and flour. Let rise to double. Pinch off and place in greased pan. Let rise and bake in hot 400° oven about 15 minutes.

Glenda Henderson
Ozona

Ice Box Rolls

1 quart milk
1 cup shortening
1⅔ cups sugar
2 yeast cakes
2 teaspoons baking powder
½ teaspoon baking soda
5 teaspoons salt
8-10 cups flour

Put milk, shortening and sugar in pan and heat to boiling point. Cool to lukewarm. Dissolve yeast cakes in ¼ cup of lukewarm mixture. Add yeast cake mixture and enough flour to make the consistency of cake batter (about 5 cups flour) to original mixture. Allow to rise in warm place for 2 hours. Then add baking powder, baking soda, salt and enough flour to make dough kneadable. Make out as many rolls as needed and refrigerate the rest. Use as needed.

Sugar and cinnamon, butter and raisins may be added to dough to make cinnamon rolls. Cook all rolls 10 to 15 minutes at 350°.

Marolyn Bean
Ozona

Superb Potato Rolls

2 packages dry yeast
½ cup warm water
2¼ cups warm milk (heat to 105°)
1 cup instant potato flakes
½ cup butter
½ cup sugar
1 teaspoon salt
2 egg yolks
6½ cups all-purpose flour (about)

Dissolve yeast in warm water. Heat milk and butter in saucepan; stir in potato flakes, sugar, and salt. Add to yeast mixture, stirring well. Add egg yolks, and ¾ cup of flour. Cover and let rise for 30 minutes, or until batter looks spongy. Gradually stir in remaining flour. Cover and let rise 45 minutes to 1 hour. Punch down. Turn onto lightly floured surface and roll out. Cut into desired shape and place on greased cookie sheet. Bake at 400° 12 to 15 minutes or until golden brown.

Francine Fields Hardeman
Sonora

Indian Bread

3 cups flour
½ tablespoon salt
1 tablespoon baking powder
¼ cup powdered milk
1⅔ cups lukewarm water

Mix well, roll up and fry.

Mary Elizabeth Baker
Rocksprings

Orange Butter for Hot Rolls
¼ cup frozen orange juice concentrate
1⅓ sticks butter or oleo
1 box powdered sugar

Cream the above together and put in covered container. Spread on warm rolls, toast or other breads.
Mrs. Richard Mayer
San Angelo

On the Santo Domingo reservation back in the 1960's, an old Indian squaw gave me this recipe in a conversation through her school age child. She also told me when there is a ring around the moon - it will rain in 3 days.

The 06 Ranch is a Texas "Century Ranch". The 06 brand was acquired around 1837 by David L. Kokernot, landowner and scout for Sam Houston during the battle of San Jacinto. Representing six generations in the ranching business, the grandson of Herbert Kokernot, Jr., Chris Lacy, is now managing the ranch for his mother, Mary Ann Kokernot Lacy. Still running the 06 brand, Chris and Diane continue the tradition of working cattle with a chuck wagon and a large remuda of registered quarter horses.

Diane's Biscuits

4 cups flour
3 teaspoons baking powder
1 teaspoon salt
1 teaspoon sugar
¾ cup butter (or ½ cup shortening + ¼ cup butter)
1¾ cups milk

Sift flour and dry ingredients in mixing bowl, add shortening and milk. Work with your hands on lightly floured board. Roll out and cut with biscuit cutter. Bake in preheated oven at 400° for 10 to 12 minutes, or until lightly brown. Makes 20 large biscuits.

Chris and Diane Lacy
06 Ranch
Fort Davis

Yeast Biscuits

6 cups flour
2 teaspoons salt
4 teaspoons baking powder
6 tablespoons sugar
10 tablespoons oil
2 yeast cakes in warm water
2 cups buttermilk (warm)

Sift together the flour, salt, baking powder, and sugar. Combine the oil, water, and buttermilk and add to the sifted ingredients, mix well, then roll out. Cut with biscuit cutter and let rise for 1 hour. Bake at 375° to 400° for 10 to 15 minutes or until golden brown on top.

Betsy Smith Coffey
San Angelo

Eddie Smith's Camp Bread

1¼ cups self rising flour
1 pint whipping cream

Mix together, adding a little more flour if sticky. Pat into hot cast iron skillet with a little oil in bottom. Bake at 450° until it looks brown on top.

This recipe is easy and probably should be doubled because its so good. It is great with anything, especially red beans. If by chance you have any left over, split and toast for breakfast the next day.

Eddie Smith
Sonora

Carolyn Wilson uses 4 tablespoons mayonnaise and 1 cup milk instead of the whipping cream and cooks the rolls in muffin tins at 425° for 12 to 15 minutes.

Cast Iron Skillet Cornbread

1½ cups cornmeal
½ cup flour
1 tablespoon sugar
2 teaspoons baking powder
¼ cup shortening (corn oil is best)
½ teaspoon salt
2 eggs
1¼ cups milk

Mix all ingredients together. Put the skillet (very important to use a cast iron skillet) on top of the stove and melt enough shortening to cover the bottom. Sprinkle a bit of cornmeal in the skillet. Pour in the batter. Sprinkle a bit of cornmeal on the top of batter. Bake at 400° for about 20 to 25 minutes.

This makes a generous serving.

Crystelle Childress
Ozona

James and Cyrstelle Carson Childress were married in 1941 in Ozona, Texas. They both came from ranching families. They have 2 children, Bob Childress and Carmen Childress Sutton.

Butane gas heating, lights, and stoves for cooking was a way of life in the 1940's. A wringer washing machine, making butter in a butter mold, chicken, eggs, a milk cow, and hound dogs were all luxuries on the Childress Ranch. Left over corn bread was fed to the hunting hounds.

My grandmother on my mother's side was Maude Brule, we called her Me-ma. She always told me the way to a man's heart is through his stomach. I spent part of one summer with her so she could teach me a few of her secrets of the kitchen. We always had this fried cornbread with greens or black-eyed peas. Robert loves it too. Maybe some of her recipes helped me get my man! Thank you Me-ma.

This recipe was given to my mother, Mrs. George T. (Virginia) Halsell, by a cattle ranchers wife who was living in Craig, Colo. We often had these muffins because they could be varied, the dough was always ready and there was always enough for company.

Me-ma's Fried Cornbread

1 cup cornmeal
1 teaspoon salt
boiling water

Heat meal and salt. Shake and stir while heating. Do not brown. Pour in enough boiling water to make batter thick but not too stiff. Make into patties in wet hands. Fry the patties in about ½ inch hot oil over medium heat. Drain on paper towels and serve hot with lots of butter. Be sure to make plenty.

Mimi Allison

Six Weeks Muffins

2½ cups sugar
1½ cups shortening
4 eggs
1 quart buttermilk
6 cups flour
5 teaspoons baking soda
2 teaspoons salt
2 cups bran cereal
4 cups bran buds (or use 1 cup Grapenuts +
3 cups buds)
2 cups boiling water

Mix the 4 cups bran buds with the boiling water and let stand. Cream shortening and sugar and add eggs. Mix flour, baking soda, and salt together; add with buttermilk. (You can use powdered buttermilk). Add cereals. Store in refrigerator and keep covered. When making a batch of muffins add a pinch (⅛ to ¼ teaspoons per 6 muffins of baking powder). Fill muffin pans ⅔ full. Bake at 350° for 10 to 15 minutes.

These muffins can be varied by adding raisins, nuts, dried fruit to the batch you're making. Dough will last 6 weeks in the refrigerator.

Judy Jarrett
Del Rio

Hush Puppies

¾ cup cornmeal
⅓ cup flour
1½ teaspoons baking powder
1 egg
½ large onion, grated
1 8-ounce can cream style corn
½ teaspoon salt

Mix all ingredients well. Drop by spoonfuls in hot grease.

Margaret Davis
Uvalde

Refrigerator Bran Muffins

1 cup bran cereal
⅔ cup boiling water
2 cups oatmeal (regular or 3 minute)
1 cup whole wheat flour
1 cup all-purpose flour
1 cup granulated sugar
2½ teaspoons baking soda
½ teaspoon salt
3 eggs (or 4 egg whites)
2 cups buttermilk
½ cup canola oil
½ cup each: chopped dried apricots,
chopped dates, coconut, chopped pecans and
raisins.

Add bran cereal to water, set aside to cool. Combine oats, flours, sugar, baking soda and salt. Add liquid ingredients mixed with cooled bran. Gently stir in fruits and nuts. Fill greased muffin pans ⅔ full. Bake at 375° for 15 to 20 minutes.

Doris Whitworth Kensing
Menard

Keep batter in the refrigerator for several weeks or freeze. Originally these muffins were very plain. I added the whole wheat flour, fruits and nuts. They are excellent to make in advance, and reheat in the microwave for a quick, nutritious breakfast.

This is my mother's recipe and the family today still enjoys it just as I did as a little girl. She was Pearl Hirst Pouncey, a pioneer resident of Fort Stockton and Pecos County.

For today's needs, I use vegetable shortening and either egg beaters or two egg whites. Sometimes, I use brandy and water instead of sour milk; omit baking soda and add ½ teaspoon baking powder. Simple to make - always good especially warm form the oven.

Holiday Tip: Double the recipe and bake in 4 smaller loaf pans. Ideal for friends and neighbors.

Banana Nut Bread

8 tablespoons shortening
1½ cups sugar
2 well beaten eggs
1 cup mashed bananas
¼ cups sour milk
½ teaspoon baking soda
2 cups flour
½ teaspoon salt
1 teaspoon vanilla
1 cups chopped nuts

Cream together the shortening and sugar. Add the beaten eggs, mashed bananas, sour milk, and baking soda. Then add the dry ingredients. Finally add the vanilla and chopped nuts. Bake in a loaf pan at about 350° for 1 hour.

Peggy Harral (Mrs. W. Alpheus)
Fort Stockton

Cherry Pecan Bread

¾ cup sugar
½ cup butter
2 eggs
2 cups sifted all-purpose flour
1 teaspoon baking soda
½ teaspoon salt
1 cup buttermilk
1 cup chopped pecans
1 10-ounce jar maraschino cherries, drained & chopped
1 teaspoon vanilla

This bread is good sliced and toasted for breakfast. We like this especially during the Christmas season.

Cream together sugar, butter, & eggs until light & fluffy. Sift together flour, baking soda, and salt. Add to creamed mixture with the buttermilk. Beat until blended. Stir in nuts, cherries and vanilla. Pour batter into greased 9x5x3 loaf pan. Bake in 350° oven for 55 to 60 minutes. Remove from pan, cool. Glaze with powdered sugar icing, if desired.

Molly Allison
San Angelo

The old-timers kept cows and consumed lots of dairy products. They butchered their own hogs and hung the hams, sausages, and bacon sides in the smokehouse. Lard was the shortening for frying and biscuits and butter was for the cakes. Eggs were plentiful and eaten often. There was a large productive vegetable garden and creamed potatoes were prepared with real cream— what's "Cholesterol?"

Apricot Bread

1 6-ounce package chopped dried apricots
1¼ cups sugar
2 tablespoons margarine
1 egg, beaten
2 cups sifted flour
2 teaspoons baking powder
½ teaspoon baking soda
½ teaspoon salt
1 cup nuts
½ cup orange juice
½ teaspoon orange extract

Pour boiling water over chopped apricots, allow to sit 20 to 30 minutes and drain. Cream sugar and margarine. Add remaining ingredients and mix. Do not over mix! Pour into bread pans and bake at 350° for 30 to 40 minutes or until done.

We eat this bread for breakfast or for dessert. It will keep for several days - if it lasts that long!

Ashley Johnson
Eldorado

Zucchini Bread

This is wonderful to fix when you have all that squash running out your ears in the summertime.

3 eggs
1 cup oil
2 cups sugar
2 cups grated zucchini
1 teaspoon vanilla
3 cups flour
1 teaspoon salt
3 teaspoons cinnamon
1 teaspoon baking soda
¼ teaspoon baking powder
1 cup chopped nuts

Beat eggs, sugar, and oil together. Add vanilla, stir in zucchini. Stir next 5 ingredients into first mixture. Fold in nuts. Pour into 2 well greased 9x5x3-inch loaf pans. Bake at 325° for 60 to 75 minutes.

Mimi Allison
San Angelo

My Favorite Recipe

Mimi Allison

I have a bad reputation about this dish. One night, I fixed a pan of this for dinner with Mary Ann and Richard Blake. We had a lovely dinner and the chicken was especially good so that we all had seconds. After dinner as I was cleaning up and putting away the leftovers, I noticed my chicken broth still in the jar in the ice box. I was curious as to how I could have made my sauce if I didn't use my broth. So I got to looking around in the ice box and found another container of broth. Upon closer inspection, I found that I had instead used my container of clothes starch! Well I didn't say a word to Mary Ann who was in the kitchen visiting with me. I very quietly walked around the corner to read the starch bottle for poison directions, or whatever, only to find the bottle didn't say anything about ingestion. When we went into the living room with the men and I very calmly asked how everyone was feeling; they immediately became suspicious and wanted to know why. As I was telling them what I had done to them, Richard, Mary Ann and I became hysterical. But Robert thought I was just awful and insisted I call the Poison Control. When I called, the lady on that end got to laughing and could hardly talk to me. She finally decided that starch is only made out of potatoes and that it shouldn't hurt any of us. After we settled down I confessed that the starch was used-I had already wrung out all the clothes in it! Now whenever I fix this dish the family wants to know if it has starch in it. It did make the prettiest, smoothest sauce ever!

Chicken Divine

1 chicken
4 stalks broccoli
4 tablespoons butter
4 tablespoons flour
1½ cups chicken stock
½ cup milk
½ teaspoon salt
¼ teaspoon pepper
2 eggs
1 tablespoon lemon juice
2 teaspoons curry powder
1 tablespoon grated
Parmesan cheese
½ cup grated yellow cheese

In large saucepan, stew chicken until tender. Skin, bone and chop. Split broccoli spears, cook and drain. Place broccoli spears in oblong baking dish cover with the chicken and set aside. Melt butter in saucepan and stir in flour. Slowly stir in stock and cook until thickened. Slowly add milk, salt, and pepper. Remove from heat. Stir some of the sauce into the lightly beaten eggs and then add the mixture to saucepan. Add lemon juice and curry powder. Pour over broccoli and chicken. Sprinkle with Parmesan and yellow cheese. Bake at 325° for 25 to 30 minutes.

Always check your container to make sure it contains what you think it contains!

You can use any "heat" of Mexican Velveeta: "mild" is nice for your Northern guests, "medium" for your acquaintances, and "hot" for your friends!

Muy Bueno Queso

1 chopped tomato
1 chopped bell pepper
1 chopped onion
1½ cups water
1 pound Mexican Velveeta cheese
½ cup oil
½ cup flour
garlic powder

Heat oil, mix in flour together stirring well. Don't brown! Stir in onion, pepper, tomato and water. Bring mixture to a boil. (Will be thick.) Reduce heat and add Mexican Velveeta cheese. Cover and let cheese melt on low. Stir occasionally.

Wendy Wardlaw
San Antonio

Tomato-Chipotle Salsa

2 pounds tomatoes
¼ cup olive oil
½ onion, peeled and chopped
4 teaspoons finely minced roasted garlic
½ cup minced fresh cilantro
2 canned chipotle chilies in adobo, chopped
¼ cup red wine vinegar
1 tablespoon salt
1 teaspoon sugar

Chipotle chilies are dried, smoked jalapeños. Canned "chipotles en adobo" are reconstituted chipotles and are available in most supermarkets.

Broil tomatoes (preferably over open flame on grill) until blackened. Reserve. In sauté pan set over medium flame, heat olive oil until lightly smoking. Add onion and sauté until caramelized, about 10 minutes. Remove from heat. In electric blender or food processor, combine onions, garlic and half of tomatoes. Pulse until finely chopped but not pureed. Add cilantro and chipotle chilies. Pulse again to mix. Peel, seed and chop remaining tomatoes. Fold into salsa with remaining olive oil, vinegar, salt and sugar. Yield: about 4 cups

Brad Johnson
Chicago, Illinois

Salsa

6-8 serrano peppers
chopped cilantro to taste
1 teaspoon salt
1 can diced tomatoes
diced onion or garlic to taste

Put 6 to 8 serrano peppers in water in a small saucepan and heat to boiling. Use number of peppers according to your own taste, whether you want it hot-hot or just tangy. After water reaches boiling, remove from stove and pull stems from peppers. Place whole peppers, chopped cilantro, and 1 teaspoon of salt in small electric food chopper and chop finely. (We like a lot of cilantro so we use about ¾ cup of coarsely-chopped cilantro.) Be careful not to run food chopper too long resulting in a foamy mixture. Only run it long enough to chop and mix ingredients adequately. Add tomatoes and chop again for only a short time. If you like, add a small amount of onion or garlic according to your own taste.

Jonella R. Pride
Robertson Ranch
Comstock

Pico de Gallo

2 finely diced large tomatoes
1 finely chopped large onion
3 finely chopped serrano chilies
¼ cup finely chopped parsley
¼ cup chopped cilantro
1 chopped clove garlic
1 teaspoon salt
black pepper to taste
juice of one lemon or lime
1 tablespoon salad oil
1 chopped avocado if desired

Combine, allow taste to blend, then serve.

Mary Ellen McEntire
Del Rio

*B*uy serrano peppers that are shiny-skinned. This will give you a more consistent pepper that is fresh and hot.
This is great on anything and adds a lot of zest to whatever you are eating.

Guacamole I
2 avocados
1 8-ounce package cream cheese
1 package green onion dip mix
1 teaspoon garlic powder
⅛ teaspoon oregano
1 teaspoon salt
1 tablespoon lemon juice
½ finely chopped onion

Combine all ingredients in mixing bowl and beat with mixer until smooth and creamy. Serve as a salad on lettuce leaf or as a dip.

Ground green hot pepper may be added for taste.
Betsy Smith Coffey
San Angelo

Guacamole

3-5 avocados
1-2 diced tomatoes
1 teaspoon salt
2 teaspoons lemon juice
Tabasco
2 tablespoons minced
    onion

Peel, seed, and mash avocados in bowl. Add salt, tomato, lemon juice, a few dashes of Tabasco, onion and mix thoroughly. Use amount of Tabasco to suit your own taste. Better to refrigerate until cold before serving.

Jonella R. Pride
Robertson Ranch
Comstock

Lemon juice should keep mixture from turning black while in refrigerator. Can also leave avocado seeds in mixture until serving to keep from darkening.

*M*y mother and father always have fresh canned New Mexico Chilies for us under the Christmas tree. They ranch in Southern New Mexico, as well as, west of Ft. Stockton. Jimmy and Suanne Delk are their neighbors in New Mexico.

Mexican Corn Bread

1 pound lean ground beef
1 teaspoon garlic salt
1 can cream style corn
½ cup buttermilk
½ cup liquid corn oil
3 slightly beaten eggs
1 cup yellow cornmeal
½ teaspoon baking soda
1 teaspoon baking powder
1 teaspoon salt
1 4-ounce can chopped green chilies
1½ cups grated Cheddar cheese

Brown ground beef, drain and season with 1 teaspoon garlic salt. Set aside. Mix all remaining ingredients except meat and cheese. In a large 9x13 inch greased pan, place ½ batter, a layer of cheese, ground meat, a layer of cheese, and top with remaining batter. Bake at 375° for 45 to 55 minutes.

Apryl McDonald
San Angelo

Suanne's Green Chilies

1 large can of green chilies (New Mexico's are the best)
1 pint of sour cream
garlic salt
cheese

Layer chilies, sour cream, and garlic salt in baking dish. Repeat until chilies are all used. Top with cheese. Bake at 350° for 10 to 15 minutes.

Molly Allison
San Angelo

These chilies go great with pinto beans. Being quick and easy, I take it to pot luck dinners where it's always a hit.

Healthy Whole Wheat Tortillas

2 cups white flour
1 cup whole wheat flour
1½ teaspoons baking powder
½ teaspoon salt
⅓ cup applesauce
1 cup warm water

Mix flour, baking powder, and salt together in a large bowl. Make a dip in the center of these dry ingredients; add applesauce and warm water. Knead with hands for about 5 minutes to form dough and let stand covered for 25 minutes. Form about 20 balls out of the dough and let rest for 5 more minutes. Roll out each ball to about 4 or 5 inches round on a lightly floured board. Cook each side on a hot griddle or skillet for 1 to 2 minutes or until covered with bubbles. If the bubbles get too big, press them down with a dry, clean dish cloth.

Elaine Wardlaw
Del Rio

Using applesauce instead of lard or oil reduces most of the fat.

Spanish Dressing

2 packages Mexican mix and bake cornbread
1 can mushroom soup - no water
1 medium onion
1 stick oleo
6-8 cooked and drained yellow squash or zucchini
1 small jar pimentos
1 pound grated Mexican Mild Velveeta cheese

Mix and bake cornbread according to package directions. Sauté the onion in the oleo. Mix squash that has been well drained with cornbread along with the onion. Add remaining ingredients and bake at 350° for 30 to 45 minutes or until it bubbles. This freezes well.

Erica Morriss
Sonora

This recipe was given to me by my sister-in-law from Dilley Texas. It is a family favorite.

A favorite at our house that freezes well. If you want only a mild hot taste use only 2 peppers. Do not cut them up.

Mexican Stew

1 4-6 pound roast (beef or mutton)
2 cans whole tomatoes
1 large onion
3 cups chopped potatoes
2 large stalks chopped celery
2 cups baby carrots
2-4 whole jalapeño peppers

Salt and pepper meat. Brown meat very brown. Remove from pan and cut into 1 to 2 inch chunks. Return to Dutch oven and add tomatoes, onion and some water and stew for 45 minutes. Add celery and carrots and stew for another 20 minutes. Now add potatoes and peppers and stew all until done. Thicken slightly with cornstarch.

LaVerne Reeh
Doss

To me, a warm bowl of chili and home just goes together. Mom made the best-and her mother before her! Mom said my grandmother clipped this recipe from a San Antonio paper 40 years ago. It has since been modified to suit my family's own taste and it is a long-time favorite! When chili is done you can add a can of tomatoes, chopped, and/or 2 cans ranch style beans - yummy!

San Antonio Chili

3 pounds ground beef
6-8 cups water
3 cloves chopped garlic
2 tablespoons sugar
1½ teaspoons oregano
¼ cup oil
6 tablespoons chili powder
1½ teaspoons ground cumin
½-1 teaspoon cayenne pepper
3 tablespoons paprika
3 teaspoons salt
4 tablespoons cornmeal
2 tablespoons flour

Heat oil in large pot. Add meat and sear over high heat until gray (not brown). Add garlic and water. Cover and cook at a bubbling simmer 1½-2 hours. Add all remaining ingredients except cornmeal and flour. Cook 30 minutes at same simmer. Mix cornmeal and flour together then sprinkle in slowly as you stir with the additional cup of water. If chili is too thick, adjust accordingly with more water. Cook 5 minutes.

Nan Chandler
Dryden

Guiso

1 round steak, cubed (small)
1 can Rotel tomatoes
½ cup cilantro
1 small garlic pod
3 green chilies
4 tablespoons flour

Brown steak in skillet with a little oil or bacon drippings. Turn temperature down and add half full skillet of water. Cover and simmer until water turns brown and add flour to thicken. May need to add a little more water. Cook 30 minutes. Blend in blender 1 can Rotel tomatoes, ½ cup cilantro, garlic, and green chilies. Add to meat mixture and cook 30 more minutes or until meat is tender.

Nancy Johnson
Sonora

This authentic recipe came from a lovely Mexican lady who brought it to a church dinner. I wish I knew her name, because she should get the credit.

Mexican Casserole

1 pound ground meat
1 tablespoon chili powder
1 can ranch style beans
1 can stewed tomatoes
1 cup uncooked rice
1 cup cheese

Brown meat; add chili powder, then beans, tomatoes (mashed or blended), and 1 can full of water from the bean and tomato cans. Then add uncooked rice. Pour into a large casserole dish, allowing room for rice to expand. Cook until rice is done at 350°. Put cheese on top before serving. This is good with picante sauce and tortilla chips.

Most men like this quick and easy main dish.

Freida Davenport
Sheffield

Never be afraid to have guests for a meal. If they are unexpected just add water to the gravy.

Shared by a lifelong friend also in the ranching business in the Rio Grande Valley. Jonnye Glee was my roommate at Texas Tech and we have shared many good times and good meals together in the past. I fixed this for a bunch of high school kids at a fajita supper and it disappeared fast! — Mimi

Spanish Rice

½ cup brown or white rice
onion rings
bell pepper rings
salt, pepper, garlic powder, cumin
chicken broth powder
1 cup water
fresh or canned tomatoes

Cover bottom of casserole or skillet with oil. Brown the rice until it is wheat-like. Add a few onion rings and bell pepper rings. Add salt, pepper, garlic powder and cumin. Fry a little more. Immediately add chicken broth powder mixed with 1 cup water. Stir; add tomatoes and more water if necessary and cover. Do not stir until done.

You may substitute carrots, peas, etc. for vegetables.

Jonnye Glee Dooley
Uvalde

Fried Mexican Rice

1 cup uncooked white rice
1 chopped onion
1 clove garlic
1 teaspoon salt
black pepper
1-2 tomatoes
1 hot green pepper
2-3 tablespoons bacon fat

Brown raw rice in hot fat. Add other ingredients. Mix together well. Add enough hot water to cover rice. Cover. Cook slowly without stirring, about 30 minutes or until rice has absorbed the liquid.

Can use canned tomatoes instead of fresh.

Mary W. Brumley
Del Rio

Shearing Day or Shade Tree Burritos

1-2 pounds ground meat
1 can stewed tomatoes or Rotel tomatoes
1 can drained corn
2 cans pinto beans or homemade
1 can Cheddar cheese soup or nacho cheese soup
12-30 regular size flour tortillas or 10-12 extra large size

optional:
cooked rice or vermicelli
black olives
chopped onions

Brown meat and drain. In large pot stir in all other ingredients and heat until mixed well. Fill each flour tortilla with a large spoonful of mixture.

I have tried many different combinations and they are all good. I usually make the burritos the night before by filling them, wrapping each one in foil and refrigerating. Early the next morning, I heat them in a jelly-roll pan in the oven just until hot. I then load them into a good clean ice chest where they stay warm until lunch. Take along another ice chest with hot sauce and cokes for a good picnic.

Carolyn Earwood
Sonora

This is such an easy meal that pleases a diverse group of people from our ranch hands to my little girls. We have one place we shear on the ranch that does not have a house or any facilities besides a hose to wash our hands and a shade tree. Plan on 4 small or 3 large burritos per man, less for women or children.

The Dunbars came to Texas in 1817 when William Elliot Dunbar, my great, great, great-grandfather, moved to Ellis County where he ranched for thirty years. Since then his many descendants have ranched in several counties around the Edwards Plateau. The Dunbars continue to work their livestock as a close family. My sister and brother, Tonya and Ned Allan, and I pooled our money and bought two Registered Angora nannies to build our own business and herd.

Quickie Burritos

1 pound ground meat
1 can Ranch style beans
1 can Cheddar cheese soup
chili powder to taste
garlic salt to taste

Brown the ground meat and add ranch style beans. Add Cheddar Cheese soup, chili powder and garlic salt.

Serve with tortillas, lettuce, tomatoes and picante sauce.

Tyann Dunbar

Portuguese Tortillas

1 onion
1 bell pepper
1 poblano pepper if desired
1 can diced tomatoes
seasonings: chili powder, oregano, garlic powder, comino
cheeses: Monterey Jack and enchilada cheese
corn tortillas

Cut up onion and bell pepper in strips or small pieces. Sauté in small amount of oil in skillet. Can also add some strips of poblano pepper if you desire. Sauté until tender and add chili powder (2 tablespoons), oregano, garlic powder, and comino to taste. Shred Monterey jack and enchilada cheeses—need about ½ to 1 pound total of cheese. Add to mixture in skillet and stir until melted. Add 1 can diced tomatoes to mixture and let simmer. Slice 12 to 16 corn tortillas into narrow strips. Fry in hot oil until crisp and drain on paper towels. Put tortillas strips onto platter and pour cheese mixture over the strips. Should place in 350° oven until heated through and serve.

Good with guacamole and pinto beans.

Jonella R. Pride
Del Rio

Sauce for Chicken Portuguese a la Siesta

1 cup chopped onion
1 cup chopped bell pepper
3 tablespoons cooking oil
2 cans whole tomatoes
1 tablespoon salt
½ tablespoon pepper
½ tablespoon ground comino
1 tablespoon garlic powder
1 tablespoon chili powder

Sear onion and bell pepper in oil. Chop the tomatoes and add to the onions and bell pepper along with remaining ingredients. Pour sauce over breast of chicken that has been baked, poached, or broiled. Cover with grated or sliced cheese and slip under broiler until cheese is melted.

Portuguese Tortillas are made by pouring sauce over tortillas that have been cut in strips and fried crisp.

Mary Ellen McEntire
San Angelo

Back in the days when Mrs. Crosby's Restaurant was flourishing in Ciudad Acuna across the river from Del Rio, everyone loved to go over and eat her Chicken Portuguese. A friend of mine wheedled the sauce recipe out of the chef at La Siesta Motel.

Mexico's Delicious Bean Loaf

Submitted in memory of my mother, Mrs. W.R. Nicks, of Eldorado and my aunt, Mrs. R.V. Sewell, of Sonora. I am a retired Spanish teacher and studied in Mexico. This recipe was served among the elite in Mexico City.

2 tablespoons oil
2 cups pinto beans, cooked, drain and mashed
1 medium onion, sliced thin
1 garlic clove, chopped
1 tablespoon chili powder
1 tablespoon sugar
1 tablespoon pepper sauce
1 tablespoon comino seed
1 tablespoon oregano
salt to taste
6-8 chili petine peppers
2 plantain bananas
½ pound grated Cheddar cheese

Put 1 tablespoon of oil in a skillet and lightly fry onion and garlic. Remove and mash the two together. Add chili powder, sugar, pepper sauce, comino seed, oregano, salt, chili petine peppers, and mashed pinto beans. Mix well with hands and form into 4 small loaves or 1 large loaf. Return to skillet to heat flipping over and over. This will form into a shape like a football. Remove and put slit in top of loaf, open up a little and add cheese. Split bananas in half and sauté them in 1 tablespoon oil. Put bananas on top of loaves and place in a preheated oven at 350° until cheese melts and bananas are slightly brown.

Willie Ruth Meckel
San Angelo
1916-1995

Texas Chalupa Beans

1 pound pinto beans (uncooked)
1½ pounds lean pork roast
7 cups water
1 tablespoon cumin
1 tablespoon chili powder
1 tablespoon salt (or to taste)
2 cloves garlic
1 tablespoon oregano
½ cup chopped onion
1 4-ounce can chopped green chilies
1 large jar pimentos

Clean the beans and cut the roast in about four large pieces. Put all together in large pot. Cook a long time until beans are done and meat cooks to pieces. Spoon into bowls over fritos. Serve topped with chopped onion, tomato, avocado, and grated cheese.

Savannah Mayfield
San Angelo

Chilies Rellenos

1 can chopped green chilies
8 ounces grated sharp cheese
½ cup milk
½ teaspoon dry mustard
4 eggs
½ teaspoon salt

Beat eggs well. Add milk, salt, and dry mustard. Layer chili and cheese in baking dish sprayed with non-stick vegetable spray. Pour egg mixture over top. Bake at 350° for 35 minutes.

Mary W. Balch
Sonora

These chili rellenos are excellent served with roast or ham. Can be used for brunch or supper dish.

This recipe is from Alice Locke who died in 1949. Even though my mother-in-law probably never set foot on the Bluebonnet Trail, she was quite a pioneer and raised ten children on her Tamale Pie. A recipe handed down from a previous generation, been a regular in our home, and passed on down to the next generation.

My recipes come from the three most important and influential women in my life. All are excellent cooks; they all cater too. The enchilada recipe was passed on to me by my mother and cooked successfully the first try. This is pretty easy to make and delicious to eat.

Tom's Mother's Tamale Pie

1½ pounds ground beef
1 large chopped onion
1 minced clove garlic
1 can whole kernel corn
1 can tomato sauce
1 cup cornmeal
3 beaten eggs
2 cups milk
2 teaspoons chili powder
salt and pepper to taste
1 can pitted olives

Brown beef, onion, and garlic together. Add corn and tomato sauce and cook for about 15 minutes. Mix meal with eggs and milk and add to first mixture with the remaining ingredients. Mix together and bake 1 hour at 325° in a casserole dish.

Paula Woodard Locke
Alamo Ranch, Kimble Co.
Kerrville

Cream Chicken Tacos

1 medium chopped onion
2 cans cream of chicken soup
1 large can evaporated milk
2 cans chopped green chili
1 can Rotel
½ pound Velveeta cheese
2 dozen corn tortillas
1 package boiled boneless chicken breasts

Sauté onion in a little butter. Add the other ingredients and heat until cheese melts. Cut tortillas into quarters and layer with soup mixture in a casserole dish. Bake at 350° for 45 minutes.

Sheri White
San Angelo

Enchilada Sauce

1 stick oleo
½ cup flour
3 cups water
3 tablespoons chili powder
1 tablespoon salt or less
1 tablespoon garlic powder
1 tablespoon cumin
½ teaspoon black pepper

Melt oleo and slowly stir in flour to make a thick paste. Slowly add water to flour mixture. Add chili powder, salt, garlic powder, cumin, and pepper. Cook until thick.

This is one to try, especially if you like enchilada sauce from your favorite restaurant.

Cheese Enchiladas
1-2 pounds grated Longhorn cheese and
Monterey Jack (mix 1:1)
12 corn tortillas
1 onion chopped
cooking oil

Add the chopped onion to the grated cheese. Dip 1 tortilla at a time in hot oil, pat on paper towel to remove excess oil, and place in long pan with sides. Put 1 tablespoon or more of onion and cheese mixture in tortilla roll up tight with seam side down. Pour enchilada sauce over top. Sprinkle with cheese and bake at 350° until cheese melts.

Nancy Johnson
Sonora

A wonderful chef at the Driskill Hotel in Austin shared this with me. I had never been able to fix good enchiladas until this recipe. If my family knew I was going to fix MY ENCHILADAS, they always found another place to eat! This one is worth trying.

These are the enchiladas Robert likes best. He will eat them for any meal of the day and especially likes them with an egg or two on the top. One time my brother, Clay, was eating at a Mexican food restaurant in College Station and ordered flat enchiladas. The cook obviously did not understand his request. When his plate came you could tell the rolled enchiladas had just been smashed down flat. We laughed all night about it! He now only orders flat enchiladas in West Texas. —Anita

Old Style Flat Enchiladas

1 recipe enchilada sauce
12 corn tortillas
1 small diced onion
2 cups grated cheese

In small iron skillet heat about ½ inch oil. Briefly dip each tortilla in the hot oil to soften. After heating in oil, dip each tortilla in enchilada sauce. As you dip the tortillas you will stack them with a layer of grated cheese, diced onions and spoonful of sauce between each layer. Stack enchiladas 3 deep and top off with some sauce. Slip into oven only long enough to melt the cheese. For a real treat top the stack off with a fried egg.

Deep Red Enchilada Sauce
4 tablespoons shortening or bacon drippings
2 tablespoons flour
1 8-ounce can tomato sauce
8 tablespoons ground chili powder
¼ teaspoon garlic powder
salt to taste

Brown the flour in the shortening. Add tomato sauce, chili powder, garlic powder, and salt. Cook about 15 minutes at very low heat. Add hot water if the sauce becomes too thick.

Mimi Allison

Enchiladas

1½ pounds ground beef
1 cup chopped onion
1½ teaspoons ground cumin
4 teaspoons chili powder
1 cup water
2 crushed cloves garlic
1½ teaspoons salt
½ teaspoon pepper
1 cup sour cream
2 cups taco sauce
12 corn tortillas
1 pound grated Monterey Jack cheese

Brown meat and onions; drain. Add the next 6 ingredients. Simmer 10 minutes uncovered. Stir until most of the liquid is gone. Grease a 9x13 baking dish. Pour ½ cup taco sauce on bottom of pan and arrange 6 tortillas to cover. Pour another ½ cup sauce evenly over tortillas. Add beef mixture that has been mixed with sour cream, sprinkle on ½ of the Jack cheese and add 6 tortillas lightly on top of cheese. Add remaining taco sauce and cheese. Cover with foil. Bake at 350° for 40 minutes. Remove foil and continue baking 5 minutes.

Shirley Martin Menzies
San Angelo

This recipe was given to me by a very good friend a long time ago.

Georgia Miers Paul's Enchiladas

Gebhart's Enchilada Sauce (use only Gebhart's)
browned hamburger meat
Velveeta cheese cut in small sticks
grated Cheddar cheese
corn tortillas
chopped onion

Soften tortillas in hot grease and dip into heated enchilada sauce; fill with meat, piece of Velveeta cheese, and onions. Roll and put in pan. Cover with sauce, grated cheese and onions. Bake at 300° for 20-30 minutes.

Susan McBee
Del Rio

This was a specialty of Georgia's and a favorite of her children and their friends. The ingredients are the key to this recipe's success. DO NOT SUBSTITUTE!

These enchiladas are legendary! This recipe comes very close to the secret recipe dad uses; however, his are always better! Enjoy!

Dad's Enchiladas

2 pounds ground beef
1 chopped onion
1 tablespoon chili powder
1 teaspoon comino
1 teaspoon garlic powder
½ teaspoon thyme
½ teaspoon oregano
¼ teaspoon pepper
1 teaspoon salt
4 tablespoon cornstarch
4 cups water
corn tortillas
grated American cheese

Brown and drain the ground beef. Mix the cornstarch with the water to make a paste. Mix all the ingredients, except for the tortillas and cheese, together with ½ the meat and heat over medium-high heat to a soft boil. Soft fry your tortillas (fold in enchilada shape as you fry and don't fry too long). Fill with meat mixture and grated American cheese. Top with sauce and more cheese. Put in oven to melt cheese.

I have used this sauce with chicken and plain cheese enchiladas and they are excellent. I have also substituted with flour tortillas and added refried beans and they are awesome!

Wendy Wardlaw

San Antonio

Baked Guacamole Enchiladas

3 peeled and mashed avocados
juice of ½ lemon
salt and pepper to taste
½ onion, finely minced
2 tablespoons canned mashed tomatoes
garlic flavoring if desired
12 corn tortillas

Dip tortillas in hot oil until just softened. Mash tomatoes and mix with other ingredients; place a portion on each tortilla. Roll or fold over and arrange in a baking dish. Cover with sour cream and grated Longhorn cheese. Bake at 350° for thirty minutes.

Mary Martha Gearhart
Marfa

This came from a dear old friend who had traveled all over the world. Her husband was in the British Diplomatic Service. She said one of the thrills of her life came when Douglas MacArthur asked her to dance. He said he liked her long legs!

On a horse the cowboys hoped would be a bucking exhibition, the notorious Booger Red just leaned forward and didn't do a thing as the horse pitched with him. Seeing a very disappointed youngster, Red leaned back, crossed his leg in front of the horn, looked over his shoulder and said. " I thought you said this horse might buck."

101

Sour Cream Chicken Enchiladas

12 corn tortillas
½ cup cooking oil
1 cup chopped cooked chicken
¾ cup chopped onion
2 cups grated Monterey Jack cheese
4 jalapeño peppers (seeded and cut into strips)
¼ cup margarine
¼ cup flour
2 cups chicken broth
1 cup sour cream

Sauté peppers in margarine in saucepan. Add flour, stirring until smooth. Add broth gradually. Cook over low heat until thick and bubbly, stirring constantly. Stir in sour cream until heated thoroughly. Soften tortillas one at a time in hot oil for 15 seconds on each side. Combine chicken, onion and 1 cup cheese in a bowl. Spoon 3 tablespoons of chicken mixture onto each tortilla. Roll to enclose filling, place seam side down in a baking dish, and pour sauce over enchiladas. Bake at 425° for 20 minutes. Sprinkle with remaining cup of cheese and bake 5 minutes longer. Makes 4 servings.

Brett Johnson
San Angelo

Pico De Gallo

4 roma tomatoes
3 bell peppers
2 onions
salt, pepper and garlic salt to taste

Chop vegetables and add seasonings; stir well. Add chopped jalapeño if you like it hot. You may add chopped avocados to this as well, for a really different taste.

Donna Kaye Herring
Ozona

Use this as a dip, put it on beans, or use with fajitas. The longer it sits, it will become juicy and really good.

Growing up on a ranch, we always had a garden and this is best made from fresh garden tomatoes. We usually had a few extra for dinner or supper and Mama always had a pot of beans and this could be made up really quick.

Tony's Green Enchiladas

1 bunch of cilantro
fresh garlic
2-2½ pounds tomatillos, wash and remove
husks
1 large yellow onion
6 chicken breasts
corn tortillas (white corn tortillas roll easily,
yellow ones crumble when cooked)
white cheese (mozzarella)
chicken bouillon
2-3 jalapeños

Boil chicken in stew pot with onion and garlic clove for about 1 hour. Remove chicken. Boil tomatillos with 1-2 jalapeños in the chicken broth. Boil about 30 minutes until they break open. Blend cilantro and fresh garlic. Pour the tomatillos on top and fill blender. Dice, not too much. Brown chopped onion. Add tomatillo sauce and add chicken bouillon. Drain and cool chicken breast. Tear into small pieces, shred. Soften tortillas in oil (too hot makes them crispy). Fill tortilla with small amount of chicken and sauce, then roll. Arrange in pan. Pour remaining sauce on tortillas and top with shredded mozzarella cheese. Bake at 350° for about 30 minutes or until hot throughout.

These freeze nicely. Keep some of the sauce to add later if needed.

Molly Allison
San Angelo

These are so good. Tony has made these for us for years. I asked her to tell me how so that I could actually cook these when Tony wasn't available.

This family favorite recipe was given to me by the late Mrs. Modell Tisdale of Eldorado several years ago.

Enchilada Casserole

1 pound hamburger meat
½ stick oleo
1 large chopped onion
2 cans cream of chicken soup
1 large can evaporated milk
1 can Rotel
1 can chopped green chilies
8-10 corn tortillas
lots of grated cheese

Brown the meat, oleo and onion in a large skillet. Add the next 4 ingredients. Cut tortillas in fourths and place in bottom of 9x13 inch Pyrex dish. Cover with mixture and continue layering until mixture is used. Bake at 350° until bubbly. Top with grated cheese.

Freezes nicely.

Ora Deal (Mrs. Otis)
Eldorado

Sulema Martinez of Ozona follows the New Years tradition of giving these wonderful buñuelos to the Ingham family. Many of us have picked up various customs from the different cultures around us and have made them part of our families to pass on.

Buñuelos

4 cups flour
½ cup sugar
1 teaspoon baking powder
pinch of salt
2 eggs
1 cup milk
2 cups vegetable oil
¾ cup sugar
cinnamon to taste

Mix first six ingredients together. Make into small balls as you do for tortillas. Roll out paper thin. Heat the oil until hot and brown the rolled bunuelas on both sides. Drain on paper towels and sprinkle each with sugar and cinnamon mixture.

Phyllis Ingham
Ozona

Field Dressing A Deer

There are two old wives' tales taught to hunters with regard to field dressing.

1) Don't bother cutting the jugular. This will mess up a trophy. Field dressing will remove the blood if the bullet hasn't.

2) Don't bother cutting off the tarsal glands because during the rut you may transfer a foul scent to the meat while field dressing.

Of course, if your hunting buddies are like mine you will pay a big price (maybe even kitchen duty) for such a bold act. A way to avoid this unfounded ridicule is to wait until you've completely finished field dressing, then carefully cut off the glands. This way you won't insult anyone and hopefully will leave more time for the more important things—like measuring the spread of your trophy buck.

The field dressing procedure is the same for whitetail, axis or mule deer. All that is necessary is a drop point, lock back knife with at least a 3½-inch blade.

Many old timers recommend splitting the deer from stem to stern in the field. This isn't necessary in most West Texas situations, nor desirable. Splitting the pelvic and completely opening the chest cavity is better done in camp for two reasons. You will protect the meat from contamination and the job will be easier in camp where you will have better tools and facilities for hanging the carcass.

1) Prop the deer with its legs in the air, head uphill. Use stones to raise the hips and shoulders.

2) Remove genitalia.

3) Starting at the base of the sternum, pinch the skin and gently insert the knife blade, making a two inch cut. Slip two fingers into this cut, lifting the hide away from belly muscles, and slowly pull the hide away, exposing the belly muscle sheath. Cut down and around the genital area. The whole idea is to make the cut without puncturing the pouch and intestines.

4) Now using the same two fingers as a guide, carefully cut open the thin layer of belly muscle from base of sternum to pelvis. The intestines will begin to bulge outward.

6) Slice the diaphragm away from the chest wall, then reach up into the neck area as far as possible and cut the windpipe free. Pull outward releasing the esophagus, heart, lungs and liver.

7) Slice down between the hams to the pelvic girdle, then cut a two inch circle around the anus. Carefully core the pelvic canal, remembering that the bladder is inside. Core away all connecting tissue. Next, core around the bladder itself until you've connected with your other cuts. Now you can remove the entire excretory tract.

8) Roll the deer on its side and pull away all the innards.

9) Prop the deer - head up to allow drainage. Transport back to camp. Rinse cavity with hose if available.

Brett Carpenter

At one time, the ranchers of the highland area ran thousands of sheep and goats. This era ended in the 60's when predators became too much too handle. Here is a recipe that is a family favorite.

Great for goat, too! Takes awhile, but well worth it!

Grandmother Mitchell's Baked Lamb

lamb
salt, dry mustard, black pepper, garlic
vinegar
lemon
onion

Remove all fat and loose skin from the lamb. Sprinkle liberally with salt, dry mustard, black pepper and some garlic. Pour some vinegar all over the lamb and put into covered pan on a rack. Bake at 275° for 3 hours. Drain off all liquid and put back into pan. Pour some more vinegar onto the meat and squeeze the juice of a lemon all over. Cut up the lemon into small pieces and lay over meat. Do the same with an onion. Cover, and place in a 250° oven for about 10 hours or overnight. Drain again, bone and add a little more mustard and lemon juice along with a small amount of ketchup. Return to oven and cook uncovered for about 30 minutes.

Adele W. Coffee, Elaine Crawford
and Laura West Whitley
Mertzon

This recipe was handed down from many generations. I learned this from my mother-in-law, Mrs. E.A. Sieker, when she managed the "Sieker Hotel" of Menardville, Texas, about 1915. I was 21 years old at that time. It was handed down to her from her mother.

Roast Leg of Lamb Sieker Style

Remove bone, add strip of bacon, roll up and tie with string. Soak overnight in lightly salted water. Add cloves, a tablespoon of rosemary, sprinkle with black pepper, then bake at low heat for about three hours in the water under a cover. Remove from water, place on rack in oven and roast until brown. Serve on platter garnished with parsley.

Ruby Spiller Sieker
Menard

Baked Leg of Lamb

1 5-6 pound leg of lamb
4 cloves garlic
2 teaspoons salt
2 teaspoons crushed oregano
½ teaspoon pepper
1 cup cooking claret
¼ cup sliced green onions
2 tablespoons lemon juice

Cut deep slits in the leg of lamb at 2-inch intervals. Crush garlic, together with salt, crushed oregano, and pepper; press into slits. Place lamb, fat side up, on rack in open roasting pan. Mix cooking claret, sliced green onions, and lemon juice. Reserve ½ cup of this mixture for gravy, brush part of remainder over meat. Brush often with claret mixture. Roast meat at 300° for 30 to 35 minutes per pound.

Leg of lamb cooked this way is eaten by people who don't like lamb.

Allie Halbert Askew
Sonora

Gyro-Burger

1 pound lean ground American lamb
1 teaspoon dried crushed oregano
½ teaspoon garlic powder
½ teaspoon ground black pepper
¼ teaspoon salt
2 pita bread rounds, halved crosswise
1 cup chopped fresh spinach or lettuce

Combine oregano, garlic powder, pepper, onion powder, cumin, and salt in a bowl. Add lamb; mix well. Form into 4 patties, about ¾-inch thick. Grill over medium coals or broil about 5 minutes on each side or to desired doneness. Split open each pita half forming a pocket. Place gyro-burger, in each pocket; top with chopped spinach and yogurt mixture.

American Lamb Council

Yummy Yogurt Sauce
¼ teaspoon onion powder
¼ teaspoon ground cumin
¾ cup plain lowfat yogurt
½ medium cucumber
2 thinly sliced green onions
1 tablespoon snipped fresh mint (or 1 teaspoon dried)
¼ teaspoon sugar
¼ teaspoon powdered garlic
salt optional

While meat is cooking; stir together yogurt, peeled, seeded, and chopped cucumber, sliced green onion, mint, and sugar.

My husband, H. Allen Belk, and I live on our stock farm in Runnels County near Winters. We raise wool, mohair, lamb, beef, wheat, and oats. As a child, my mother and Grandmother Earwood prepared lamb for their families, and I have followed in their footsteps by raising my three children on lots of delicious lamb.

My daughter won a 4-H Lamb contest with this recipe.

Lamb Stew

4 pounds lamb
1 tablespoon salad oil
1 large onion
3 medium-size white potatoes
6 carrots
1 28-ounce can tomatoes in puree
1 beef-flavored bouillon cube
1 cup cooked rice

Cut lamb into bite size pieces. In a 5-quart Dutch oven brown lamb and chopped onions in oil. Remove lamb to let fat drain as much as possible. Cut potatoes and peeled carrots into chunks. Return the lamb to Dutch oven. Add 4 cups of water and remaining ingredients; except tomatoes. Heat until bubbling then reduce heat to low; cover and simmer until lamb and vegetables are very tender, about 2 hours. More water can be added if necessary. Add tomato puree and pre-cooked rice. Total cooking time about 2½ hours.

I don't remember Mom using the rice, but my sons like the added thickness and taste.

Elsie Belk
Winters

Award Winning Mexicali Stew

1½ pounds ground lamb
1 package onion soup
1 tablespoon minced garlic
1 can Rotel
1 can ranch style beans
2 cans minestrone soup

Brown the lamb with the soup and garlic. Drain. Add remaining ingredients without draining tomatoes or beans. Simmer for 30 minutes or on low in crock pot until ready to serve.

This is not as good if you substitute lamb for beef or turkey.

Kathy Kohls
Garden City

Lamb and Green Bean Stew

(Lub Yeh'Blah'M)

> 2 pounds fresh snapped green beans
> 1½ pounds cubed lamb leg or beef
> 3 tablespoons butter
> 1 large chopped onion
> 1 can tomato sauce or tomatoes
> dash cinnamon and allspice
> salt and pepper to taste
> pinch of sugar
> ½ clove crushed garlic - optional

Melt butter in large kettle, brown meat and onions over medium heat. Add remaining ingredients. Cover and cook stirring occasionally until beans are done. Serve over rice (Shireeya).

Buttered Rice (Shireeya)

> 2 cups rice
> 4½ cups water
> 2 teaspoons salt
> ½ cup melted butter
> ½ cup seed Roni or broken vermicelli

Wash and drain rice. Brown seed Roni with butter in 3 quart saucepan until light brown. Add rice, water and salt; stir; cover and cook 5 minutes. Stir, cover tightly and cook 20 minutes or until rice is done. Leave covered 10 minutes before serving.

Laurice Solomon Rogers
Kerrville

One of the many recipes I had to learn by trial and error. My grandparents were born in Lebanon. They came to Texas in the Early 1900's. My mother, Sadie Stevens Solomon, learned to cook from her mother, as I did - by word of month and a good sense of how it was supposed to taste.

Lamb Sirloin With Honey Mustard Sauce

1 pound American lamb sirloin steaks, ¾-inch thick
¼ teaspoon salt
¼ teaspoon pepper
Sprinkle lamb steaks with salt and black pepper. Broil or grill 4 inches from heat for 3 to 5 minutes. Turn and continue cooking 3 to 5 minutes or until desired doneness. Serve sauce with lamb steaks.

Honey Mustard Sauce
1 slice firm-textured whole wheat bread
¼ cup plain lowfat yogurt
2 tablespoons brown stone-ground mustard
1 tablespoon honey
1 teaspoon prepared horseradish
1 teaspoon snipped parsley
1-2 tablespoons water

Tear the bread into small pieces into a medium bowl. Stir in the yogurt until mixture is fairly smooth. Stir in mustard, honey, horseradish and parsley; mix well. Stir in 1 to 2 tablespoons water as necessary to desired consistency and refrigerate until serving time.

American Lamb Council

Cabrito Guisado

8 pounds cabrito - about ½ whole cabrito
¼ cup oil
3 tablespoons salt
⅔ cup oil
¾ cup flour
3 large skinned and diced tomatoes
1 sliced green bell pepper
1 large sliced onion
10 cloves garlic
2 teaspoons ground cumin
1½ teaspoons pepper
1 teaspoon whole oregano
8 cups cold tap water - 1 cup at a time

Wash meat well. Cut meat into ½ to 1 inch cubes. In a large Dutch oven, heat ¼ cup oil at medium heat. Place meat and salt in heated oil. Cook for about 60 minutes stirring occasionally. Remove from heat and set aside. In a large skillet heat ⅔ cup oil. Add flour and brown well. Turn off heat, add water, 1 cup at a time to make gravy. Add vegetables and spices to meat, mix well. Simmer 25 to 35 minutes at medium heat until meat and vegetables are tender. Serves 10 to 12.

Use a garlic press or molicajete to crush the garlic cloves.

Teodora M. Hinojosa
Submitted by Texas Sheep and Goat Raisers
Association

I serve it with mashed potatoes and/or Mexican rice with raisins, lettuce, tomatoes and onion salad, iced tea and hot corn tortillas.

This has been a Fourth of July "Family Tradition" since my family and I moved to Austin in 1965 - when the children entered college. I could always depend on lots of "drop in guests" so to be safe I would do two. How delighted I was to discover that Bill Christopher enjoyed it as much as we—so now that I live in beautiful West Texas, it continues to be a tradition. Not only the Fourth-but Easter, also. Bon Appetit!

Family Cabrito

1 12-ounce jar Grandma's Molasses
6 ounces cider vinegar
½ cup salt
1 tablespoon pepper
½ cup oil

Place small goat in roasting bag with 3 tablespoons flour. Cover with the above sauce, tie bag securely and bake slowly for 2½ hours. Let set in bag overnight. The next morning, carefully remove from bag and save sauce to baste for the two hours that it is on the SMOKER END of barbecue pit. Remove from smoker and "YUM-YUM"!

I prefer to use Bertelli olive oil.

Billie Marie Christopher
Marfa

Round-up Goat Meat

Put your goat meat on rack in a roasting pan. Cover the bottom of pan with water (not touching meat). Season meat with favorite seasonings - brisket or fajita rub. Cover with lid. Cook in slow oven at 275° for 6 hours. For the last 30 minutes remove foil and brown meat.

If you are in a hurry, just put it under the broiler and brown quickly.

Nan Beckwith
Progreso

Great for coming in after round-up.

Cabrito con Fideo

1½ pounds cabrito
2 tablespoons oil
1 box or 5-ounces fideo (vermicelli)
1 small diced onion
1 diced bell pepper
½ tablespoon whole black pepper
1 tablespoon comino seed
3 small cloves garlic
2 diced fresh tomatoes

Cut cabrito into bite sized cubes and brown in skillet with two tablespoons oil until well done, about 20 to 30 minutes. Combine onion and bell pepper. Set aside. In blender, grind comino seed, black pepper and garlic cloves until pulverized. Add spices and mix well. Add fideo and enough water to cover entire mixture, then add the tomatoes. Cover and bring to a slow simmer. Cook approximately 15 minutes or until fideo is tender. Do not stir until ready to serve.

I recommend a large and well aged cast-iron skillet for this dish.

Hubert Adami
Submitted by Texas Sheep
and Goat Raisers Association

Like all good South Texas recipes, ingredients can be increased or decreased to suit individual tastes. A good batch of hot home made tortillas will add to your enjoyment of this recipe. Good eating , Amigo!

World's First Goat Cooking Contest
Brady, Texas

Coon Dog Harris, of Eldorado says, "Cook goat by putting it on a hot fire for about 4 hours, then leaving it on another four or five to get tender. Only salt and pepper and never touch it, never turn it…it just falls of the bone. Don't use any sauce. The more gook you put on it, the more the meat will sear over and the heat won't penetrate."

Cabrito Chili

2 cups chopped onion
2 tablespoons vegetable oil
1 tablespoon ground oregano
2 tablespoons ground cumin
1 teaspoon garlic powder
2 teaspoons salt
3 pounds lean ground goat meat
½ cup + 2 tablespoons chili powder
cayenne pepper to taste - optional
½ cup flour
8 cups boiling water

In a heavy pot, sauté onions in cooking oil, add oregano, cumin, garlic powder and salt. Cook until onions are almost clear. Add ground meat; cook and stir until crumbly and almost gray. Add chili powder, cayenne pepper and flour, stirring until well blended. Add boiling water, bring mixture back to boil, simmer for less than 1 hour.

Seasonings may be adjusted to individual taste. Serve cooked pinto beans as a side dish.

Texas Department of Agriculture

Fried Goat Stew

goat meat
flour
salt and pepper
potatoes
onions

Flour, salt and pepper the cubed goat meat. Fry until done and set aside. Add more shortening to pan to fry the potato and onion slices. Set aside. Make milk gravy in pan and add goat meat, potato and onion slices. Salt and pepper if needed.

Can use venison or beef with equally good results.

Carolyn Wilson
Ozona

Fried Venison

venison
salt, pepper and garlic powder
flour

Cut meat into half-inch slices against the grain. Generously salt, pepper and garlic powder the meat. Dredge in flour; fry until golden.

Soaking the meat in buttermilk before flouring is good to take out the wild taste.

The backstrap is the best!

Marcella Anderson
Rocksprings

Val Verde "Buckhorn" Chili

6-7 pounds coarse ground venison
7 onions
5 bell peppers
4 1-pound cans stewed tomatoes
½ can Rotel tomatoes
6 cups water
½ teaspoon minced garlic or 4 whole cloves
2 teaspoons celery seed
2 teaspoons cayenne pepper
6 bay leaves
1 teaspoon basil
6 teaspoons salt
6 tablespoons chili powder
1 cup flour

Mince onions and bell peppers very fine. Sauté onions and garlic in butter until brown; add meat to onions and cook until well done. Puree tomatoes in blender. Add tomatoes, water, bell pepper, and spices to meat mixture. Bring to a boil then simmer on very low heat overnight or for 24 hours (if possible). About an hour before serving, add flour and water to thicken.

Can add cooked red beans and/or jalapeños to chili just before serving.

Brett Carpenter
San Angelo

Lots of our city cousins don't know how to properly gut, skin and process deer meat; so they think the meat is "gamey". Learn this fine art and you'll enjoy your game so much more. It doesn't all have to be ground up as sausage! (Please see Field Dressing.)

Baked Deer Ham
deer ham
red wine
tart apple
peach jam
bacon slices

Cook your deer ham in a roasting pan. You may place the bacon over the ham and mix the other ingredients to baste the meat as it cooks. Bake at 325-350° for 3 to 4 hours.

Leg of lamb is also good cooked in this manner.
Alma Ingham Smart
Rocksprings

The Venison Beer Stew is one of my favorites as we eat a lot of venison.

Venison Beer Stew

4 slices bacon
2 pounds venison
¼ cup flour
1 16-ounce can cut up tomatoes
1 can beer
1 medium chopped onion
minced garlic - optional
2 teaspoons instant beef bouillon granules
1 teaspoon sugar
½ teaspoon crushed thyme
¼ teaspoon black pepper
⅛ teaspoon red pepper
3 medium carrots
2 small turnips
1 stalk celery
1 cup frozen peas

Cook bacon until crisp, drain and reserve 2 tablespoons drippings. Crumble bacon and set aside. Coat 1 inch cubes of venison with flour and brown. Add undrained tomatoes, beer, onion, bouillon, sugar, thyme, black and red peppers. Bring to boil; reduce heat, cover and simmer 1¼ hours. Cut carrots and celery into 1-inch pieces; peel turnips and cut into wedges, add these to pot and simmer 30 minutes more. Stir in frozen peas, cook 5 minutes. Stir in the crumbled bacon. Makes 6 servings.

Sadie Puckitt
San Angelo

Crockett County Venison Fajitas

1½ pounds venison ham
6 limes
2 minced cloves garlic
2 minced green chili peppers
1 thinly sliced onion
fresh chopped cilantro leaves (remove stems)
freshly ground pepper
2 cans beer
salt to taste

Slice the venison ham into slices ½-inch thick. Place one layer venison slices in deep glass baking dish and cover with lime juice, some garlic, onion, cilantro, peppers and freshly ground black pepper. Repeat with a second layer of the same ingredients. Add your favorite beer to almost fill the pan. Cover and marinate overnight. Remove from marinate and cook over hot mesquite fire, turning only once. Do not over cook. Salt to taste. Cut diagonally into very thin strips. Wrap fajita style in flour tortillas with guacamole, sour cream, pico de gallo shredded cheese and refried beans.

Brett Carpenter
San Angelo

"Fajita" means "little girdle" and typically describes the thin girdle of meat at the bottom of a steers rib cage. With beef, the traditional fajitas are cut from skirt steak, but with venison, it's best to use a better cut, even from a ham. I typically slice off ½-inch thick pieces from a boned out ham as a starting place when using venison.

The isolated ranches along our bluebonnet trail were some of the last parts of our country to be modernized. In our mothers day, they still used wood for cooking and heating, and kerosene lamps for light. What a day when a windcharger might be erected to charge batteries for lights and a radio. A Servel kerosene refrigerator might be the most exciting purchase of the year. The telephone was the oak box "ring Central" type. And the road to town was usually up one rocky ledge and down another. When REA came to the country, life changed! The road to town is still up one rocky ledge and down another, but that pickup is usually air-conditioned! A satellite dish in the back yard, a water cooler in the window, and a private phone line makes us right up town. Some days you can really miss the fun of that old party line.

I found the original recipe to this in "Southern Living" when I first married 9 years ago and use it often for any kind of red meat, not only venison.

Venison Shish Kebobs

2 pounds venison sirloin
2-3 cups vegetable oil
¼ cup burgundy
2 tablespoons cider vinegar
1½ tablespoons liquid smoke
2 teaspoons salt
1 teaspoon white pepper
1 teaspoon garlic powder
1 teaspoon onion juice
cherry tomatoes, fresh mushrooms, onion chunks, green pepper, whole jalapeños

Place meat in large shallow container. Combine oil and next 7 ingredients; pour over meat. Cover and refrigerate 24 to 48 hours, stirring occasionally. Remove meat from marinade, reserving marinade. Alternate meat and vegetables on skewers brush with marinade. Grill over medium hot coals about 15 minutes turning and basting frequently with marinade. Serves 8.

This is great served with rice.

Mary Ann Ham
Big Lake

Pheasant in Mushroom Soup

1 pheasant
1 can mushroom soup

Bone pheasant and cut into small pieces. Sauté in small amount of oil. Mix mushroom soup with about ¼ cup water and add to pheasant. Cook until pheasant is done, about 30 to 40 minutes.

I simmer this in an electric skillet and serve over rice.

Fast, simple and delicious!

Linda Hayes
Ivanhoe

 Game

Chicken Fried Duck

Bone duck breast and cut into strips. Dip strips into mixture of beaten egg and milk, shake in baggy with flour and fry in oil until done. Make gravy out of the drippings.

Linda Hayes
Ivanhoe

My family really likes duck this way. It tastes like fried dove.

Roast Duck

ducks
onion
1 can sauerkraut
bacon, optional

Stuff duck with sauerkraut and chopped onion. Place 2 strips of bacon on duck breast and place in roaster breast side down. Add about ½-inch water. Cover and bake at 325° for about 3 hours or until done.

Serve with cornbread dressing.

Linda Hayes
Ivanhoe

Being married to an avid duck hunter for 33 years, I have cooked many ducks. This is the only way I roast it now. The sauerkraut tenderizes and modifies the wild flavor. Cooking it breast down keeps the breast from getting dry. It does not taste at all like sauerkraut.

This is my husband, Jerry's, favorite dish! M-M-M-Texas eating at its best!

Try our Jalapeño Gravy with this dish!

I keep my spices mixed up all the time so I'm always ready to whip out this family favorite. Make your favorite pan gravy to go with the steak.

Texas' Famous Chicken Fried Steak

1½-2 pounds tenderized cube steak
1 egg
1 cup milk
1 cup flour
1 teaspoon salt
1 teaspoon pepper
1 teaspoon garlic salt
½ teaspoon MSG (optional)
½ cup cooking oil
1 tablespoon flour
2 tablespoons garlic powder

Blend egg and milk together in a small bowl. Put 1 cup flour in dinner plate to dip meat in. Dip meat first in flour, then dip in egg mixture and the back in flour, shaking off excess. Cook in hot oil and season with, salt, pepper, garlic salt, and MSG mixed together. Mix 1 tablespoon flour with 2 tablespoons garlic powder and sprinkle over cooking steak. Turn steak after browning on one side and continue cooking to brown the other side. Total cooking time is 7 to 9 minutes.

Nancy Johnson

Brisket

1 6-pound brisket
2 tablespoons liquid smoke
2 tablespoons garlic salt
2 tablespoons celery salt
2 tablespoons liquid smoke
2 tablespoons Worcestershire sauce
pinch of salt

Trim fat from the brisket. Rub the next three ingredients well into the meat, wrap with foil and refrigerate overnight. The next day rub with the liquid smoke, Worcestershire sauce, and salt. Wrap airtight in foil and place in pan. Bake at 300° for 5 to 6 hours.

Zackie Dutton Dunbar
Rocksprings

Marfa Beef Loin

1 3-pound beef loin
1 cup low-sodium soy sauce
½ cup lemon juice
4 tablespoons soft margarine
4 stems fresh dill
freshly ground black pepper

Trim the meat and place in a glass baking dish. Combine the soy sauce, lemon juice, and margarine in a microwave-safe dish and microwave on high for 20 seconds, or until the margarine is melted. Pour the marinade over the meat. Place 2 stems of fresh dill on top of the meat and a stem on each side. Cover and refrigerate for 24 hours. Drain and reserve the marinade from the meat. Sprinkle with black pepper. Grill over medium coals, occasionally brushing with the reserved marinade, for 30 to 40 minutes, or until an instant meat thermometer reads 150° for medium-rare or 160° for medium. Serves 6.

Billie Christopher
Marfa

Billie Christopher is the owner of La Tejana, "The Texas Woman", a gift shop in a beautifully restored old hotel in Marfa. Be sure to stop in when in Marfa. - Mimi

Marfa Lights

The mysterious lights appearing at night on the plains a few miles east of Marfa defy explanation although they have been studied by scientists, geologists, and uranium seekers. Reports of the mysterious lights go way back to the Indians. In the 1880's, cowboys reported strange lights that glowed, glided and bobbed a few feet above the ground, and early settlers reported strange pulsating globes of light. Many of us who have occasion to visit the Marfa area have seen these lights for ourselves. There is seldom an evening that people aren't parked in the viewing area hoping to see this phenomena for themselves, we have even witnessed cars stopped in the daytime with people looking off into the distance hoping for a glimpse. You can see the lights anytime of the year and in all kinds of weather but, you won't get close to them. They have always managed to keep their distance. The Marfa lights are truly a Texas mystery!

Roast Beef - White Style

Use a rib, rump, or rolled roast, at room temperature. Preheat oven to 325°. Note weight of roast. Rub roast well with salt and pepper on all sides. Place in an open, uncovered pan in oven for 25 minutes per pound for medium-rare roast. For example, a six pound roast is ready in 2½ hours.

Jane Brite White
Marfa

Beef Roll-Ups

My daughter, Caroline Hight, gave me this recipe. It has been a family favorite for generations. Fred's mother, Ruth Case, gave it to me, but I never wrote it down. I'm happy to have it, too. There are many ways you can change it or add to it.

½ pound sliced bacon
1½ pounds tenderized round steak
2-3 tablespoons mustard
3-6 dill pickle wedges
¼ cup chopped onions
6 slices of cheese
1 can cream of mushroom soup

In skillet cook bacon until crisp. Remove bacon from pan but leave bacon grease in skillet. Cut the tenderized steak into 4 to 6 rectangular pieces (a serving size). Spread mustard on each piece of steak. Place a pickle, some chopped onions, a slice of cheese, and a piece or 2 of bacon on each piece of steak. Start at narrow end of meat and roll up. Secure with a toothpick. Dip the rolled up meat in flour, and brown in the bacon drippings until the meat is browned on all sides. Drain the bacon drippings after browning. Mix the cream of mushroom soup and 1 can of water and pour into the pan of browned meat. Cover skillet and simmer over low heat for 1 hour to 1 hour and fifteen minutes. Stir occasionally to keep from sticking to pan. If gravy starts to thicken, then add a small amount of water to thin. Makes 4 to 6 servings.

Nicky Case
Eldorado

Beef

Flank Steak with Cilantro Sauce

1½ pounds flank steak
2 cloves garlic, peeled and thinly sliced lengthwise
2 tablespoons olive oil
½ cup dry red wine, preferably Merlot
2 loaves fresh flatbread, warmed in the oven

Place flank steak in large dish. Combine garlic, olive oil, and wine and pour over meat. Let marinate at room temperature for at least 30 minutes or overnight in refrigerator. (Combine all ingredients for sauce, season to taste, let set at room temperature at least 30 minutes.) Prepare grill. Remove meat from marinade and grill until done to your liking about 10 minutes for rare, turning meat once while cooking. Remove meat from grill and dice diagonally, against the grain. To serve, place half a warmed flatbread on each plate and cover with overlapping slices of meat. Drizzle with cilantro sauce.

Cilantro Sauce
1 cup coarsely chopped fresh cilantro
⅓ cup olive oil
1 tablespoon very finely minced red onion
salt and freshly ground black pepper

Combine ingredients for sauce together, season to taste, let sit at room temperature for at least 30 minutes.

Preccia Miller
Dallas

Gourmet Pot Roast

A silk purse recipe - looks and tastes expensive but isn't.

1 4-5 pounds chuck roast cut into 1½-inch cubes
½ cup olive oil
1½ cups water
1 cup catsup
½ cup sherry (or more to taste)
2-3 cloves minced garlic
1 large onion, cut into large pieces
1 teaspoon dry mustard
1 teaspoon marjoram
1 teaspoon rosemary
1 teaspoon thyme
2 bay leaves
1 8-ounce can mushrooms

Brown cubed meat in olive oil. Add onions and cook in oil for several minutes. Stir in remaining ingredients, except mushrooms, and simmer until tender (1 to 1½ hours). Add mushrooms and thicken with a water and flour mixture.

Francine Hardeman
Sonora

Sterling County

By the 1870's, when the early settlers came to ranch on the open ranges of West Texas the buffalo were already gone. There were many deer, wild turkey, quail, a few prairie chickens, and herds of antelope- the streams of the Concho River were alive with fish. Besides game and wild horses, there were also in this area many lobo wolves, coyotes, panthers, bobcats, and wildcats. One last herd of buffaloes came through this area in 1883 or 1884. One of the last Indian battles between the Commanches and a force of Rangers and cowboys occurred in Sterling County. The danger of Indians had not completely disappeared by 1880 because of the absence of fences.

Zesty Beef Bourguignonne

¼ pound bacon, diced or cut into lardons (thin strips)
¼ cup cognac
½ cup fresh chopped parsley
½ teaspoon fresh or coarse ground pepper
¼ teaspoon cayenne pepper
2 teaspoons salt
⅔ cup flour
1 3-pound cubed round steak or roast
1 stick butter
2 cups chopped onion
2-3 cups beef stock, canned or cubes
1½ cups Burgundy wine (or a dry red Texas Cabernet)
½ teaspoon dried crushed thyme or 1 teaspoon fresh
½ teaspoon dried marjoram
1 pound fresh mushrooms
1 carton tiny onions or 18-20 boiling onions

This may be frozen and heated in the oven. Good for crowds.

Marinate bacon and parsley and ¼ teaspoon pepper in cognac 2 to 3 hours. Season flour with salt, pepper, and cayenne. Trim beef of all fat, cube and coat with seasoned flour. Melt 4 tablespoons butter in a heavy skillet and brown beef on all sides. Add chopped onions and brown. Transfer beef and onions to a large oven proof casserole. Drain bacon, reserving liquid. Brown bacon in 1 teaspoon butter then add to beef. Deglaze skillet with marinade and ½ cup beef stock. Add to beef. Add wine, thyme and marjoram and enough stock to cover beef. Cover and bake in a 300° oven for 3 hours. If mushrooms are small, use whole; if large, cut in half or quarters. Sauté mushrooms in 2 tablespoons butter until barely done. Parboil onions 3 to 5 minutes, drain well and sauté in 1 tablespoon butter until lightly browned. Add mushrooms and onions to meat and cook 30 minutes longer also adding more wine or stock if needed. Serves 8.

Clara Winters
Brady

125

Jake Wardlaw used to say that the best way to survive the drought is to watch the magnificent sunsets, eat good barbecue, listen to Frank Meadows strike up lively tunes on the banjo and to have Sonny Noelke tell his famous tales!

Mother's Beef Stroganoff

1½ pounds tenderloin or sirloin
3 tablespoons butter
1 large chopped onion
2 tablespoons flour
1 cup sliced mushrooms
2 cups beef consommé
2 tablespoons tomato paste
1 teaspoon dry mustard
3 tablespoons sherry, optional
⅔ cup sour cream

Slice beef into strips and generously salt and pepper. Brown beef in butter and add onion, cooking until onions are clear. Stir in flour. Slowly add consommé. Add mushrooms, tomato paste, dry mustard, and sherry. Cook on medium heat about 30 minutes or until sauce thickens. Before serving add sour cream and stir. Serve over noodles or rice. Serves 4 to 6.

H.R. Wardlaw III
San Angelo

This is Chris' specialty when it's cold outside or when friends or family come.
Tenderloin tips are also wonderful!

Chris' Stew

2 steaks cut in small pieces
4 large cubed potatoes
1 chopped onion
2 tablespoons oil
seasonings: garlic, salt, dash cayenne pepper
water
2 large crushed tomatoes
1-2 seeded and chopped long green peppers
1 can tomato sauce
grated Cheddar cheese

Cook potatoes and onions in oil. Add the meat and stir until browned. Add salt, garlic, and cayenne seasonings. Add tomatoes, green peppers, and water. Simmer. Add tomato sauce and continue to simmer. Put grated cheese on top and let melt.

Chris Lacy
06 Ranch
Fort Davis

Gladie's Brown Stew

2 pounds sirloin
2 tablespoons oil
4 cups boiling water
1 teaspoon lemon juice
1 teaspoon Worcestershire sauce
1 clove garlic
1 medium onion
2 bay leaves
1 tablespoon salt
½ teaspoon pepper
½ teaspoon paprika
1 teaspoon sugar
6 carrots
1 pound small onions

Cut meat into bite size pieces. Brown meat in oil. Add water, lemon juice, Worcestershire sauce, garlic, onion, bay leaves, and all seasonings. Simmer 2 hours stirring occasionally. Add carrots and onions. Cook until tender. Thicken the liquid for gravy.

Marjorie Davis
Sterling City

This recipe came from my mother-in-law, Gladie McKnight (Mrs. Jeff) Davis.

Salisbury Steak

1 can cream of mushroom soup
1 pound ground beef
⅓ cup dry bread crumbs
1 egg beaten
¼ cup finely chopped onion
1½ cups sliced mushrooms

In bowl, mix ½ cup of the soup, beef, bread crumbs, egg and onion. Shape firmly into 6 patties. In skillet, over medium-high heat, cook patties a few at a time until browned on both sides. Spoon off fat. Stir in remaining soup and mushrooms, return patties to skillet. Reduce heat to low. Cover, simmer 20 minutes or until done turning patties occasionally.

Sherry Wipff
San Angelo

I remember my mother making this dish when we were kids.
And I remember Carol making this dish for us when we lived on neighboring ranches in Sutton County raising our kids together. What fun we used to have and the meals we shared! - Mimi

Great served over rice as a main dish.

Sweet and Sour Beef Balls

1 pound ground beef
1 egg
4 tablespoons cornstarch
2 tablespoons chopped onion
1 teaspoon salt
cooking oil
1 cup pineapple juice
1 tablespoon soy sauce
3 tablespoons vinegar
6 tablespoons water
½ cup sugar
4 slices pineapple cut in pieces
3 green peppers cut in strips

Mix beef, egg, 1 tablespoon cornstarch, salt, and onion; form into 18 or more balls. Brown in a small amount of oil; drain. Combine 1 tablespoon oil and the pineapple juice and cook over low heat for a few minutes. Add mixture of 3 tablespoons cornstarch, the soy sauce, vinegar, water and sugar. Cook until juice thickens, stirring constantly. Add meat balls, pineapple and green peppers. Heat thoroughly and serve hot. Serves 6 to 8.

Carol Love
Sonora

Century Ranches

The Family Land Heritage Registry contains information on families who have held the land for agricultural production for 100 years or more. For the most part, it is a body of personal histories, remembrances passed from parents to children which, taken as a whole, create a panorama of our pioneer heritage. It is such memories which have formed the images of another day and shaped the attitudes of present owners. You will find recipes contributed by Century Ranches of Texas throughout this book.

West of the Pecos

2 pounds ground beef
1 large diced onion
1 diced green pepper
1 cup diced celery
2 teaspoons chili powder
½ cup Worcestershire sauce
1 can mushrooms
1 can tomato soup
1 can cream style corn
1 can Rotel tomatoes
1 package medium egg noodles
1 pound grated American or Longhorn
cheese

Boil noodles according to directions on package, drain and rinse with cold water. Sear beef (can be rinsed to reduce fat) and add remaining ingredients, including noodles. Heat on top of the stove and serve cheese on the side. This recipe can be baked at 375° for one hour, but we prefer the vegetables crisp and unbaked. Your choice!

Also, this recipe can be prepared the day before - omitting noodles. Add noodles after the dish has been reheated and just prior to serving to keep them from overcooking.

Serve with a fresh green salad and Mexican cornbread.

> *Ruth Caldwell (Mrs. Lee)*
> *U Ranch*
> *Sterling City*

After a delightful and delicious patio brunch at her home some thirty years ago, this recipe was given to me by a very special lady, Bennie Sue Thomas, who ranches West of the Pecos. There's no telling how many times I've prepared and served it since. The U Ranch on the North Concho in Sterling County was founded in 1876 and acquired by W.R. McEntire, a Civil War Veteran, in 1880. It is now owned and operated by his great-granddaughter, Ruth McEntire Caldwell and her husband Lee.

Our Favorite Casserole

1 pound ground beef
salt, pepper, and garlic
1 package cooked wide egg noodles
1 small carton sour cream
1 small carton small curd cottage cheese
3-4 chopped green onions
1 large jar of your favorite spaghetti sauce
Parmesan cheese

Brown ground beef; add salt, pepper, and garlic to taste and set aside to drain. Mix sour cream, cottage cheese, and green onions together. In casserole dish, layer ingredients: noodles, meat, cheese/onion mixture and sauce. Sprinkle generous amount of Parmesan cheese on top of casserole. Bake 30 minutes at 350°. Serves 4 to 6.

This can be made a day ahead. Also freezes very well for baking later.

Pat Andrews
San Antonio

Sherried Beef

2-3 pounds lean bite size stew meat
2 cans mushroom, chicken or celery soup,
mix as you like
½ package onion soup mix
½ cup sherry

Place beef in casserole, cover with remaining ingredients, and cover with lid or foil - do not seal. Bake at 350° for 3 hours. Serve over rice or noodles.

Martha Lee Meador
Eldorado

Roast Turkey

Kill and dress turkey; when perfectly cold, rub well inside and out with salt; let stand overnight. When ready to roast, rinse in cold water. Place in pan with breast down, add one cup hot water and cover and bake at temperature 350° to 400° or at 15 to 25 minutes per pound according to heat until tender. Remove cover and brown (An apple placed in the breast gives it a nice flavor). Meanwhile boil the giblets in water, use this for gravy and dressing. Make dressing of about 1-3 or better of cornbread and 2-3 biscuit moistened with part of water that giblets were cooked in. Add rest of hot water to make it the right consistency, about 5 or 6 raw eggs, salt, pepper, butter or bacon grease; add onion, celery and sage to taste. Cook on top of stove until it is well mixed, then place in pan with turkey.

Mrs. C. B. Wardlaw
Cookbook of Tried Recipes, early 1940's
Del Rio
Submitted by Tennille Wardlaw Smith

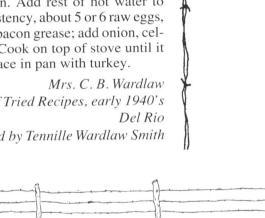

I remember as a child all the wonderful smells that came from my Grandmother's kitchen on Christmas morning. My mother was in charge of stirring the dressing on the stove and my aunt Mary and Rachel were busy preparing other goodies. All the while the 10 grandchildren had the run of the house, waiting for Santa to arrive, so we could open our gifts. As was traditional in our family, Santa arrived and ask if we had been good, gave us our gift and as he would leave he always fell to the ground in a frightening fit. It was the grandchildren who had to get Santa up and on his way. With that done, all 21 or more sat down to a wonderful Christmas meal.

This recipe of Turkey and Dressing comes from my grandmother, Faye Kirby Drake (Mrs. Bruce Drake). She taught my mother, Dorothy, how to prepare and cook it. We have enjoyed this for many years during Thanksgiving, Christmas, New Year's and Easter time.

Grandmother's Turkey and Dressing

Prepare turkey as usual-remove parts from inside, wash and clean, and sprinkle with salt. Cook slowly in covered pan to which has been added several cups water. Mom starts the turkey at 4:00 A.M.

Giblet Gravy
   giblets cooked in as much water as needed
   ¼ cup melted butter
   ¼ cup flour
   ½ teaspoon salt
   2 cups chicken broth or juice from cooked turkey
   water as needed
   2 heaping tablespoons of the cooked dressing

Blend together the butter, flour, and salt in a large saucepan. Add the finely chopped gizzard and liver, broth, water, and dressing. Stir constantly until well blended, then cook until desired thickness.

Cornbread Dressing
   1 package cornbread as directed, omitting sugar
   several slices white bread
   sage
   poultry seasoning
   salt and pepper

Crumble together the cornbread, white bread, sage or poultry seasoning and salt and pepper to taste. Prepare this part several days ahead of time.

   1 large finely chopped onion
   1 cup chopped celery
   4-6 hard boiled eggs

The night before prepare the onion, celery, and eggs.

Cool eggs in fridge and grate with cheese grater. Mix all the ingredients and add juice from the cooked turkey. Bake at 350°-400° until cooked and browned on top.

We like it moist, not hard or dry.

Glenda McMullan
Iraan

132

Turkey Pot Pie

1 cup diced carrots
½ cup diced celery
½ cup chopped onion
1½ cups cooked turkey
⅛ teaspoon pepper
1 can each of mushroom, chicken and celery soup
½ can water
1 box frozen snow peas
½ cup sliced mushrooms
1 recipe double pie crust

In a small amount of water, sauté carrots, celery and onions. Add turkey, soup and water, remaining vegetables and seasonings; set aside. Roll out pastry dough. Line one deep large pie pan with ½ of the dough. Fill with turkey filling. Adjust top crust, tuck edges under and flute. Cut steam holes. Bake at 400° for 20 minutes or until lightly browned.

Linda Hayes
Ivanhoe

Use a pie crust made with oil and it will be low in cholesterol. The snow peas really add to this recipe. Do not over cook the vegetables. It is great for leftover turkey, or you may use chicken.

And now for the rest of the story…

Paul Harvey said on the radio the other day that we don't have to worry about those little cactus thorns that get under your skin any more. He said you can get the little ones (not the big ones - but the little stingers) out by applying some Elmer's glue to the spot, letting it dry, and then peeling it off. Not any of this bunch will volunteer to try it out but for what it's worth you might want to put it under your bonnet to pull out some day.

Award Winning Turkey Tamale Pie

1 pound ground turkey
1 medium onion, finely chopped
2 garlic cloves, minced
1 green bell pepper, chopped
1 cup frozen corn, thawed
1 14-ounce can whole tomatoes, drained
1 teaspoon ground cumin
1½ teaspoons salt, divided
2½ cups milk
2 tablespoons butter or margarine
¾ cup cornmeal
2 cups grated Cheddar cheese, divided
½ cup chopped scallions
2 plum tomatoes, thinly sliced

Preheat oven to 350°. Lightly grease 13x9x2-inch glass baking dish. In large non-stick skillet, over medium-high heat, sauté turkey, onion and garlic 5 to 6 minutes or until turkey is no longer pink. Stir in green pepper, corn, tomatoes, cumin and 1 teaspoon salt. Reduce heat to low and simmer, uncovered, 10 minutes. Remove pan from heat. In medium saucepan, over high heat, combine milk, butter and remaining salt; bring to a boil. Slowly add cornmeal; whisking constantly. Reduce heat to low and simmer 5 minutes. Remove pan form heat and stir in 1 cup of cheese. Line sides and bottom of baking dish with ¾ of the cornmeal mixture. Pour in meat mixture and spread remaining cornmeal over top. Sprinkle with scallions and 1 cup of remaining cheese. Arrange tomato slices over top and bake 40 minutes or until cheese is bubbly.

Sofya Radelet
Submitted by the Poultry Council

Braised Chicken Breasts

4-6 chicken breasts
salt and pepper to taste
lemon-pepper (generously)
½ teaspoon celery salt
½ teaspoon onion salt
½ teaspoon garlic salt
¼ cup oleo
juice of 1 lemon
½ teaspoon Worcestershire sauce
¼ cup water

Skin breasts of chicken, season with salt, pepper and lemon pepper. Sprinkle with celery, onion and garlic salt. Melt oleo in heavy skillet. Brown breast slowly on both sides. Add lemon juice, with Worcestershire sauce and water. Cover tightly. Simmer for 45 minutes or until tender.

Anna Belle Eldin
Channing

Curried Breast of Chicken

1 apple, chopped
1 onion, chopped
1 tablespoon curry sauce
1 can cream of mushroom soup
1 cup coffee cream
2 tablespoons butter
4 chicken breasts

Brown apple in butter, add onion, curry, mushroom soup, and coffee cream. Pour this over the chicken breasts and bake at 350° for 1 hour, or until chicken is done. Serve over rice when ready to serve.

Virginia M. Wilkinson
Burnet

This recipe is fool proof and easy, besides being very good.

135

Sweet and Sour Chicken

4-6 boned chicken breasts or any other chicken parts
1 bottle French dressing
1 8-ounce jar apricot preserves
1 package onion soup mix
¼ cup pineapple chunks

Mix the above ingredients together and pour over chicken and marinate in refrigerator overnight.

Bake in 400° oven for 45 minutes.

Serve with rice and sauce.

Mrs. Richard Mayer
San Angelo

Aunt Clara's Chicken and Rice

This recipe was given to me years ago by my Great Aunt Clara. Aunt Clara was a wonderful cook. She knew how much I enjoyed cooking and sent many recipes. This one proved to be a great favorite of ours, even for my not-so-chicken-loving boys.

1 fryer, cut up
1 cup rice
1 can beef bouillon
1½ cans water

Put small amount of oil in large iron skillet and quickly brown chicken pieces. Remove the chicken and lightly brown the rice in the skillet. Arrange the chicken pieces over the rice. Pour over all the can of beef bouillon and 1½ cans of water. Salt and pepper to taste. Cover with lid or foil and bake at 350° for about 45 minutes or until done.

Brown one chopped onion with the rice and stir in one can chopped green chilies.

Mimi Allison

Company Chicken and Crabmeat Rosemary

3 cups cooked, diced chicken
2 6-ounce cans crabmeat, drained
2 cups sour cream
2 cups chicken broth
1 teaspoon paprika
½ teaspoon salt
1 teaspoon dried rosemary
½ cup flour
2 tablespoons chopped onion
1 stick butter or margarine
1 tablespoon lemon juice
2 medium avocados, peeled and chopped
1 cup soft bread crumbs

Preheat oven to 350°. Grease a 2-quart baking dish. In a large pan, melt butter or margarine. Add onion and cook until translucent. Stir in flour and cook 2 minutes, stirring constantly. Add seasoning and chicken broth. Reduce heat and simmer until thickened about 5 minutes. Remove from heat and add sour cream, chicken, crabmeat and avocado which were covered with the lemon juice. Pour into dish. Toss bread crumbs with melted butter and sprinkle on top or use potato chips instead. Cook for 30 minutes at 350°. Serves 6 to 8 people.

A very old tried and true recipe and truly a special company recipe. It is very easy to make.

Martha Wallace
Sonora

Something grandparents should do: Love them at all times. Try not to be judgmental! I have 10 grandchildren, and I try to make each one think they are the special one.

A favorite with our family. One I put together myself based on other popular ones, but suited to our taste. It is quick and easy.

Serve with rice, green salad and Italian bread.

Chicken Cacciatore

4 boneless chicken breasts
2 tablespoons cooking oil
2 bell peppers, cut in strips
1 large onion, sliced and halved into rings
½ teaspoon garlic salt
small jar sliced mushrooms or fresh
1 large can stewed tomatoes
½ cup water or white wine
3 teaspoons Italian herbs seasoning
1 teaspoon sugar
1-2 tablespoons picante sauce

Brown chicken breast in oil; add peppers, onions and mushrooms. Add wine or water, tomatoes with juice, and sprinkle on sugar and seasonings. Simmer about 20 to 30 minutes.

Jeannie Lewis
Del Rio

Serve with buttered fettuccini and salad.

Chicken Marsala

2 chicken breast halves, skinned and boned
2 tablespoons butter
6 large mushrooms, sliced
1 cup Marsala wine
½ teaspoon salt
dash of pepper
1 teaspoon lemon juice
3 green onions, chopped
2 teaspoons fresh parsley, chopped
instant rice

Place each piece of chicken between 2 sheets of wax paper. Using a meat mallet, or rolling pin, pound chicken to ¼" thickness. Melt butter in a medium skillet. Add chicken. Over low heat, cook each side of chicken until tender and golden brown. Remove chicken breasts and place on serving platter. Add next 6 ingredients to skillet. Cook until mushrooms are tender. Pour wine mixture over chicken. Sprinkle with parsley. Place the chicken back into skillet after wine mixture is done and add instant rice to it and let simmer 5 to 10 minutes; then serve from the skillet.

Leslie Lewis Dunbar
Brackettville

Chicken or Eggplant Parmesan

6 boneless, skinless chicken breasts or 3 eggplants
2 eggs
2 tablespoons water
2 tablespoons oil
1 cup flour
1 cup Italian bread crumbs (or crushed Italian croutons)
1 cup grated Parmesan cheese
1 teaspoon oregano
1 teaspoon salt
1 teaspoon pepper
½ stick margarine
2 cups finely grated mozzarella cheese
4 cups Marinara Italian Sauce

I devised this after eating at the Olive Garden (too many times). It is my families favorite! It is also a popular dish at the Allison Ranch during shearing (when Stephanie is fixing it)!

In a small bowl, mix well the eggs, water and oil. In another medium bowl, mix the flour, bread crumbs, cheese and seasonings. Melt butter in glass baking dish and set aside. If using eggplant, peel and slice in ¼ inch slices. Quickly dip chicken or eggplant slices in dry mixture, then egg mixture, then dry mixture again. (This is messy!) Arrange chicken or eggplant in pan so that the breading is not disturbed. (If making both at the same time use two different dishes, one for eggplant and one for chicken, because the eggplant sometimes cooks slower.) Bake at 350° for 35 to 45 minutes. Use toothpick to check tenderness. Place marinara sauce in saucepan and slowly bring to a low simmer. Five minutes prior to being completely baked, remove pans and top each breast or eggplant with fancy grated mozzarella cheese. Replace in oven and let cheese melt until bubbly. Remove immediately. Top individual servings with ¼-½ cup marinara sauce.

You can use the same recipe to make either of these or you can make half and half. This recipe easily doubles. It is easier than it sounds and almost 100% fool proof.

Stephanie Elliot
San Angelo

My maternal great-grandparents came to Texas from Germany and Denmark in the 1840's and ranched between Fredricksburg and New Braunfels. This is an old German recipe they brought and handed down through twelve children, so I'm sure many people carried the recipe through Texas. My grandmother, Emily Franzer Carr, made this for me when I visited her because I loved it so much!

German Dumplings and Chicken

2 cups flour
½ teaspoon salt
½ cup shortening
¼ cup milk
1 egg
1 stewed chicken

Cut shortening into flour and salt. Add beaten egg and milk. Mix well, roll on floured board, roll thin and cut in pieces. Let this dry, if possible for several hours.

My mother used a cut up chicken and left the pieces whole. I boil 5 chicken breast (boned) and cut in bite size pieces. Remove chicken from pan, drop dumpling pieces in chicken stock and boil gently 1 to 1½ hours. Add cooked chicken to warm.

I add ½ teaspoon oregano and 2 chicken bouillon cubes and sometimes 2 chopped boiled eggs.

Lee Bennett

Marfa

Gillis Family Chicken and Dumplings

    1 large chicken
    1 bay leaf
    ½ onion, sliced
    2 celery stalks
    6 peppercorns
    salt to taste
    3 tablespoons parsley, chopped

Boil chicken and other ingredients in water until chicken is tender. Remove chicken and keep warm. Remove onions and celery and discard. Reserve liquid to cook dumplings.

Dumplings:
    2 cups flour
    ½ teaspoon baking powder
    1 teaspoon salt
    ¼ cup shortening
    1 egg

Sift together dry ingredients and cut in shortening. Add egg and enough milk to make a fairly stiff dough. Roll thinly and cut 1 x 2-inch. Dust lightly with flour. Drop one by one in boiling chicken stock and simmer gently until done. about 30 to 45 minutes. Add salt and pepper to taste while cooking. The stock should thicken as dumplings cook.

Susan McBee

Del Rio

When I was young, my grandmother Gillis always had a special family dinner on each relative's birthday. The dinner traditionally featured chicken and dumplings. Thus, I grew up thinking this was the most special, elegant dish there was, to be enjoyed only on the most festive occasions!

Country Club Hot Chicken Salad

I like to leave off the cheese and cover with crushed buttery crackers, crushed corn flakes or crushed potato chips.

4 cups chicken, cooked and chopped (about 2 chickens)
2 cups celery, chopped
4 eggs, hard-cooked, chopped
1 2-ounce jar diced pimentos, drained
2 tablespoons finely chopped onion
1 cup mayonnaise
2 tablespoons lemon juice
¼ teaspoon salt
1 cup shredded Cheddar cheese
⅔ cup sliced almonds, toasted

Combine first 8 ingredients, mix well. Spoon into a slightly greased 12x8x2-inch baking dish; cover and bake at 350° for 20 minutes. Sprinkle cheese over casserole; top with almonds. Bake uncovered, an additional 3 minutes or until cheese melts. Makes 6 to 8 servings.

Erlene McKinney
San Angelo

King Ranch Chicken Casserole

This is a great dish to take on a weekend trip with your friends. You can freeze it and take it all the way to Ruidoso to supply a great supper after a day at the horse races! - Anita

1 chicken
1 small onion chopped
1 can cream of mushroom soup
1 can cream of chicken soup
½ pound Cheddar cheese
1 can Rotel tomatoes
12 corn or flour tortillas
½-1 cup of chicken broth

Boil chicken in 2 quarts of salted water until tender, about 1 hour. Skin and bone chicken and set aside. In a medium saucepan mix onion, mushroom soup, chicken soup, Rotel tomatoes, and ½ to 1 cup of chicken broth. Chop chicken and mix well with sauce, layer tortillas, sauce, tortillas, etc. Sprinkle cheese on top and bake in 350° for about 30 minutes, or until cheese melts.

Nancy Johnson
Sonora

Del Rio Chicken Spaghetti

2 cans (3 pounds, 4 ounces each) whole chicken in broth
1 package (1 pound) spaghetti, broken in thirds
¼ cup margarine
3 bell peppers, diced
3 onions, diced
3 cups diced celery
2 4-ounce jars pimentos, diced
1 8-ounce can mushrooms, sliced
4 10¾-ounce cans cream of mushroom soup
1 pound American cheese, grated
salt and pepper to taste

Drain chicken, saving broth. Cook spaghetti in broth until pasta is al dente. There should be some broth left in the pot after cooking. Sauté diced vegetables in margarine until soft. Skin and bone chicken and chop into pieces. Mix all ingredients together in large bowl or pot. If mixture seems too dry, add a little extra chicken broth. Pour into dishes and bake at 350° for 30 to 45 minutes.

This recipe fills two 3 quart and one 2 quart Pyrex dishes, or 1 oven roaster. It freezes beautifully. It's lovely to have in your freezer for quick and easy entertaining.

> *Susan Gurley McBee*
> *Del Rio*

Susan Gurley McBee, 1969, Texas House of Representatives, District 70.

This recipe may be doubled or tripled for a large gathering. Serve with curried peach halves, garlic bread and a green salad.

You have to learn from the mistakes of others. You will never live long enough to make them all yourself.

Chicken Spaghetti Casserole

2 large chicken breasts
4 stalks of celery, chopped
1 small onion, chopped
1 small bell pepper
1 small can chopped black olives
1 pound Velveeta cheese
1 small red pepper
salt and pepper to taste
1 small package elbow spaghetti
2 cans tomatoes

Cook chicken the night before and put in refrigerator. Cook spaghetti, combine onion, celery and bell peppers and sauté in chicken fat - add oil if needed. Add 2 cans of drained chopped tomatoes. Add broken up chicken and chopped olives; mix. Add cooked spaghetti and mix. Then layer spaghetti and slices of Velveeta cheese ending with cheese. Slightly thicken chicken broth and pour about an inch in bottom of pan. Bake at 350° for 1 hour.

Mrs. Warren Hemphill
Sonora

Chicken Casserole

3 cups cooked chicken, chopped
1 can cream of chicken soup
2 tablespoons lemon juice
1 large carton sour cream
½ cup mayonnaise
3 cups grated Cheddar or Longhorn cheese
2 cups cooked rice
3 cups chopped broccoli
1 cup grated carrots
salt and pepper to taste

Cook rice and set aside. Grate cheese. Boil chicken and chop. Mix cooked rice, broccoli, carrots and 1 cup of cheese. Spread in bottom of 9x13-inch casserole dish. Mix chopped chicken, cream of chicken soup, lemon juice, sour cream, mayonnaise and one cup of cheese and spread on top of rice mixture and top with remainder of cheese. Bake covered for 30 minutes at 350° - uncovered for last 5 minutes.

Enjoy! This recipe is great for Church dinners. Even better if made the day before.

Carolyn Pennington
Farmington, New Mexico

Chile Chicken Casserole

1 chicken
1 cup diced celery
½ diced onion
1 package chicken soup mix
1 package tostadas
1 medium can green chilies, chopped

Cook chicken in salty water until done about 1 hour. Remove skin and bones from the chicken, reserving the broth. Add celery, onions and soup mix to broth and simmer until tender. Place alternate layers of tostadas, chicken, chilies and broth mixture in a greased casserole. Cook at 375° for 30 minutes.

Mary Brumley
Del Rio

In order to realize the worth of the anchor, we need to feel the stress of the storm!

145

Pork Tenderloin

1 2¼-pound pork tenderloin
½ teaspoon coarse salt
½ teaspoon freshly ground black pepper
5 bay leaves
3 sprigs fresh thyme
2 tablespoons olive oil
¼ cup fresh tangerine or orange juice

Place tenderloin in a baking dish and rub with salt, pepper, bay leaves, and thyme. Let rest at room temperature for 30 minutes. Preheat oven to 375°. Scrape marinade off the pork; reserve. Heat olive oil in a large skillet and add tenderloin. Sear the meat quickly over high heat until well browned on all sides. Place the seared meat in a foil-lined roasting pan. Rub the reserved marinade back onto the meat and pour tangerine juice over it. Tightly close the foil and cook for 20 minutes. Remove the tenderloin from oven and loosen the foil to allow any steam to escape. Return to oven for 30 to 40 minutes, or until meat registers 160° on a meat thermometer. Let rest at least 10 minutes before slicing. While tenderloin is roasting, make the conserve. Cut the tenderloin into slices and serve with the warm conserve.

Onion-Raisin Conserve
½ cup raisins
½ cup fresh tangerine or orange juice
3 tablespoons unsalted butter
½ red onion
1 small bulb fennel
1 teaspoon sugar
salt and freshly ground black pepper

Combine raisins and the tangerine or orange juice and let macerate for 30 minutes. Peel, halve and thinly slice the red onion lengthwise; halve, core and thinly slice the fennel lengthwise. Melt 2 tablespoons of the butter in a large skillet and sauté the onion slowly for 5 minutes. When the onion has softened, add the fennel. Cook over medium heat for 5 minutes. Add the raisins, juice, and the remaining 1 tablespoon butter. Stir in sugar and season to taste. Serve with pork tenderloin.

Preccia Miller
Dallas

Pork Chops

4 center cut pork chops
1 small can chopped green chilies
1 can undiluted mushroom soup
noodles or rice

Brown the pork chops and transfer to a 10½x6¾-inch baking dish. Smother them with the green chilies and mushroom soup (use the whole can). Bake in 325° to 350° oven. Serve with noodles or rice and steamed broccoli and/or squash.

When the noodles or rice are ready, the chops will be, too. Good quick 30 minute meal.

Pat Shurley
San Angelo

Beer-Grilled Chops

4 boneless pork loin chops - about 1 pound
¼ cup soy sauce
1 cup beer
2 tablespoons brown sugar
2 teaspoons grated fresh ginger root

Combine marinade ingredients together well; place trimmed chops in plastic bag and pour marinade over, seal bag and refrigerate 4 to 24 hours. Prepare medium-hot coals in grill. Remove chops from marinade; grill over medium-hot coals 7 to 8 minutes per side, turning once.

National Pork Producers Council

Barbecued Baby Back Ribs

4 pounds pork back ribs
your favorite barbecue sauce

Place ribs in shallow roasting pan. Cover with foil and bake at 300° for 2 hours. Finish on grill by turning and basting ribs with barbecue sauce for 15 to 20 minutes. Serves 4.

National Pork Council

When using charcoal briquettes, start the fire 20 to 30 minutes before placing your meat on the grill. Pile the briquettes in a pyramid in the center of the grill. Ignite with charcoal lighter fluid or an electric starter. The coals are ready for cooking when ash-covered and glowing.

Tips for Cooking Pork

Don't sauce too soon. Wait until the last 30 minutes of cooking to add sauce to ribs.

Take it slow. Cook ribs slowly over low heat, usually for at least an hour, to produce the best flavor and tenderness.

Is it done yet? Ribs are considered "done" when you can just wiggle the meat from the bone.

147

This is better if sauerkraut portion is done a day or two before, reheated and meats added in final cooking.

My family, the Wilhelm Family, has ranched in Menard and McCulloch counties since 1881. I have used this recipe in cooking classes and demonstrations in the past.

Choucroute Garni Á Lalsacienne

Braised Pork and Sauerkraut

2 pounds sauerkraut (fresh or in a jar)
½ pound bacon cut into lardons
2 tablespoons butter
½ cup thinly sliced carrots
1 cup diced onions
1 peeled and diced apple
1 cup dry white wine or champagne
bouquet garni: 4-5 parsley sprigs, 1 bay leaf, 8 peppercorns, 10 juniper berries (or ½ cup gin if you don't have juniper berries)
2-3 cups light stock; chicken or beef or a mix
pork loin roast or pork chops
3-4 knockwurst, bratwurst, smoked bratwurst, or weinerwurst
game birds (pheasant, duck, or goose), optional

Drain and rinse sauerkraut. (If using canned, rinse 2 times.) In a large casserole, melt butter, sauté bacon and onions until onions wilt. Add carrots and apple, cook 8 to 10 minutes but do not brown. Stir in sauerkraut, cook 5 to 6 minutes, stirring constantly. Make bouquet garni, tying herbs and aromatics together in cheesecloth or tying herbs and crushing peppercorns and juniper berries. Bury bouquet in sauerkraut. Pour in wine and bouillon to cover, bring to a simmer. Cover with buttered waxed paper or parchment to "sweat." Place in a 300° oven for 3 to 3½ hours. Check occasionally to see if more stock is needed.

Pork Loin Roast: brown pork loin roast in skillet, add to sauerkraut last 1 to 1½ hour of cooking in oven. Do the same with pork chops if using, adding to sauerkraut last hour of cooking.

Sausages: Pierce casing several places, poach in water on top of stove for 30 minutes; add to sauerkraut last ½ to 1 hour of cooking. Or just slice, sauté and drain.

Game birds: brown on stove top or smoke, add to sauerkraut last hour of cooking.

Clara Winter
Brady

Pork Ribs and Gravy

pork ribs or chops
8-10 potatoes
2-3 onions
1 can sauerkraut

Cut pork ribs in small pieces (trim off any excess fat) and place in boiling water and cook until about ⅔ done. Scrape or peel and cut up the potatoes. Cook the potatoes and onions in the pot with the pork until done. Add a can of shredded kraut to the pot and cook about 15 minutes. Salt and pepper to taste. Serve with cornbread, Cream Cornmeal Gravy and a tossed salad.

I prefer the Bush Bavarian Style Kraut - it has a sweet flavor.

This recipe is over 100 years old and is for those who really like sauerkraut and will change the minds of those who think they don't like it.

Cream Cornmeal Gravy
3 tablespoons oil
salt and pepper
2 tablespoons cornmeal
milk or water

Pour the oil in the pan; add salt and pepper to taste and stir. Add the cornmeal and stir constantly until browned, then pour in milk or water or a combination of milk and water. Let boil for about 2 minutes. If too thick, add extra liquid.

Cornmeal gravy is made the same as regular cream gravy except you use cornmeal instead of flour.

Henrye Evans
Fort McKavett

If you've never eaten cornmeal gravy with cornbread—you've missed a "real treat". It's delicious!

Crab Quiche

1 unbaked pie shell
4 ounces Swiss cheese, grated
2 green onions with tops, chopped
4½ ounces canned crabmeat
½ teaspoon grated lemon peel
½ teaspoon salt
½ teaspoon dry mustard
3 eggs, beaten
¾ cup light or heavy cream
¼ cup slivered almonds

Bake pie crust for 5 minutes at 450°. Arrange cheese on bottom of pie shell, sprinkle onion on the top of cheese. Combine the rest of the ingredients. Pour over cheese and onions. Top with slivered almonds. Bake at 325° for 40 minutes. Remove from oven and let sit for 10 minutes.

Cindy Rink
Saudi Arabia

Shrimp Curry

My dear friend, Mary Eleanor Cartall, was one of Del Rio's best cooks, and she gave me her shrimp curry recipe years ago. It's the only one I ever use.

2 pounds fresh shrimp
1 cup chopped onion
3 tablespoons salad oil
½ teaspoon salt
3½ teaspoons curry powder
1 teaspoon vinegar
1 teaspoon sugar
1 teaspoon Worcestershire sauce
¾ cup water
2 cups tomato soup
1 tablespoon A-1 sauce

Cook shrimp in boiling salted water. Do not over-cook. Prepare sauce by sautéing onions in hot oil until golden brown. Add all other ingredients. Simmer, uncovered for 10 minutes. Add shrimp and heat thoroughly. Serve over steamed rice.

This dish is more delicious if made the day before.

Mary Ellen McEntire
San Angelo

Shrimp and Chicken Casserole

3 cups cooked, cubed chicken breast
1 teaspoon salt
1½ pounds cooked peeled shrimp
2 pounds fresh or frozen broccoli, cut up
½ cup fat free mayonnaise
1 can cream of chicken soup, fat free
1 can cream of celery soup, fat free
3 tablespoons lemon or fresh lime juice
½ cup fresh brown bread crumbs
1 cup grated, low fat white cheese

Spread broccoli evenly over a lightly greased 13x9-inch baking dish, set aside. Combine mayonnaise and next four ingredients and spread ⅓ of this mixture over broccoli. Combine chicken and shrimp. Spread evenly over casserole and top with remaining sauce. Cover tightly with foil and chill overnight. Bake at 350° for 30 minutes. Uncover, sprinkle with cheese and bake 15 minutes more. Sprinkle with paprika. Makes 10 servings.

Mary Beth Ince
Mason

Education is what a fellow gets from reading the fine print. Experience is what he gets if he doesn't read it.

Shrimp Fettuccine

3 ounces spinach fettuccine
2 cups fresh sliced mushrooms
½ cup chicken bouillon
¼ cup light sour cream
1 pound shrimp, steamed and peeled
2 tablespoons green onions, chopped
½ cup plain nonfat yogurt
¼ teaspoon salt
¼ teaspoon paprika
⅛ teaspoon crushed oregano
⅛ teaspoon onion powder
⅛ teaspoon red, white and black pepper
⅛ teaspoon thyme

Sauté mushrooms and onions. Set aside. Boil chicken broth and add shrimp. Stir constantly. Set aside. Heat sour cream, yogurt, and 1 tablespoon flour (or cornstarch). Add spices and mix with sour cream. Stir until well blended and add broth and shrimp. Serve on top of fettuccine.

Serve with green salad, fruit and French bread.

Ro'Re Stokes
McKinney

Grilled Shrimp

1 pound jumbo shrimp
¼ cup butter
1 teaspoon garlic juice
1 tablespoon minced parsley
dash cayenne pepper
4 tablespoons white wine

Melt butter, garlic, parsley and cayenne pepper, cook for 3 minutes. Stir in wine, heat do not boil. Thread shrimp on skewer and grill over medium hot coals. Turn often for about 6 to 7 minutes. Baste with sauce. Makes 2 servings. Up to 4 people if you serve with a big steak.

Joan Tucker
San Angelo

Shrimp Creole

¾ cup chopped onion
1 clove minced garlic
1 medium finely chopped green pepper
½ cup finely chopped celery
2 tablespoons butter
1 8-ounce can tomato sauce
½ cup water
1 crushed bay leaf
1 teaspoon minced fresh parsley
½ teaspoon salt
⅛ scant teaspoon cayenne pepper
1 8-ounce package deveined shrimp
fluffy white rice

Sauté onion, garlic, green pepper, and celery in butter for 5 minutes or until tender. Stir in tomato sauce, water, bay leaf, parsley, salt, and pepper. Simmer for 10 minutes. Add more water if needed. Add shrimp, and bring to a boil. Cook 5 minutes. Serve over rice. Makes 2 servings and is easily doubled.

Mary K. Elliot
San Angelo

This recipe was my first meal to make for company after my wedding! Still a favorite!

Shrimp Steamed with Beer

1 12-ounce can of beer
1 tablespoon seafood seasoning
juice of 1 lemon
1 pound large shrimp, unpeeled

In a large saucepan, combine the beer, seafood seasoning to taste, and lemon juice. Bring to a boil. Place the shrimp in a steamer basket, place basket in saucepan, cover, and steam shrimp over the liquid just until they are pink and done, 3 to 5 minutes. The shrimp can also be boiled right in the liquid. Remove the shrimp from the pan and serve hot, warm, or cold.

Preccia Miller
Dallas

Chipotle chilies are dried, smoked jalapeño peppers. Canned "chipotles in adobo" are reconstituted chipotles and are available in most supermarkets.

Chipotle Dipping Sauce
2 chipotle chilies in adobo sauce
1 egg yolk
1 tablespoon sherry vinegar
2 teaspoons mustard
1 tablespoon lemon juice
salt to taste
1 cup canola oil

In blender or food processor, combine chilies, yolk, vinegar, mustard, lemon juice, and salt. With motor running, add oil slowly in fine stream. Emulsify.

This sauce/mayo is good for just about anything, from burgers to grilled seafood.

Texas Gulf Shrimp Fritters

3 separated eggs
1½ cups all purpose flour
1 teaspoon olive oil
½ cup cold water
½ cup cold milk
1 tablespoon finely diced red bell pepper
1 tablespoon finely diced green bell pepper
1 tablespoon finely diced yellow bell pepper
½ cup frozen corn kernels
1 tablespoon chopped fresh cilantro
12 medium shrimp, cleaned, chopped
salt, cayenne pepper, and paprika to taste

Whip egg whites to stiff peaks; set aside. In mixing bowl, combine yolks, flour, olive oil, water, and milk; mix until smooth. Add diced peppers, corn, cilantro, and shrimp. Season with salt, cayenne, and paprika to taste. Fold in whipped egg whites. Fry spoonfuls of batter (about 2 tablespoons each) in hot oil 3 to 5 minutes or until golden brown. Serve with chipotle dipping sauce.

Brad Johnson
Chicago, Illinois

Chipotle Grilled Shrimp

8 wooden skewers soaked in water
32 medium-sized shrimp, peeled and deveined
1 tablespoon olive oil
salt and pepper to taste
chipotle dipping sauce
chopped parsley as needed for garnish

Place 4 shrimp on each skewer, making sure shrimp stay flat. Brush with olive oil and season with salt and pepper to taste. Grill over hot coals, approximately 1 minute each side. Serve with chipotle mayo dipping sauce. Garnish with parsley.

Brad Johnson
Chicago, Illinois

Fresh Italian Pasta Sauce

1 stick of butter
6-8 whole garlic pods, peeled
8-10 fresh tomatoes, peeled and chopped
1-2 cups water
1 tablespoon fresh parsley, chopped
1 tablespoon basil, chopped
1 tablespoon oregano, chopped
2-3 grated carrots
2-3 grated zucchini and or yellow squash
½ cup chopped celery leaves
½ cup chopped mushrooms
1 teaspoon salt
1 teaspoon white pepper

In a large saucepan melt butter then sauté garlic, until it starts browning. Add tomatoes and water. While simmering add all the other ingredients. Continue to simmer at least 1 hour. Serve over any pasta.

Dawn Kothman
Ozona

Even my "Meat and Potatoes" husband loves this one! You can double the recipe and freeze some of the sauce for a later use.

Fettuccine Pasta with Chorizo and Jalapeño Cream Sauce

1 8-ounce package fettuccine, cooked, and drained
¼ pound chorizo, crumbled
2 tablespoons fresh jalapeños, chopped
1½ cups heavy cream
¾ cup grated Asiago or Parmesan cheese

Brown chorizo with jalapeños; drain. Add cream; heat over low about 5 minutes, until lightly reduced. Stir in cheese. Serve over warm pasta. Top with extra cheese if desired.

Brad Johnson
Chicago

My mother's cooking always filled our home and our stomachs with fresh, natural foods. Our plates, she said "Should look like a rainbow" (with a variety of different colors). From golden corn, and fresh greens to rich gravies. It is not unusual on holiday's to feast on 2 to 3 different meats and close to 7 or 8 different vegetables to choose from. The recipes here are passed down from my grandmother. Today, my brother Anthony and I try to keep alive the memories and traditions and of course, I tell my five year old daughter, Lisa, "Your plate should look like a rainbow", full of colorful and healthy foods.

Mama Lisa's Special Italian Gravy with Meatballs and Sausage

Gravy

2 large cans of crushed tomatoes
1 small can of tomato paste
1 small clove of garlic
1 fresh basil leaf
1 tablespoon of olive oil
1 tablespoon of fresh chopped parsley
1 teaspoon of dried oregano

Place both cans of crushed tomatoes in an electric blender for 30 seconds. Set aside. In a large sauce pot place olive oil and chopped garlic. Brown lightly. Add blended crushed tomatoes, basil, parsley, salt to taste, and oregano. Bring to a simmer for 1 hour. Add 1 can of tomato paste. Add cooked meatballs and sausage. Cook on a low flame for additional 1 hour. If gravy is too thick, add ½ cup of water. Cook 15 minutes.

Meatballs

1 pound sirloin chopped meat
1 tablespoon chopped parsley
1 tablespoon grated Parmesan cheese
½ teaspoon salt
¾ cup of plain bread crumbs
1 egg
¼ cup of water
¼ teaspoon garlic powder

Place all ingredients in a large mixing bowl. Blend together until mixed completely and evenly. Take out small amounts and roll between palms of hand to form a meatball. Place on a platter. Continue until all meat is done. In a large frying pan, heat 2 tablespoons of olive oil and fry meatballs until brown on all sides. Place meatballs in gravy and let cook for 1 hour.

Continued on next page

**Mama Lisa's Special Italian Gravy with
Meatballs and Sausage (continued)**

Italian Sausage:
  6 Italian sausage
  2 tablespoons olive oil

Heat olive oil in frying pan. Pierce sausage once
with fork. Place in frying pan and cook on all sides
until completely done and browned. If there is any
cooking fat in frying pan, take 1 to 2 tablespoons
and place in gravy. Place all sausage in gravy and
cook for 1 hour.

Madeline Daddiego
Director of Promotion
Mohair Council of America, New York Office

Sausage and Meatballs
can be placed in Gravy at
the same time. When
finished cooking, remove
Sausage and Meatballs
and place on a serving
platter. Place Gravy over
your favorite pasta.
Please use only olive oil
for these recipes. This is
one flavor that cannot be
substituted.

Lemon and Asparagus Fettuccine

  1 pound thin asparagus
  2 tablespoons butter or margarine
  1 cup heavy cream or evaporated skim milk
  2 tablespoons extra virgin olive oil
  juice of 1 lemon
  freshly ground black pepper to taste
  zest of 1 lemon
  freshly grated Parmesan cheese

Cook asparagus spears in steamer until stems are
just crisp. Blanch in cold running water and drain,
then slice spears diagonally into 3 or 4 pieces. Cook
fettuccine according to package directions, and
drain well. In a large skillet melt margarine and
sauté asparagus, add cream or evaporated skim
milk; stir in lemon juice and pepper. Combine pasta
to cream and asparagus mixture and toss well.
Sprinkle with lemon zest and serve with freshly
grated Parmesan cheese. Makes 4 to 5 servings.

Vicki Rees
San Angelo

I substitute evaporated
skim milk in place of the
heavy cream for a lighter
dish. To make this a main
meal I like to steam fresh
salmon and add it to the
pasta dish. Prepare a
fresh garden salad and
dinner is ready.

I can remember having this at least once a week growing up. My mother was from Germany, and I believe this was her own invention. I have altered it very little.

Ellen's Spaghetti

2 pounds ground beef
1 onion
2 garlic cloves
1 bell pepper
1 carrot, grated
5 tomatoes
1 teaspoon thyme
1 teaspoon pepper
dash Tabasco sauce
¼ cup red wine
1 bay leaf
4 ounces grated fresh Parmesan cheese
2 cans tomato sauce
2 tablespoons brown sugar
1 tablespoon Worcestershire sauce
1 tablespoon lemon juice
1 tablespoon oregano

Brown meat until almost all the pink is gone. Add in onions, garlic, bell pepper, mushrooms, and tomatoes. Sauté until onions are soft. Add in tomato sauce, brown sugar, lemon juice and the rest of the ingredients; except for 1-ounce of Parmesan. Simmer one hour; remove bay leaf. Serve over pasta and sprinkle with the remaining 1 ounce Parmesan cheese. Great meal with a large salad and French bread.

Kimberly Kothman
Sanderson

My MeMe's Chicken Spaghetti

1 boiled and boned hen or fryer
1 bell pepper
1 onion
2 stalks celery
1 small clove garlic
1 can Italian tomato paste
1 tablespoon sugar
salt and pepper to taste
2 small cans hot tomato sauce (optional)

Melt shortening in large pan. Fry chopped onions, peppers, celery, and garlic until browned. Add tomato paste, tomato sauce, sugar, salt, and pepper. Simmer until sauce is thick. Add chicken pieces at any time after sauce has been completed. Better when you start to simmer - the taste has time to cook through the chicken. Serve over cooked spaghetti.

Angela Crittendon
Sonora

This recipe was given to me by my grand-mother, Ruth Brotherton Luckett. When my mom, Camille Luckett Green, needs something special, she gets this—it is her favorite.

Spaghetti a la Zilker

1½ pounds hamburger, browned and drained
1 teaspoon oregano, slightly rounded
12 ounce can tomato paste
2 large cans tomato sauce
1½ large cans of water
½ teaspoon anise
1 teaspoon sugar
2 bay leaves
1 clove garlic
1 teaspoon salt
1 tablespoon Accent
1 tablespoon minced onion
1 can or 1 package frozen artichoke hearts, halved
½ pound fresh sliced mushrooms

Combine all ingredients and simmer for 30 to 60 minutes. Serve over spaghetti

Marilyn Leinweber
Mountain Home

This is an elegant, but easy recipe. My husband can't understand why I throw in the "Live Oak" leaves.

Lasagna Noodle Casserole

1 large onion
2 garlic cloves
1 teaspoon dried parsley
¼ cup olive oil
1 number 2 can tomato paste
2 bay leaves
½ cup water
1 pound ground meat

Sauté onion, garlic, parsley, salt, pepper, and meat in oil. Add rest of ingredients and simmer for 45 minutes. Remove bay leaf after cooking.

Cheese Sauce
1 small onion
4 tablespoons butter
3 tablespoons flour
2 cups milk
2 egg yolks
¾ cup grated Parmesan cheese
1 large package lasagna noodles

Chop onions, cook in butter then add flour and milk to make thick sauce. Add the egg yolks and cook a bit longer. Add cheese. Boil lasagna noodles until tender. Layer noodles, meat sauce, and cheese sauce in long pan. Heat in 350° oven until bubbly.

Laura C. McMullan
Iraan

Texas Field Hand Chili

1½ pounds lean ground meat
1 large chopped onion
1 can ranch style chili beans
1 can pinto beans
1 can ranch style beans with jalapeños
1 can diced Rotel tomatoes
1 can stewed tomatoes
1 can creamed or whole corn
1 small package dry ranch dressing mix
1 package taco seasoning

Sauté meat and onion; drain on paper towels to remove fat. Put in large crock pot or other large pot with remaining ingredients. Mix well and simmer all day.

Great to have ready when you come in from working all day!

Elaine Wardlaw
Del Rio

This was given to me by Alice Cauthorn.

Chili

Where in the world did it come from?

Chili is not Mexican food. It originated with the cowboys, when a chuck wagon cook ran our of black pepper while preparing stew, he had to settle for red pepper which was offered by the Indians in Southwest Texas. When the cowhands complained about their spicy food, the cook said it was "Chile", a term applied to red pepper from Indian natives. So now you know where we got the dish called CHILI!

When the cook works in the pasture or pens, this is an easy and filling supper or quick breakfast that sticks to your ribs.

Fifty miles in the country, no phone and you hear company driving up at meal time. Don't worry, fresh air, fresh eggs and fresh milk helps to make plain food taste great! - Mrs. Ray Dulnap, Ozona 1898 - 1994

This was the winning entry at the 1992 Texas Lamb and Wool Days Lamb Cook-Off.

Gopher Supper

2 pounds sausage
1 large pan milk gravy
1 large pan fresh biscuits

Fry up sausage patties, make pan of milk gravy (from sausage drippings), bake fresh biscuits, put on table and "go-for-it"!

Carolyn Stuart Wilson
Ozona

Miles Messenger Messy Cookers Special Barbecue Sauce

4 18-ounce bottles catsup
½ cup white wine (cheap-o)
½ cup lemon juice (fresh or bottled)
¼ cup Worcestershire sauce
1 medium onion, yellow or white, finely chopped
1 pound brown sugar
8-10 small jalapeño peppers, finely chopped (more or less to suit your taste)

Mix all ingredients together in pot on stove, adding brown sugar last. Heat enough to melt sugar. DO NOT BOIL. Baste meat with sauce while cooking on open coals, turning often. Enjoy!

Texas Sheep and Goat Raisers Association

Meatball Sandwiches

2 slightly beaten eggs
3 tablespoons milk
½ cup fine dry breadcrumbs
¾ teaspoon salt
⅛ teaspoon pepper
1 pound ground beef
½ pound bulk Italian pork sausage
½ cup chopped onion
½ cup chopped green pepper
1 cup water
1 8-ounce can tomato sauce
1 6-ounce can tomato paste
2 teaspoons sugar
1 teaspoon garlic salt
½ teaspoon dried crushed oregano
½ teaspoon crushed parsley flakes
8 French rolls

Combine eggs, milk, breadcrumbs, salt and pepper. Add ground beef, mix well. Form into 24 1½-inch meat balls. Brown in hot skillet. Remove meatballs from skillet and drain. Add sausage, onion, and green pepper; cook until sausage is browned. Drain. Add water, tomato sauce, tomato paste, sugar, garlic, salt, oregano, and parsley flakes. Return meatballs to skillet. Cover and simmer 15 minutes stirring twice. Remove top crust from rolls, hollow out leaving a ¼-inch wall, fill rolls with 3 meatballs and some sauce. Return top crusts to sandwich. Makes 8 sandwiches. These freeze well.

A great change from the same old sandwich and they fill 'em up!

> Joan Motl Tucker
> San Angelo

Nothing brings two women closer together than the mutual dislike of a third.

Mush

1 cup boiling water
⅓ cup cornmeal
1 egg yolk
salt
hamburger, sausage, pecans - all optional

Stir meal into boiling water. Add egg, salt and browned hamburger, sausage, or pecans. Refrigerate. Slice and fry.

Carol Arledge
Arledge Ranches
Robert Lee

Depression

The Joe Wheeler Arledge Ranch began around 1900 in Coke and Nolan Counties. The fifth generation of Arledges now live on the ranch near Sanco, Texas which is operated by my brother, Dr. Joe W. Arledge, III. According to my mother, Geraldine Arledge, and my aunt, Jo Ella Arledge Leeper (now in her 90's), "MUSH" was a favorite and also a way to "stretch a dollar" during days of the Depression, the drought of the fifties, and other lean times for ranchers and their families who were struggling to hold on to their land.

One of a Kind

Rice and Sausage

1 cup brown rice
2 cups water
2 8-ounce cans tomato sauce
1 medium onion chopped fine
2 link sausages skinned and chopped fine
½ teaspoon garlic and herb seasoning

Cook rice in water until done. Skin and chop sausage fine (small pieces), put in pan and cook until light brown or most of grease is out. Discard grease- add onion and cook until soft on low temperature. Add tomato sauce and seasoning, stir well; add cooked rice and stir.

Geneva Wells Pendley
Leakey

My family likes spicy food. This recipe pleases them and it makes a complete meal when served with pinto beans.

Quick Pizza

1 loaf French bread
1 pound hamburger or sausage
1 small can mushrooms
1 small can black olives
1-2 cups spaghetti sauce
8 ounces mozzarella cheese

Slice French loaf in half lengthwise. Spread spaghetti sauce mix over cut halves of bread. Spread cooked hamburger or sausage over sauce. Sprinkle mushrooms and sliced olives over meat, then sprinkle with cheese. Other ingredients such as onion, bell pepper, pepperoni, jalapeños, etc., may be added before grated cheese. Place on cookie sheet in 400° oven until cheese bubbles and turns golden brown. Serve hot with salad. Delicious and filling. So easy to prepare that kids can help.

Mrs. Fritz Kuebel
Blanco

When I joined this family in 1946, only the men would eat this. They would have a big party and play dominoes. Today everyone loves this stew.

Son of a Gun Stew

5 pounds beef marrow gut
½ pound lean beef
1 beef tongue
1 beef heart
1 pound sweetbread
½ pound beef brains

Cut all ingredients in ½ to 1-inch bite sizes. Cook the tongue the day before; peel and cut up. Put all ingredients into a very large pot except for the brains. Salt and pepper to taste and cook 6 or 7 hours very slow. One hour before it is ready, add the chopped brains; also add some instant potatoes just to make the juice a little thicker. Add chili petine in your bowls if you like it hot.

Jo Foster
Sterling City

This was given to me by my oldest brother who enjoys barbecuing.

Bar-B-Que Sauce

1 cup butter
1 cup packed brown sugar
1 cup ketchup
¼ cup vinegar
1 cup Worcestershire sauce
1 medium onion
2 ounces Tabasco sauce
2 tablespoons mustard
1 teaspoon salt

Mix all ingredients together and cook over medium heat for about 15 minutes.

Cheryl Shipp
Iraan

Jones-Espy Barbeque Sauce

½ gallon vinegar
24 ounces mustard
12 ounces maple syrup
3 quarts catsup
1 pound butter
mellow with brown or raw sugar to taste
salt & pepper to taste

Cook slowly over medium low heat. I'm guessing
I cook it about 20 minutes.

The recipe was given to me in the large propor-
tions. Listed here are the measurements for a more
manageable size. We keep a jar in the icebox. We
especially like it on lamb chops.

1 pint vinegar
6 ounces mustard
3 ounces maple syrup
3 cups catsup
1 stick butter

Donald Allison
San Angelo

Season Salt

½ pound MSG or Accent
½ pound salt
5 tablespoons coarse ground black pepper
2 tablespoons garlic powder
1 tablespoon paprika
1 teaspoon oregano
1 teaspoon ground cumin

This comes from a popular steak house in Del Rio.
It can be used on meat, salads and all vegetables.
Really perks up cottage cheese. It is easy to mix in
a food processor but use the rubber blade or it will
be pulverized.

Frankie Lee Harlow
Del Rio

Nothing can match the barbeque served at the Jones-Espy Cook Shed during the annual Bloys Camp Meeting. The meat (leg of lamb) is started at about 2:00 a.m. and cooked slowly over live oak coals until noon. About every couple of hours the cooks come to turn and brush the sauce on the meat. The men stand over the pits, carve the lamb with their pocket knives and smother it in the barbeque sauce. Since it is only once a year, they can really put away a huge amount of barbeque.

Oven-Roasted Garlic Barbecue Glaze

½ cup unseasoned rice vinegar
½ cup cider vinegar
1 tablespoon coriander seeds
½ tablespoon whole cloves
3 allspice berries
2 tablespoons virgin olive oil
½ white onion, cut into ½-inch dice
1 head roasted garlic, peeled and sliced
¼ cup brown sugar
1 tablespoon dark molasses
½ tablespoon Worcestershire sauce
½ bottle dark beer, such as Negra Modelo, Dos Equis, or Beck's
1 14-ounce bottle ketchup (1¾ cups)
½ tablespoon salt

Place the rice and cider vinegars in a saucepan, add the coriander, cloves, and allspice; bring to a boil. Reduce the liquid by half, strain, and set aside. In a separate pan, heat the olive oil and sauté the onion and garlic for 5 minutes over medium heat. Lower the heat and stir in the sugar until it melts, about 1 minute. Add the molasses and Worcestershire sauce, and bring to a simmer, keeping the heat low so that the sugars in the glaze do not caramelize and burn. Deglaze the pan with the beer and reserved vinegar mixture. Reduce heat to low and simmer for 30 minutes. Add the ketchup, and simmer for 15 minutes longer. Strain through a fine sieve, pushing down on the garlic to extract the juices.

Use as sauce or glaze. Good with chicken, ribs, or burgers. Keeps in refrigerator up to 2 weeks. Yields about 4 cups.

Chris Davis
Dallas

168

Safe Spot

As I sit here and ponder the realities of life,

the heartaches and pain,

happiness and strife.

I realize the pleasure that someone like you can bring.

Your open honesty is sincere like a clean fresh running spring.

Words can only paint pictures in someone's minds eye,

but words without feelings come easy for those that don't ever try.

I look at my good fortune and thank you for always being there.

A utopia of safety from the everyday ware and tare.

Like a queen within a castle or a ruler that reigns on high.

Your walls are indestructible but compassionate for a strangers crying eye.

I take this time to thank you for your friendship,

and the closeness that we share,

for life isn't always easy and pain really has no care.

It is vicious like a rattler,

that's suffered a stepped on tail,

not being opinionated or selective in its choice,

striking with deadly accuracy upon both the strong or frail.

Like a hospital full of nurses ready upon request,

your friendship is always there,

that safety is the best.

Sometimes it is taken for granted,

and often threatened to be replaced,

but the things that we have shared are an oasis within God's saving grace.

Thank you for always being there.

Merry Christmas and God bless you!

Russell Rogers

Our good friend, Joseph Decker, gave us this recipe. He said that you stir them every time you pass the stove!

Let them know that you love them more than anything, but make them mind; then they'll respect you and others.

Mrs. Peggy Harral (Mimi to her grandchildren), has served her delicious beans to countless work crews and her family and friends for many years. They are a family favorite.

Always be sure to pick through your beans to remove rocks and mud clods. Many new brides don't know to do this, and the groom can't figure why her beans taste like mud!

West Texas Beans

3 cups dry pinto beans
1 pound bacon or salt pork
1 large onion
2-3 fresh jalapeño peppers
1 8-ounce can tomato sauce

Pick over and wash 3 cups pinto beans. Soak an hour or two before boiling. (Use a pot about 3 times as large as beans.) Cover beans about 2 inches with water. Add the chopped salt pork or bacon, bring to a boil and cook slowly for about 2 hours (or until soft). Then add chopped onion, seeded and chopped jalapeño peppers and tomato sauce. About 30 minutes before serving, add salt to taste.

Good with a barbecue meal or just plain cornbread.

Anys Godfrey
Menard

Mimi's Pinto Beans

4 cups pinto beans
1 chopped onion
4 slices salt pork
1 tablespoon pepper
1 tablespoon salt
1 15-ounce can whole tomatoes

Wash beans and pick out any rocks! Put in a large pot and fill with water until ¾ full. Cook at rolling boil with top on for 30 minutes; turn heat off for 45 minutes. Add water until ¾ full again and cook, covered on low heat 1 and ½ hours. Add chopped onion, chopped salt pork, salt, pepper, and whole tomatoes. Cook 2 hours adding water as necessary. Take top off and cook 30 minutes more. Eat and enjoy!

At times, Peggy substitutes little smokie sausages for the salt pork.

Angela Harral
Fort Stockton

Big Mom's Red Beans

3 cups pinto beans, picked and washed
¾ pot full of water
¼ pound salt pork
2 little green chilies, chopped
2 garlic pods, chopped

Always start red beans in cold water. Cut salt pork 3 or 4 times through middle and add to the beans and water. Cook on high until the beans start to boil. Reduce the heat and cook 2 to 3 hours, stirring every time you pass the stove. Add the green chilies, garlic. Add salt as needed during the last hour of cooking. If water gets low, ALWAYS ADD BOILING WATER, to your beans (never cold). Continue to cook until done.

To cook in a pressure cooker: Use same procedure as above. Cook on high heat until clicker goes to clicking, turn down to medium heat and cook for one hour. Turn off heat to release all the pressure slowly. Be sure to release all pressure before removing lid.

Substitute ham or bacon if you don't have salt pork.

> *Zilla Miller*
> *Ozona*
> *Submitted by Miles R. Miller*
> *San Antonio*

Big Mom made a fresh pot of red beans everyday, you could always go by her house and have beans and cornbread. She always said her secret to a long life was to eat a lot of garlic, chilies, peppers, and beans. She lived to be 101 years old, and is missed every day by her family.

Rice Dressing

2 cups cooked rice
3 large onions
4 stalks celery
1 green pepper
½ cup butter
1 tablespoon salt
1 tablespoon poultry seasoning
2 eggs
1 cup chopped nuts
½ cup chopped parsley
3 fresh sliced mushrooms
canned water chestnuts, chopped

Sauté the chopped vegetables; mix with rice; add the eggs, seasonings, and remaining ingredients. Bake at 350° for ½ hour. Makes 8 cups - enough for 16 people.

Nancy Peyton
Rio Medina

Fried Rice

3 cups raw long grain white rice (12 cups cooked)
¾ cup salad oil or peanut oil
6 eggs
¾ cup chopped green onion
⅓ cup soy sauce
salt and pepper

Cook rice, following package label directions for cooking firm rice. Refrigerate, covered, overnight. Next day; heat oil in 12-inch skillet. Add rice and cook, turning frequently with spatula to separate grains and coat with oil, until heated through. Add green onions, soy sauce, 1½ teaspoons salt, and a dash of pepper. Mix lightly until well blended. Keep warm over low heat. In a small bowl, with fork, beat eggs with 2 tablespoons water, ½ teaspoon salt, and a dash of pepper. Push rice to side of skillet, to make a circular space 6 inches in diameter. Pour egg mixture into center; cook, stirring egg mixture until it is set but soft. Toss lightly with rice and serve immediately. Makes 12 servings or more.

Jana Thornton
Abilene

Sweet Potato Casserole

3 cups mashed cooked sweet potatoes
¾ stick margarine
1 cup canned milk
1½ cups sugar
2 eggs
½ teaspoon nutmeg
½ teaspoon vanilla
½ teaspoon cinnamon

Mix all ingredients together well. Pour into baking dish and bake 15 minutes at 425°.

Topping
1 cup crushed cornflakes
½ cup light-brown sugar
½ cup chopped nuts
¾ stick margarine

Melt margarine. Add sugar, nuts, and cornflakes to margarine and mix well. Spread over top of potatoes and bake an additional 15 minutes at 400°.

Amy Elizabeth Fields
Sonora

Tabasco Potatoes

6 medium potatoes
⅔ cup milk
½ teaspoon Tabasco sauce
1½ teaspoons salt
1 can chopped green chilies
1 tablespoon butter
¼ cup shredded Longhorn cheese
¼ cup shredded Monterey Jack cheese

Slice potatoes like French fries and place in greased shallow pan. Combine the milk, Tabasco sauce, salt, and chopped green chilies. Pour over the potatoes and dot with butter. Cover and bake at 425°. After 40 minutes top with cheese and bake uncovered until cheese is melted.

Jean Owens
Iraan

I am currently attending nursing school at Texas Tech University, and every year that I am away from Sonora and the family ranch, I realize that my heritage is inextricably interwoven with Sutton County, mohair, and beef.

This is good to serve when you are cooking for a bunch of hungry men at shearing time.

The person who smiles when everything goes wrong has already thought of someone he can blame it on.

Uncle Art's Favorite Pasta

1 package tri-colored pasta
1 small bottle Robust or Zesty Italian dressing
chopped cauliflower, broccoli, carrots, bell peppers, green onions or any mix of vegetables

Cook the pasta and drain well. Pour dressing over the pasta while warm and let it sit while you chop vegetables. Toss chopped vegetables into pasta, cover and chill in icebox. Best if chilled overnight. This will keep for days.

This recipe may be used as a side dish or as a salad served on a lettuce leaf.

Great for the family or the church picnic.

Nan Beckwith
Progresso

Ranchers Round-Up Vermicelli

1 package vermicelli
1 can diced tomatoes (Italian or Mexican style)
canola oil

Brown vermicelli in a little oil in an iron skillet until a nice golden color. Add tomatoes and stir well. Cover and let sit until ready to serve.

Be careful when browning the vermicelli as it burns quickly.

Nan Beckwith
Progreso

Creamy Hungarian Noodles

8 ounces fine noodles
2 cups sour cream
1 cup small curd cottage cheese
1 teaspoon minced garlic
1 teaspoon Worcestershire sauce
dash Tabasco sauce
½ cup chopped green onion, including tops
2 teaspoons poppy seeds
salt and pepper to taste
paprika
freshly grated Parmesan cheese

Cook noodles according to package directions, drain well. Process cottage cheese and sour cream with onions, garlic, and seasonings. Combine noodles with cream mixture. Put into a buttered casserole and top with paprika and Parmesan. Bake 30 to 40 minutes, until hot. Serves 8.

This dish freezes well and is great served with Zesty Beef Bourguignonne.

Clara Winters
Brady

Cheese Bake

3 cups milk
4 eggs
¼-½ pound butter, melted
1 loaf white bread (cut off crusts and cube)
1 pound sharp cheese
salt and pepper to taste
¾ teaspoon dry mustard

Mix milk and eggs well, add dry mustard to this. Pour eggs and milk mixture over layer of bread. Pour melted butter over everything. Let stand in refrigerator for 2 hours or overnight. Bake uncovered at 350° for 1 hour. Makes 12 servings.

This makes a good buffet dish along with ham and curried fruit bake. Delicious and festive!

Eva Rink (Mrs. Wilson)
San Angelo

For my family, this is a must when we are having ham. Sometimes I think this is the main dish, and the ham goes on the side. I don't remember where I obtained this one, but it has been a hit with my bunch for many years.

Pineapple Surprise

2 cups sugar
½ cup butter
3 eggs
1 number 2½ can crushed pineapple
4 cups cubed bread slices
½ cup milk

Cream sugar and butter. Add beaten eggs and pineapple. Moisten bread cubes with milk and mix all together. Bake one hour in greased casserole at 350°.

Mimi Allison

Hot Baked Fruit

1 1-pound package pitted prunes
½ 11-ounce package dried apricots
1 can pineapple chunks
1 can cherry pie filling
1½ cups water
¼ cup dry sherry
⅓ cup roasted slivered almonds
½ cup sugar plus 2 packages Equal
almond extract

Place prunes, apricots, and pineapples in a deep 9 inch casserole. Combine cherry pie filling, water, sherry, and pour over fruit. Mix well. Stir in almonds along with sugar, equal, and almond extract. Bake at 350° for 1½ hours.

This freezes beautifully.

Jana Thornton
Abilene

Val Verde 4-H Club Hominy

3 pounds salt pork
7 large onions
2-3 cloves garlic (more or less to taste)
2 pounds bell peppers
3 hot peppers
9 1-pound cans tomatoes
3 gallons hominy
coarse ground pepper

You will need to use a large 18 quart roaster. Cut the salt pork into small pieces and fry until crisp and brown. Sauté the chopped onions and garlic after the pork has browned. Stir in the chopped bell peppers, the chopped hot peppers or jalapeños, tomatoes, and drained hominy. Simmer for 2 to 3 hours.

Some of you may find it easier to brown the salt pork and onions in a large iron skillet before adding to roaster with the other ingredients.

I have successfully substituted Rotel tomatoes and chilies for the hot pepper; use your own judgment, according to how hot you prefer.

I have successfully cut this down to crock pot size and love to make it for my own back yard cookouts. Recently I even added some chopped zucchini, and it was wonderful. If you have any left, I think it is better the next day.

Joy Carruthers
Sanderson

I never prepare and serve this dish without being asked for the recipe. I'm not surprised that we had two contributors for this wonderful dish. I remember as a little girl my mother, Mary Ellen McEntire, and my Aunt Mattey Wardlaw making this for the 4-H barbecue. They would get together to make their roasters full so they could visit and help each other with all the chopping. The whole house smelled heavenly. This dish is the reason I can, say "Yes, I do like hominy." - Mimi

Hominy Casserole

½ **cup butter or oleo**
1 **onion**
1 **small can whole corn**
1 **30-ounce can drained hominy**
1 **cup sour cream**
1 **small jar chopped pimentos**
1 **small can chopped green chilies**

Melt butter or oleo in a casserole and mix in other ingredients. Bake at 325° for 30 minutes.

Dorothy Friend
Ozona

Asparagus Casserole

2 **cups green asparagus spears**
1 **7-ounce can sliced mushrooms**
3 **tablespoons sliced almonds**
2 **ounces chopped pimentos**
salt and pepper
1½ **cups medium white sauce**
grated cheese
paprika

Place asparagus in greased casserole. Combine mushrooms, almonds, pimentos, salt and pepper with white sauce; pour over asparagus. Top with cheese; sprinkle with paprika. Bake at 350° until cheese melts. Yield: 6 servings.

To make a white sauce: stir about 3 tablespoons flour into about 4 tablespoons melted butter. Slowly add about 1½ cups milk stirring constantly. Cook until desired consistency, stirring constantly. Remove from heat.

Eva Clare Dooley
Brackettville

Eva Clare is my college roommate, Jonnye Glee's, mother. I remember Mrs. Dooley as being a wonderful cook from the meals I shared at their Laguna Ranch home. - Mimi

Buy asparagus with firm green stalks with hard-closed tips.

Creole Green Beans

2 cans French style green beans
1 small green pepper, chopped
1 medium onion, chopped
1 small pod garlic, chopped
2 small cans tomato sauce
4 slices bacon
1 small can mushrooms

Cook bacon crisp, lay aside. In the drippings, cook onions and peppers until clear. Add tomato sauce and garlic. Cook until well blended and thick. Add mushrooms, salt, and pepper to taste. Last, add the crisp bacon, crushed. Pour this sauce over the green beans which have been drained. Serve very hot.

This is also very good served over fresh beans.

Mimi Allison

Dutch Green Beans

4 strips bacon
½ chopped onion
¼ cup sugar
¼ cup apple cider vinegar
1 can French style green beans
mushrooms or water chestnuts (optional)

Fry the 4 strips of bacon, remove from skillet. Add the chopped onion and sauté for a few minutes. Add sugar, vinegar and drained green beans. You may add mushrooms or water chestnuts if you like. Heat until ready to serve.

Martha Lee Meador
Eldorado

Robert's Uncle Jack McDermott was living in Sonora when we married and moved there. He quickly become a very important part of our little family. Uncle Jack had a wonderful collection of recipes that he had gathered from many friends from all over. He used to come out to the ranch, with recipes in hand, and tell me where each came from as I prepared each dish. He never hesitated to tell me exactly how to do it and to tell me if I messed up. However, he was just as quick to brag on my accomplishments as well. Uncle Jack was a great encourager in my endeavors in the kitchen.

Gourmet Green Beans

2-3 cans Italian green beans
1 cup sour cream
3 tablespoons butter, melted
3 tablespoons chopped chives (can use dried)
2 teaspoons dill weed

Melt butter, stir in chives, sour cream, and dill weed. Pour over hot beans. Makes 8 servings.

A nice and different way to serve green beans.

Tracey Ferguson
Sonora

Cabbage Casserole

1 large head cabbage, shredded (12-13 cups)
5 tablespoons oleo
1 onion, chopped
1 10-ounce can cream of mushroom soup
8 ounces processed American cheese, cubed
salt and pepper to taste
⅓ cup dry bread crumbs
1 tablespoon oleo

Cook cabbage in boiling salted water until tender, drain thoroughly. In large skillet sauté onions and 5 tablespoons oleo until tender. Add soup and mix well. Add cheese; heat and stir until melted. Remove from heat and stir in cabbage, salt, and pepper. Pour into ungreased 2-quart baking dish. In small skillet sauté crumbs and 1 tablespoon oleo until lightly browned. Sprinkle over cabbage. Bake uncovered at 350° for 20 to 30 minutes or until heated through.

One slice of sandwich bread will make enough crumbs.

Sue Arledge
Ozona

Broccoli Supreme

1 slightly beaten egg
1 10-ounce package frozen chopped broccoli-
partially thawed
1 8½-ounce can cream style corn
1 tablespoon grated onion
1 tablespoon grated cheese
¼ teaspoon salt
dash pepper
3 tablespoons butter or margarine
1 cup herb seasoned stuffing mix

In mixing bowl, combine egg, broccoli, corn, onion, cheese, salt, and pepper. In small saucepan melt butter; add herb seasoned stuffing mix, tossing to coat. Stir in ¼ cup of buttered stuffing mix into vegetable mixture. Turn into ungreased 1 quart casserole. Sprinkle with remaining ¼ cup stuffing mix. Bake, uncovered, in 350° oven for 35 to 40 minutes. Makes 4 to 6 servings.

Dorothy Dennis
Borden County Ranch
Snyder

Buy broccoli that is a rich, dark green with tightly closed buds.

Eggplant Parmigiana

1 large eggplant
8 ounces thinly sliced mozzarella cheese
15½ ounces spaghetti sauce of your choice
Parmesan cheese
olive oil

Slice eggplant about ¼ inch thick. Place on broiler tray. Brush one side with olive oil. Brown until golden. Turn, brush and brown until golden. Repeat with remaining eggplant. In bottom of 10x6x2-inch baking dish or larger, spread ½ cup of the sauce. Layer ½ of the eggplant slices, ½ of the cheese and ½ of the remaining spaghetti sauce. Repeat layer ending with sauce on top. Sprinkle with Parmesan cheese. Bake uncovered in a 350° oven for 20 to 30 minutes.

Kaye Pfluger
San Angelo

This is great and good for you without the battered and fried eggplant.

Buy the heavier eggplant; these are the best ones.

This recipe originally stems from the region of Schwaben in Germany. It was modified by my husband who added some Tex-Mex touches after he arrived in Texas.

"Zwiebel Kuchen" Onion Pie

2 cups flour
1 stick butter
few tablespoons water
salt
3-4 pounds yellow onions (1015's when in season)
1 cup sour cream
2 eggs
salt
1 tablespoon caraway seed
1½ tablespoons sweet chili powder
3 strips bacon

Make pie crust out of the first 4 ingredients, place in 10 inch pie shell and keep in refrigerator unbaked. Mix eggs, sour cream, caraway seeds and chili powder in bowl. Cut onions as small as you have the patience. Put cut onions in large saucepan and mix with plenty of salt. Put lid on and cook over moderate heat while stirring occasionally until onions are soft and pulpy. Take off fire and let cool. Mix in the mixture of sour cream, eggs and spices. Add all into the cold pie crust. Bake in oven at 350° to 400° for 30 minutes. Sprinkle pie with pieces of fried bacon.

Preferably served with red wine.

Laura K. Hawkins
Austin

Turnips

This is an East Texas recipe from my aunt, Mary Jule Baggett of Lufkin.

3 pounds white turnips
1 8-ounce package cream cheese
1 stick butter
¼ cup sugar
salt and pepper to taste

Cook turnips until soft. Mash to get out the water. Season with above ingredients and blend in a food processor. Crumble crackers on top and bake 20 or 30 minutes at 350°. Serves 6 to 8.

Betty Baggett Miller
San Angelo

Spinach

1 large or 2 small cans spinach
1 large onion
1 small can whole tomatoes
3-4 slices breakfast bacon

Drain spinach thoroughly and chop. Place in a casserole dish that has been sprayed with a non stick vegetable spray. Slice the onion into thick slices and leave whole; place over the chopped spinach. Mash the tomatoes and place over the other ingredients. Place the bacon on top of the spinach, onion, and tomato layers. DO NOT USE SALT PORK. Cover the casserole dish, and bake in moderate oven (350°) until the bacon is done. You may watch and turn the bacon half way through the cooking time. Total cooking time should be about 45 minutes. You may remove the lid if you wish the bacon to be crisp.

This is great with goat meat, beans and cornbread.

Ruth Anne Hutto
Del Rio

Our family ate a lot of this spinach recipe during the Great Depression in the 1930's: The spinach and tomatoes were grown in our garden, so we were able to have it all winter long.

Gigi's Carrot Casserole

2 pounds sliced carrots
½ stick butter or more
½ large onion
2 tablespoons fresh parsley
2 tablespoons flour
2 cups milk
½ pound grated American cheese
cornflakes

Cook the carrots for about 7 minutes. Sauté onions and parsley in butter. Add flour and milk to make white sauce; then melt cheese into the sauce stirring well. Throw carrots into a large baking dish and cover with sauce. Top with buttered cornflakes and bake at 350° until bubbly. It's Awesome!

Wendy Wardlaw
San Antonio

I couldn't wait to get to Gigi's for holiday eats! This dish has always been one of my favorites. When I finally started experimenting in the kitchen this was one of the first recipes I requested. (It's also one of the few fool proof ones I have run across as well!) It's so easy and delicious - I serve it all the time!

Baked Carrots

6 carrots grated
1½ cups orange juice
3 eggs
½ cup flour
½ teaspoon salt
¼ teaspoon Tabasco sauce
1 cup sugar

Mix well together. Bake in a salad mold ring for 1 hour at 300°.

After taking out of oven fill ring with peas and decorate with mandarin orange slices.

Blanche Walker (Mrs. C.O.)
Ozona

Squash Tampico

4 slices chopped bacon
1 large chopped onion
2-2½ pounds zucchini
1 can whole kernel corn
1 scant cup catsup
1 cup buttered cracker crumbs
1 cup grated sharp cheese
salt and pepper

Sauté onion with chopped bacon until bacon is crisp and onion is soft. Add the thinly sliced zucchini, corn and catsup. Cook until zucchini is tender. Season to taste. Pour in a baking dish or casserole. Sprinkle crumbs and cheese on top. Bake at 350° until cheese melts.

Very good with yellow squash or calavasa too.

Alice Cauthorn
Comstock

Calabacita Rellena

4 medium zucchini squash
2 cups fresh or frozen corn
½ teaspoon salt
½ teaspoon pepper
6 ounces grated Monterey Jack cheese
2 eggs
3 medium tomatoes
¼ cup chopped onion
1 clove garlic
¼ teaspoon salt
2 tablespoons oil
green chilies to taste

 olly was the first one to send in her recipe. And it is a good one. We just couldn't wait to try it.
- Cookbook Committee

Cut the zucchini in half lengthwise. Scoop out seeds and pulp leaving ½ inch shell. These will resemble little boats. Place these in a greased large baking dish and set aside. Salt and pepper zucchini shell. Puree the corn and eggs in blender. Transfer corn puree to mixing bowl and add cheese, mixing well. Spoon into zucchini. Cover and bake at 350° for 45 minutes. Broil tomatoes until the skin starts to turn black and the tomatoes begin to shrivel. Put tomatoes (including skin), onion and garlic in blender and process until smooth. Add green chilies. Heat oil in skillet and add tomato sauce. Heat 8 to 10 minutes until thick. Pour tomato sauce over zucchini and serve promptly. Garnish with additional cheese.

I slice a small portion off the bottom of the shells to make them flat so they will sit in the cooking pan without rolling from side to side.

Holly Griffin (Mrs. Kirk)
Eldorado

This is a very old recipe that Robert's grandmother, Pearl Lee Shurley passed along to me. My kids all think it is the only way to fix zucchini. Pearl Lee was a wonderful cook but, like all good cooks, she didn't have many recipes written down. You had to learn from her by standing at her elbow. These kinds of cooks sure would laugh at you when you wanted to stop and measure everything out while they were showing you how to cook something.

Granny's Squash

1 slice bacon, browned and crumbled
1 small chopped onion
3 cups sliced zucchini
1 diced tomato
½ cup brown sugar
2 slices cubed toast
salt to taste
½ cup grated cheese

Sauté onion in the bacon drippings. Stir in the zucchini, cover and cook until tender over moderately low heat. Stir in the tomato and brown sugar and cook just enough to mix in well. Stir in the bacon crumbles and cubed toast, sprinkle grated cheese over all and cover until cheese melts.

Mimi Allison

Baked Macaroni and Cheese

2 cups macaroni
1½ teaspoons salt
4 cups hot water
⅛ teaspoon pepper
2 tablespoons butter
2 eggs, slightly beaten
½ cup milk
½ cup grated cheese

Add 1 teaspoon salt and macaroni to hot water and boil until tender. Drain, add butter and stir until melted. Add remaining ½ teaspoon salt, pepper, cheese, and milk to eggs. Mix well and add to macaroni. Pour into buttered casserole (6x10x2) and bake 20 to 30 minutes at 450°.

Mimi Allison

Stuffed Yellow Squash

2 hard-boiled eggs
8 small yellow squash
1 small onion finely chopped
½ cup chopped celery
½ cup finely chopped bell pepper
1 small jar pimentos
½ cup cracker crumbs
½ cup cream sauce

Boil squash until tender in salted water. Scoop out inside, leaving the shell. Mash squash insides and mix all ingredients to make a stuffing mixture. Fill the squash shells with mixture and place into a long baking dish. Top with grated Cheddar cheese, fill rest of dish with cream sauce. Bake at 350° for 45 minutes.

Cream Sauce
¼ cup butter
3 tablespoons flour
3 cups milk
1 teaspoon salt

Melt butter, add flour and salt to make a smooth paste, add milk and cook until thick. Stir constantly.

Elizabeth Horwood
Sterling City

This recipe came from my grandmother, Mary Elizabeth Allen, who came to Sterling County in 1886 at the age of 17 to marry William Lenard Foster. Her mother was from the South and this was a good old southern recipe. They loved fresh vegetables. At Sunday Dinner we had 4 or 5 fresh vegetables at one time. She loved having her grandchildren at one large table in the kitchen, never in the dining room.

Squash and Carrot Casserole

5 medium diced squash
6 peeled and diced carrots
1 diced onion
1 8-ounce package of cream cheese
1 can of mushroom soup
1 teaspoon salt
½ cup mayonnaise
buttered bread crumbs
Parmesan cheese

Cook squash, carrot, and onions until tender in water. Drain thoroughly, mash cream cheese, soup, salt, and mayonnaise together. Mix it with cooked vegetables in a casserole dish. Top with bread crumbs and Parmesan cheese and heat for 30 minutes at 350°.

Jo Wright
Junction
Submitted by Pierce Hoggett

Spanish Squash

3 tablespoons bacon grease
5 cups sliced yellow squash
1 large bell pepper
1 large onion
1 small can tomatoes
1 small can tomato sauce

Sauté sliced squash, chopped pepper and onion in bacon grease until tender. Add tomatoes, tomato sauce, salt, pepper and chili powder to taste.

Mrs. Sid Harkins
Sanderson

My sister-in-law, Mrs. Ernest Harkins, gave me this recipe about 40 years ago. I still use it often.

Squash Casserole

1½ cups yellow squash
½ cup undiluted mushroom soup
1 well beaten egg
1 tablespoon grated onion
½ cup grated cheese
1 tablespoon margarine
salt and pepper
⅓ cup cracker crumbs

Cook, drain and mash squash. Add egg, soup, onion, cheese, salt, and pepper. Pour into casserole dish; top with buttered cracker crumbs.

Kathryn Word Robbins
Houston
submitted by Ethel Miller

Fried Okra Charlotte

2-3 slices bacon
1 pound okra
1 medium onion
¼ cup cornmeal
salt and pepper to taste

Fry bacon until crisp. Slice okra and dice onion; mix with salt and pepper to taste. Add cornmeal to the onion and okra and toss until coated. Add to bacon and bacon grease. Cook at low heat; stirring frequently. Cover and let steam; cooking for about 30 minutes.

Kaye Pfluger
San Angelo

This was my favorite vegetable dish growing up, and it is still my favorite way to eat okra.

Cajun Queen Okra

fresh okra
diced tomatoes
diced green chilies
seasonings: Creole, garlic, rosemary, salt
and pepper

Boil fresh cut okra until tender. Add tomatoes, chilies, and seasonings to taste.

Tiffany Talley
Temple

Creole Peas

We moved here from East Texas where you get plenty of fresh peas.

Lettuce leaves absorb fat. Place a few into the pot and watch the fat cling to them. Remove the leaves along with the fat.

1 cup diced celery
1 cup diced bell pepper
2 medium diced hot peppers
1 cup diced onion
6 cups cooked black-eyed peas with juice
2 cups chopped tomatoes
2 packages frozen cut okra

Sauté the first 4 ingredients in ⅓ cup oil until tender, stirring often. Add the peas, tomatoes and okra. Bring to boil and add salt to taste. Simmer until okra is tender.

Ann Trimble
Ft. McKavett

My Favorite Recipe

Anita Allison

When I was about seven years old, I made this for 4-H. I remember winning some kind of ribbon, so I must have placed. This recipe is so good, that if it didn't win first place - it should have. Years later, I was making this again for my two older brothers when one of them bit down on something very hard in the cake. It was a whole clove. Little did I know that the cloves were suppose to be ground! Maybe that is why I don't remember winning that blue ribbon. I have always wondered why no one ever said anything sooner - someone had to be eating those cloves! Now I put in a few cloves just to keep them all on their toes.

Gingerbread with Lemon Sauce

½ cup butter or margarine
½ cup sugar
1 egg
1 cup dark cane syrup or
molasses
2½ cups flour
1½ teaspoons baking soda

1 teaspoon cinnamon
1 teaspoon ginger
½ teaspoon nutmeg
¼ teaspoon cloves
½ teaspoon salt
1 cup boiling water

Cream butter, sugar and egg. Add syrup. Sift flour, baking soda, spices, and salt together and add to first mixture. Beat well. Add boiling water. Grease and lightly flour a baking pan 14x10x2 inches. Pour in mixture and bake in 350° oven for about 25 minutes or until done. Cut in generous squares and pour on the Lemon Sauce.

Lemon Sauce:

2 whole eggs
¾ cup sugar
2 tablespoons flour
juice of 2 lemons

lemon rind of 1 lemon
pinch of salt
2 tablespoons butter
1 cup very hot water

Mix all but hot water together in saucepan. A blender does this in a snap. When well mixed, add hot water. Stir well and cook until thick, but do not boil.

You can cook the sauce in the microwave if you watch it carefully. Serve this sauce warm over the gingerbread and everyone will love it!

Anita Allison

This is very similar to that orange drink we are all familiar with in the malls. It is good with a raw egg if you are so inclined!

Orange Drink

1 small frozen orange juice
1 cup water
1 cup milk
¼ cup sugar
1 teaspoon vanilla
10 ice cubes

Mix well in blender. Drink and enjoy.

Molly Woehl
Midland

Candlestick Salad

lettuce leaf
canned pineapple slice
ripe banana
mayonnaise
maraschino cherry

Wash lettuce and let dry. Put lettuce leaf on salad plate. Arrange pineapple slice in center. Peel banana. Cut off end so banana will stand. Dip banana in pineapple juice and stand in center of pineapple ring. Tint mayonnaise pink with maraschino cherry juice. Spoon a dab of pink mayonnaise over tip of banana and let drip down the side like a melting candle. For the flame, place a maraschino cherry on top.

Madaline Barrows, 2 years old
San Angelo

Younguns

Pear Salad

1 large can pear halves
1 tablespoon honey
1 tablespoon mayonnaise
2 tablespoons peanut butter
grated cheese

Drain pears and arrange on platter cut side up. Mix the honey, mayonnaise, and peanut butter together in a little bowl and mix until smooth. Divide evenly into the pear halves. Sprinkle lightly with grated yellow cheese if desired.

Mindy Woehl
Midland

I learned this simple, fun recipe at the Allison Ranch during spring shearing, and I enjoy fixing it. Anita doesn't like the cheese on top.

Fruit Kabobs

every kind of fruit you can get!

Wash, clean, and peel the fruit. Cut off any leaves, and stems. Chop in chunks. Stick all kinds of fruits on kabob sticks.

Great before meals or as desert!

Renee Bradford
Progreso

Cheese Balls

1 pound bulk sausage
3 cups biscuit mix
10 ounces sharp cheese, grated

In a large bowl, mix all of the ingredients together using your hands. If you can't remember the last time you washed your hands, please wear plastic gloves. Roll the mixture into small balls and place on cookie sheet. Bake at 375° for 25 minutes.

Miles Donnelly
San Antonio, Age 9

This recipe makes 2 tons, so you better have room in the freezer for leftovers.

Ham and Cheese Rolls

1 can crescent rolls
2 slices ham
2 slices cheese, American or Swiss
1 beaten egg

Place crescent rolls on a cookie sheet. Pinch 2 triangles together to make a square. Cut ham and cheese into strips. Place strips of ham and cheese on edge of dough and roll up. Paint the beaten egg on the rolled up sandwich. Bake at 375° until done, about 13 minutes.

Charla Haubold
Decatur

Little Pizzas

1 slice of mozzarella cheese
1 tablespoon tomato sauce
1 tablespoon salad oil
salt and pepper (garlic salt optional)
a sprinkle of oregano

Place all of this on a toasted bun and sprinkle with grated cheese (Parmesan preferred), then place in 450° oven until cheese melts. Quick and easy for a busy day lunch and they taste surprisingly like the real thing.

Add any kinds of toppings you like: black olives, sausage, mushrooms, tomatoes, etc.

Mary Ellen McEntire
San Angelo

Beau's Soap Bubbles
½ cup Joy or Dawn
 detergent
5 cups cold, clean water
2 tablespoons glycerin
 (get at drugstore)
frying pan
coat hanger

Bend a coat hanger into a loop with a handle. The loop needs to fit into the frying pan. Mix the detergent with water in the frying pan. Measure carefully. Stir. Add glycerin. Dip coat hanger into the solution, then wave it in the air!

The longer you keep the solution the better it gets!
Beau Bradford
Progreso

Cooking and eating is fun. Kitchen and table time with your kids is quality time. What a wonderful time for one on one visits.

Allison Goulash

2 pounds ground meat, browned
1 medium yellow onion, chopped
2-3 medium potatoes, cubed
1 large can of pork & beans
1 can Rotel tomatoes
salt and pepper to taste

Brown meat with onions in large iron skillet. Drain any accumulated grease. (I use lean ground meat). Add other ingredients, including liquid. Add water to cover ingredients. Cover and cook slowly until potatoes are tender. Approximately 30 minutes.

Serve with flour tortillas. Don't plan on leftovers.

Molly Allison
San Angelo

Dipsy Doodle Hamburger Noodle Casserole

little oil
1 medium onion, finely chopped
1 pound ground beef
1 16-ounce box macaroni
1 10-ounce can Cheddar cheese soup

Brown onion in oil; add ground beef and brown. Drain off fat. Cook macaroni and drain. Add to beef mixture along with soup. Heat all together.

Rink Donnelly, age 12
San Antonio

This is Matt Allison's favorite meal. Donald taught him to cook when they were "batching". The men depend on this meal when the mom is not home to cook. It has been served at many Boy Scout cook outs and once was cooked for a very adventurous Rio Grande canoe trip. I thought it was Donald's recipe, but Donald says that it originally was Robert Allison and Pee Wee Corder's recipe when they were boys. None the less, it is the meal Matt requests when he comes home from school.

195

My daddy fixed this at Boy Scout Camp with my great grandfather, Otho E. Rink. You can cook this on a camp fire, under hot coals or bake in the oven at home. Either way it's good and simple even for a ten year old.

Boy Scout Dinner

1½ pounds lean ground meat
2 medium potatoes, cut in rounds
2 small onions, sliced
2 carrots, cut in rounds
salt and pepper to taste
little oleo

Divide the ground meat into 4 parts and shape into large patties. Cut enough foil to hold 4 large hamburger patties. Place the patties on the foil and put potato rounds, carrots, onions on top of meat. Salt and pepper, adding a little pat of oleo to each patty. Sprinkle a little water on top of each. Fold up foil and bake in oven at 350° for 1 hour. Makes 4 servings.

Jett Rink
Austin

Chewy Peanut Butter Brownies

½ cup peanut butter
⅓ cup butter or margarine
1 cup sugar
¼ cup packed brown sugar
2 eggs
1 cup flour
1 teaspoon baking powder
¼ teaspoon salt
1 6-ounce package semi-sweet chocolate chips
1 teaspoon vanilla

Beat peanut butter and margarine until blended. Gradually add sugar and beat until fluffy. Add eggs one at a time, beat well after each. Add dry ingredients and mix well. Stir in chocolate chips and vanilla. Spread in buttered 9-inch square pan. Bake at 350° for 30 to 35 minutes. Cool in pan on rack.

Jonnie Barrows
San Angelo

Big Jam Cookies

1½ cups flour
½ cup soft butter
¼ cup powdered sugar
½ teaspoon baking powder
2 tablespoons milk
1½ cups jam or pie filling - your choice

Mix flour, butter, powdered sugar, baking powder and milk (if dry, add a little more milk). Divide into 6 to 8 equal parts. Shape each into a ball. Place on an ungreased cookie sheet. Flatten in center with a large thumb print about 1½-inches in diameter and about ¾-inch deep in center. Fill the thumb print with 2½ tablespoons filling. Bake for about 20 minutes in preheated 375° oven.

Joan Tucker
San Angelo

Forgotten Cookies

2 egg whites
⅔ cup sugar
pinch of salt
1 teaspoon vanilla
1 cup chocolate chips
1 cup chopped pecans (optional)

Beat egg whites until foamy. Gradually add sugar and continue beating until stiff. Add salt and vanilla, mix well. Add chocolate chips. Preheat oven to 350°. Drop cookies by teaspoonfuls onto foiled covered cookie sheet. Place cookies in oven and immediately turn oven off. Leave cookies in closed oven overnight. Makes 2 dozen cookies.

Renee Reinke
Stanton

This recipe, a favorite of mine growing up, was passed down from my grandmother, Bernice Palowski.

Fruit Cocktail Pie

1 cooked pie shell
1 12-ounce jar strawberry preserves
1 banana
1 16-ounce can fruit cocktail
1 carton whipping cream
¼ cup sugar

Spread the preserves over the bottom of the cooked pie shell. Add sliced bananas arranged over the preserves and put the drained fruit cocktail over the bananas. Spread sweetened whipped cream over the pie and refrigerate a couple of hours.

Mary Ellen McEntire
San Angelo

Surprise Pie

1 graham cracker pie crust
1 can blueberry pie filling
2 chopped bananas
1 carton whipped cream

Slice the bananas into the pie crust. On top of that put the can of blueberry filling. Finish with the whipped cream on top. Refrigerate for a couple of hours before serving.

Mindy Woehl
Midland

Nancy and Mimi believe in getting the kids involved early. Take them shopping for their special dishes. Let them choose it, wash it, prepare it and they'll love to eat it. Then let them set the table and clean up. As you can see with Preccia and Anita, the love of cooking can be taught from an early age. And their brothers are all handy in the kitchen too. All the kids are good cooks. Make it fun!

McNeil's Fudge Pie

1 square unsweetened baking chocolate
½ cup butter
1 cup sugar
2 eggs
1 cup flour
1 teaspoon vanilla
whipped cream

Preheat oven to 350°. In a saucepan melt the butter and chocolate. Remove from heat. Into the same pan, add the sugar to the chocolate mixture and stir well. Add the eggs and vanilla and beat well. Stir in the flour and blend. Pour into buttered 9 or 10-inch pie plate and bake for 20 to 25 minutes. Do not over bake. Serve with whipped cream.

This is also very good served with ice cream.

McNeil Allison
Lubbock

Microwave Fudge

1 pound box powdered sugar
¼ cup milk
¼ cup cocoa
1 stick butter
1 teaspoon vanilla
nuts (optional)

Pour sugar into 8x8-inch square glass pan. Add cocoa, milk and butter. Slice butter into 4 or 5 pieces and dot around on mixture. Do not stir. Put into microwave for 3 or 4 minutes. Stir vigorously. Add vanilla and nuts. Refrigerate for 1 hour only. Remove, cut and enjoy!

Will Ferguson, age 8
Sonora

McNeil made this for 4-H and many times for the family. Of course he made it many times for McNeil and he could probably eat a whole pie even though it is much too rich for anyone else to do so. -Mimi

Younguns

Cereal Christmas Trees

3 tablespoons butter
32 large marshmallows
1 teaspoon vanilla
1 teaspoon green food color
4 cups Cheerios
1 small package gum drops

Heat butter and marshmallows over low heat. Remove from heat, stir in vanilla and coloring. Fold in cereal. On waxed paper shape into trees using ½ to ⅔ cup per tree. Decorate with cut gumdrops.

Anita Allison
San Angelo

Holly Candy

30 large marshmallows
1 stick butter
2 teaspoons green food coloring
1 teaspoon vanilla
5 cups corn flakes
1 package red hots candy

Melt the marshmallows with the butter. Add coloring and vanilla. Pour this mixture over the corn flakes and mix well. Drop by teaspoonfuls onto waxed paper. Place a red hot candy in the center of each. Let set for 24 hours.

Anita Allison
San Angelo

Both these Christmas recipes are so much fun to make with the kids during the holidays. The little Christmas Trees are really great for the school party. The holly is really nice to place on the platters with your "real" food.

Edens' Play Dough

1 cup white flour
½ cup salt
8-10 drops food coloring
½ cup water - a little less
2 tablespoons vegetable oil
1 teaspoon alum (from drug store)
plastic bag or air-tight container
big mixing bag

Add food coloring to the water. Mix all the other ingredients in the bowl and add the colored water just a little bit at a time until it feels like dough. Play with it on top of newspaper at first because it will be a little oily. Store in airtight container or plastic bag in refrigerator.

Edens Bradford
Progreso

Variation
1 cup flour
½ cup salt
1 cup water
1 tablespoon oil
2 teaspoons cream of tartar
food coloring

Cook fast on medium heat, stir aggressively until pulls together. Cool before allowing kids to play with it. Mix up several colors. Keeps a long time in airtight containers.

Molly Allison
San Angelo

I made this with Amy and Matt at the ranch. We all had fun at our special afternoon tea parties.

Salt your food with
  Humor
Pepper it with Wit
Sprinkle over it the charm
  of fellowship
Laughter is one of the
  greatest aids to
  digestion.

Nicole's Glob

**1 tablespoon borax (sodium borate) from
supermarket
4 fluid ounces liquid glue
distilled water
1 2-quart bowl
2 clean, empty quart jars; one with a lid**

Fill one of the jars with distilled water. Label the
jar BORAX with marker. Add 1 tablespoon of borax to the water. Put the lid on the jar and shake
vigorously. Empty a 4 fluid ounce bottle of glue
into a second jar, labeled GLUE. Fill the empty glue
bottle with distilled water and pour the water into
the jar. With a spoon, stir until the glue is thoroughly
mixed. Pour 1 measuring cup of the borax solution
into the empty bowl. Slowly pour the glue solution
into the bowl of borax. Stir as you pour. Dip the
glob out of the bowl with spoon on top of plastic
bag. Let sit for 2 minutes. Pick the glob up with
your fingers and squeeze. Transfer the glob from
one hand to the other, and squeeze until it and your
hands are dry. Squeeze it, stretch it, pull it, and have
fun with it!

Store in refrigerator in plastic bag.

Nicole Bradford
Progreso

My Favorite Recipe

Nancy Rink Johnson

This recipe is one of the only recipes I have that belonged to my mother, Ela Preccia Rink. She did most of her cooking by memory. Not too many of her recipes were ever written down. I learned early how to cook because she was so sick when I was growing up. She passed away when I was 21 years old, so most of her recipes that she gave me were from just helping her in the kitchen when I was younger. Back in the early days most of our mothers cooked the way their mothers cooked, not too many written recipes were passed around, they were too busy cooking, cleaning and taking care of the small ones at home. There wasn't too much extra money to buy something special to fix, most of it was basic, meat, potatoes and gravy. She was never famous for being the best cook in the world. I had four brothers, all older than myself and being the baby and only girl, I was treated like a Princess, now days we would call it spoiled. With my two oldest brothers, James and Wilson in World War II, mother would send my brother Pat and me to the grocery store, that's when we were using food ration coupons. We brought home a large sack of cherries, she made us take them back because it wasn't the usual food we had to live on. The memories are many, so at this time I want to thank my two oldest brothers, James and Wilson, for helping us through all those many years of hard times.

Homemade Vanilla Ice Cream

6 eggs
1½ cups sugar
1 can sweetened condensed milk

1 can evaporated milk
1½ gallons milk
2 teaspoons vanilla

Beat eggs and sugar together well with mixer. Add condensed milk, evaporated milk, and part of whole milk. Mix well. Then pour into ice cream freezer and add enough milk to fill to the line in freezer canister. Freeze according to instructions of your freezer.

This is just plain vanilla ice cream and many things can be added such as, strawberries, peaches, chocolate, bananas, etc.

Apricot Horns

½ pound butter or margarine
½ pound creamed cottage cheese
2 cups sifted flour

Blend butter, cottage cheese and flour together with hands to form dough. Add more flour if cottage cheese is watery. Shape into 1-inch balls and refrigerate overnight or at least 2 hours. (Dough may be kept in refrigerator up to 1 month.)

Filling
½ pound dried apricots
1 cup sugar

Cook apricots in small amount of water until tender (15 to 20 minutes.) Drain and puree. Add sugar while still hot. Cool.

Coating
¾ cup ground almonds (can use pecans)
½ cup confectioners sugar
¾ cup sugar
2 egg whites, slightly beaten

Mix nuts and sugar. Roll each dough ball into a 3 inch round. (Make only 10 horns at a time so dough will stay cold.) Place a teaspoon of filling in center, roll up in shape of a horn or crescent. Dip into egg white and then roll in nut and sugar mixture. Place on a greased baking sheet and bake at 375° for 12 minutes or until lightly browned. Sprinkle with confectioners sugar. Makes 4 to 5 dozen, depending on how dough is rolled. This recipe serves 20 to 25 people, a serving size is 2 horns.

Julie Childress
Ozona

Desserts

Mamaw's Apple Crisp

1 cup flour
1 cup sugar
1 teaspoon baking powder
1 well beaten egg
4 apples
⅓ cup butter
½ teaspoon cinnamon

Sift the first three ingredients together. Add the beaten egg. Peel the apples and cut them into thin slices. Spray 8x8 inch pan and add apple slices. Pour the crumbly mixture over apples. Melt butter and pour over mixture. Sprinkle cinnamon over the top. Bake at 400° for 40 minutes.

Brandi Gage
Iraan

Nanny's Nursery Plum Dessert

trim ¾ inch strips of white bread from French, Italian, or Austrian Bread - not sourdough
lots of melted unsalted butter, not oleo
plums
1 cup sugar
3 tablespoons of flour
1 tablespoon of lemon juice

You will need a glass dish or a pottery dish, 1¾-inches deep and 7-inches wide. Soak bread strips with butter and line sides and bottom of dish. Cut plums (firm ones) into eight chunks. Whisk together sugar and flour. Fill dish, adding sugar as you go. Heap plums up, sprinkle with lemon juice. Cover with more bread strips. Start baking at 325° for 30 minutes. Finish at 400° for 10 minutes or until top toasts a nice color and juice bubbles. If plums are not juicy, add a bit of orange juice mixed with apple juice. Sprinkle top with a bit of cinnamon sugar before baking.

This is also delicious with apples, peaches, blackberries, or blueberries.

Mrs. Ford Boulware
San Angelo

I entered this recipe in my first Pecos County 4-H Food Show and won First Place with it. This recipe has been in my family many years. My great-grandmother, Mrs. Delfo Clark, got the original recipe off a Gold Medal Flour box in 1927. She and my great grandfather were living in a tent in the "Standard Oil Camp" outside of Iraan, Texas during the Yates Oil Field boom.

This was my favorite up in my fourth floor nursery in London, England in 1923 to 1924.

205

This recipe is from Virgie Graves of Fort Davis. She was in a sewing group that I belonged to after we took a tailoring class together at Sul Ross State.

Cherry Crunch

red food coloring
1 can sour cherries
1 egg
1 cup sugar
1 cup flour
1 teaspoon baking powder
¾ teaspoon cinnamon
¼ teaspoon salt
½ cup chopped pecans
1 teaspoon vanilla
1 stick oleo

Topping
cherry juice
½ cup sugar
2 tablespoons flour

Add the red food coloring to the cherries. Drain the cherry juice and save. Line an 8x8 inch pan with cherries. Mix beaten egg, sugar, flour, baking powder, cinnamon and salt with fork. Add chopped pecans and vanilla. Mix and pour over cherries. Melt 1 stick of oleo and pour over the crumbs. Bake at 350° for 30 minutes or until brown. Cook cherry juice, sugar and flour until thick and pour over baked mixture.

Doris Haby
Rocksprings

206

Vinegar Roll Pie

2 cups flour
2 teaspoons baking powder
¾ teaspoon salt
¼ teaspoon baking soda
4½ tablespoons shortening
1 cup buttermilk

Mix biscuit dough together. Roll out on floured board. Roll thin and spread with melted butter, sugar and cinnamon. Roll up like a jelly roll. Press end firmly, cut in 1-inch slices (or larger if preferred). Place cut side up in greased pan. Pour ⅔ cup vinegar (more or less depending on your taste) and 3 cups water over the rolls. Pour 1 cup sugar over top and dot with butter. Bake in warm oven for 45 minutes to 1 hour at 350°.

Delicious when served warm with cream or milk.

Roy Jean Johnson
Sonora

Coconut Pie

4 eggs, well beaten
½ cup self rising flour
1¾ cups sugar
¼ cup butter
1 teaspoon vanilla
2 cups milk
7 ounces shredded coconut

Mix dry ingredients. Add wet ingredients to dry. Pour into a deep 9-inch pie shell. Bake at 375° about 30 minutes. Pie will not be completely firm, just golden on top. Chill.

This is a really easy recipe. The pie makes its own crust!

Brad Johnson
Chicago, Illinois

This recipe was given to me by my mother, Lodessa A. Pope. It was given to her by my grandmother, Susan Wilhoit, and it originated from my great-grandmother Annie Casey or "Little Momma". We enjoyed this for years as we were all growing up. I have never seen this recipe written out in cookbooks.

My momma told me in her own words to: "Make a biscuit dough - not as much baking powder as usual - little more shortening than usual - roll thin - sprinkle with sugar and cinnamon - put in cup of sugar and butter - pour ⅔ cup vinegar and 3 cups water and bake".

This is a good recipe to make a day ahead. It is delicious, but very rich!

Chocolate Delight or Sex in a Pan

1 stick butter
1 cup flour
½ cup chopped pecans

Melt butter, pour over flour and nuts. Mix and pour into bottom of greased 9x13 pan. Bake at 350° for 12 to 15 minutes. Cool.

8 ounce package cream cheese
1 cup sugar
1 cup frozen whipped topping

Mix together and spread on cooled bottom layer. Chill in refrigerator for 1 hour.

1 package chocolate pudding
1 package vanilla pudding

Make puddings according to box directions. Spread on top of second layer.

rest of container frozen whipped topping
½ cup pecans (optional)

Mix topping and pecans; spread on third layer. Chill until ready.

One large frozen whipped topping container is enough for the entire recipe.

Camille Miller Yale
Dallas

Chocolate Fluff

12 large marshmallows - or 2 cups small
½ can of 7½-ounce can chocolate syrup
½ cup butter
3 eggs (separated)
1 cup powdered sugar
pinch of salt
1 teaspoon vanilla
1 cup finely chopped pecans
12 vanilla wafers

Cut marshmallows. Pour chocolate syrup over marshmallows and let stand. Cream butter, yolks of eggs and sugar, add salt, vanilla, and pecans. Add this mixture to chocolate and marshmallows. Beat whites of eggs until stiff and fold into mixture. Crush wafers and spread in buttered pan, pour and spread the chocolate mixture over crumbs. Let set at least 6 hours. Serve with whipped cream.

Ruth Howard
Marfa

Chocolate Dessert

1 12-ounce package chocolate chips
4 egg yolks
pinch of salt
4 egg whites
2 tablespoons sugar
1 teaspoon vanilla
1 cup chopped nuts
1 pint stiffly beaten whipping cream
1 large Angel Food Cake

Melt chocolate chips in double boiler - remove from stove. Beat egg yolks well - add to chocolate mixture with a pinch of salt. Beat egg whites, add sugar and vanilla. Fold into chocolate mixture. Add chopped nuts to stiffly beaten whipped cream and fold into chocolate mixture. Tear cake into small pieces, put half into a large cake pan and pour ½ of chocolate over it then another layer of cake and the rest of the chocolate mixture.

Erlene Peters Mills
San Angelo

This keeps well in a covered pan in the refrigerator. I like to freeze it in a spring pan, take it off, and serve the dessert from a large plate.

Dredge nuts, dates and raisins with small amount of flour before adding to cake batter.

Pumpkin Roll

3 eggs (beat 5 minutes on high)
⅔ cup pumpkin
1 teaspoon ginger
¼ cup flour
2 teaspoons cinnamon
1 cup sugar
1 teaspoon lemon juice
½ teaspoon salt
1 teaspoon baking powder
½ teaspoon nutmeg
1 cup pecans

Mix all together. Pour into a 15x10x1 inch greased, floured, and wax papered cookie sheet. Top with chopped pecans. Bake at 375° for 15 minutes. Turn onto towel sprinkled with powdered sugar. Roll up and let cool.

1 cup powdered sugar
6 ounces of cream cheese
4 tablespoons water
½ teaspoon vanilla

Mix ingredients together and beat until light and smooth. Unroll cake and spread icing. Reroll. Refrigerate. Slice and serve.

This roll freezes beautifully and is great for the holidays!

Kittye Bolin
McKinney

Banana Split Cake

2 cups graham cracker crumbs
1 stick margarine

Mix together and spread in a 13x9 inch pan and chill.

1 8-ounce package softened cream cheese
1 pound powdered sugar

Mix together and spread over graham cracker crumbs

4 - 5 sliced bananas
1 large can well drained crushed pineapple
1 large container frozen whipped topping
chopped pecans
chocolate syrup
frozen whipped topping

Layer the above first three ingredients in the order they are written. Sprinkle the top with pecans and drizzle with syrup. Dot with cherries. Put in the refrigerator and chill for 8 hours.

Sherri White
Brackettville

This recipe was given to me by someone I consider my second mother, a ranchwoman from Brackettville, Craylene Frerich.

This cheesecake has won Best of Show at the Tom Green County Rodeo and Fair. It also is the first recipe my mother, Nancy Dunham gave to me.

Old Style Cheesecake

3 8-ounce packages cream cheese
1 cup sugar
4 egg yolks
2 teaspoons vanilla
2 tablespoons flour
4 egg whites, beaten stiff
½-¾ cup graham cracker crumbs

Topping
8 ounces sour cream
1 teaspoon vanilla
¼ cup sugar

Preheat oven to 350°. Cream together cheese and sugar. Add egg yolks, vanilla and flour. Fold in egg whites and gently mix until smooth. Pour into greased 9-inch springform pan with a generous layer of graham cracker crumbs on the bottom. Bake for 50 to 60 minutes, or until top is just about to crack. Remove pan from oven, increase oven to 475°, and immediately pour topping over cheesecake. Replace cheesecake in oven for 7 minutes. Remove and let cool completely before removing from pan. Top with your favorite topping such as fresh fruit, chocolate, blueberry or strawberry pie filling, shredded coconut, etc. Is best if let set in refrigerator for 24 hours.

Greg and Fawn Dunham
San Angelo

Fresh Strawberry Cheesecake

Filling
    1 32-ounce package cream cheese
    1½ cups sugar
    1 8-ounce container lite sour cream
    4 eggs
    3 teaspoons vanilla
    1½ teaspoons almond extract

With electric mixer, blend cream cheese. Slowly add sugar until well blended. Then mix in sour cream and eggs one at a time. Mix in extracts. Chill while preparing crust.

Crust
    2¼ cups graham cracker crumbs
    ¾ cup sugar
    ½ cup margarine

Mix crumbs and sugar, add margarine and blend. Grease the rim of a spring form pan. Place crumb mixture in pan and press firmly into the bottom and up the sides. Fill with chilled filling. Bake at 350° for 50 to 55 minutes until golden brown or until knife inserted into the center comes out clean. Let cool for about 30 minutes before glazing.

Topping and Glaze
    1 cup sliced fresh strawberries
    2 tablespoons orange juice
    8 ounces apricot preserves

Place strawberry slices on top and sides of cake. Bring orange juice and preserves to a boil. Cool and pour over strawberries on the cake.

Carmen Sutton
Ozona

My daughter, Stefny Sutton, won the 4-H District food show in the Dessert Division with this recipe in 1984.

Pumpkin Cheesecake

Crust
  1¼ cups graham cracker crumbs
  ½ cup finely chopped pecans
  ¼ cup brown sugar
  ¼ cup granulated sugar
  ¼ cup butter, melted

Combine all ingredients and mix well. Pat mixture firmly into bottom of a buttered 9- to 10-inch springform pan. Bake 15 minutes at 325°. Remove from oven and set aside. Reduce oven to 300°.

Filling
  ¾ cup granulated sugar
  1 cup canned pumpkin
  3 eggs
  1½ teaspoons cinnamon
  ½ teaspoon nutmeg
  ½ teaspoon ground ginger
  ½ teaspoon salt
  24 ounces cream cheese, softened
  6 tablespoons granulated sugar
  1 tablespoon cornstarch
  2 tablespoons evaporated milk or whipping cream
  1 teaspoon vanilla

Mix ¾ cup sugar, pumpkin, eggs, cinnamon, nutmeg, ginger and salt in a bowl. Set aside. Using an electric mixer, beat the cream cheese and 6 tablespoons sugar until smooth. Add cornstarch, evaporated milk, and vanilla, beating well after each addition. Add pumpkin mixture to cream cheese mixture. Mix well. Pour filling mixture into prepared springform pan, and bake 1 hour at 300° until sides have risen; the center will be soft. Turn OFF oven and let cake cook with door closed for several hours or overnight. Serve with whipped cream.

Matt Miller
Ozona

214

Eloise McKissack's Apple Spice Cake

2 cups sugar
1 cup butter or soft margarine
3 eggs
3 cups flour
1 teaspoon vanilla
½ teaspoon cinnamon
½ teaspoon nutmeg
½ teaspoon cloves
½ teaspoon allspice
½ cup of warm water
½ teaspoon baking soda
3 medium apples, thinly sliced (mealy apples are best)
⅛ teaspoon salt
1 cup of nuts, chopped

Preheat the oven to 350° and grease and flour bundt pan. Pare and slice 3 medium raw apples, add ½ teaspoon cinnamon, nutmeg, cloves, and allspice. Sift flour, add baking soda and salt, set aside. Cream ½ pound margarine and add sugar gradually, beating mixture the whole time. To margarine base; add eggs, one at a time and continue to beat during each addition. Add sifted flour mixture to margarine base. Add warm water and continue to beat. Add sliced apple mixture and chopped nuts, but do not use mix master to blend in apples and nuts. Add vanilla and blend, pour into bundt pan. Bake for 1 hour or until done.

Eloise McKissack
Submitted by: Carol Santry
San Angelo

Growing up as an only child, I can still remember the wonderful smell of Mother's traditional fresh apple cake baking for Christmas. Mother made the cake and I would leave cake and milk for Santa Clause. He always ate his cake, leaving a few crumbs and a thank you note, saying how much he loved her cake. So those of you who left something special always got something special back from Santa.

My mother, Molly Cavaness Wright, and grandmother, Bessie Newman Cavaness from Junction, began to make Applesauce Cake around Thanksgiving and on into Christmas. It was our "holiday sweet" and I have continued to do the same. It helps me not miss them so much during the holidays.

Applesauce Cake

2½ cups flour
2 cups sugar
2 cups applesauce
1 cup melted butter
2 teaspoons baking soda
2 teaspoons allspice
2 teaspoons cinnamon
1 teaspoon powdered cloves
2 cups chopped pecans
1 box chopped dates
1 package of chopped candied cherries
1 package chopped red and green pineapple
(do not buy citrus fruits)

Sprinkle the pecans, dates, cherries, and pineapples with ½ cup of flour from the original 2½ cups flour, set aside. Dissolve sugar, baking soda, allspice, cinnamon and cloves with applesauce and melted butter. Stir well and add fruit and pecans. Add remaining 2 cups of flour and stir until blended. Bake in 4 greased and floured loaf pans or 4 small round pans or 1 tube pan. Bake in preheated oven at 275° to 300° for one hour and if batter does not stick to straw, leave 10 minutes longer then remove from oven and let cool.

Ann Wright Hodge
Del Rio

 *Cakes*

Applesauce Cake

2 teaspoons baking soda
2 cups apple sauce
1 cup melted butter
2 cups sugar
3½ cups flour
2 teaspoons allspice
2 teaspoons cinnamon
1 teaspoon cloves
2 cups raisins
2 cups pecans

Dissolve the baking soda in the applesauce. Add butter, sugar, flour and then the spices. Mix thoroughly - if too stiff to mix add a little buttermilk. Bake at 350° for 1 hour 15 minutes or until straw comes out free of dough.

Lucille McMillan
Sonora

This is my grandmothers recipe - very old and very good!

Qualia Family Carrot Cake

2½ cups cake flour
2 teaspoons cinnamon
1 teaspoon salt
2 teaspoons baking soda
1½ cups Wesson oil
4 eggs
2 cups sugar
3 cups grated carrots
1 teaspoon vanilla

Grease and flour a bundt cake pan. Measure flour and sift all dry ingredients together, except the sugar. In mixer bowl, mix oil, eggs and sugar. Add dry ingredients. Add carrots and vanilla last. Bake at 350° for 35 minutes.

Susan McBee
Gurley & McBee Ranches
Del Rio

This wonderful recipe is passed down by members of the Qualia family.

Carrot Cake Icing
1 box powdered sugar
1 8-ounce package cream cheese
1 stick margarine
1 cup chopped pecans
1 teaspoon vanilla

Cream the sugar, softened cream cheese and margarine together. Stir in pecans and vanilla. Spread evenly over cooled cake. Freezes well.

217

Swedish Pineapple Cake Icing

1 8-ounce package cream
   cheese
1 stick margarine
¾ cup granulated sugar
¾ cup chopped pecans

Combine cream cheese
and margarine and put in
microwave for 1 minute
to soften. Do not use
powdered sugar. Add
remaining ingredients and
pour over hot cake.

Swedish Pineapple Cake

1 20-ounce can of crushed pineapple with
juice
2 cups sugar
1 teaspoon baking soda
1 teaspoon vanilla
2 cups flour
¾ cup chopped pecans

Mix with a spoon in a large bowl in the order listed.
Batter may foam when you add the soda. Pour into
an ungreased 13x9 inch baking pan. Bake at 350°
for 30 minutes.

Zackie Dutton Dunbar
Rocksprings

Pineapple Upside Down Cake

3 eggs, separated
1 cup sugar
8 teaspoons pineapple
1 cup flour
1 heaping teaspoon baking powder
1 stick butter
pineapple slices
maraschino cherries
1 cup brown sugar

Beat egg yolks, add sugar and pineapple juice. Sift
flour with baking powder, add to sugar mixture
gradually beating until light. Fold in stiffly beaten
egg whites. Melt butter in deep baking pan or iron
skillet. Place pineapple and cherries in bottom of
ban; cover with brown sugar and cake batter. Bake
at 375° until cake tests done (about 25 minutes.)
Let stand for 5 minutes. Turn onto cake dish.

Vallree Draper
Sonora

 *Cakes*

Prune Cake

1½ cups sugar
1 cup cooking oil
3 eggs
2 cups cake flour
1 teaspoon baking soda
1 teaspoon baking powder
½ teaspoon cloves
½ teaspoon nutmeg
½ teaspoon salt
1 teaspoon cinnamon
1 cup buttermilk
1 cup cooked prunes, seeded and finely chopped
1 cup pecans, finely chopped

Mix the sugar and oil together; add eggs. Sift together flour, baking soda, baking powder, and spices. Add the dry ingredients to the first mixture alternating with buttermilk. Mix in the prunes and the nuts. Bake in 3 greased and floured pans at 375° for 25 to 30 minutes or until done. Cool and frost.

Lou Deaton (Mrs. Buster)
Ozona

Apricot-Lemon Cake

1 package yellow cake mix
1 package lemon jello
¾ cup apricot nectar
⅔ cup Wesson oil
2 teaspoons lemon extract
4 egg yolks
4 egg whites

Combine the cake mix, jello, nectar, oil, and extract; beat for 3 minutes. Separate the eggs and beat in the egg yolks one at a time. Fold in the stiffly beaten eggs whites. Bake in a tube pan at 300° for 1 hour or longer.

Frances Armstrong
Abilene

Prune Cake Icing
¼ cup butter
1 box powdered sugar
grated rind of 1 lemon
grated rind of 1 orange

Blend and spread on cake.

This was Mrs. Elmo Arledge's mother's recipe. It was brought to Pandale from Pontotoc. This has been called Rim Rock Cake by the men of Pandale.

Lemon Icing
1½ cups powdered sugar
juice of 1½ lemons
pinch of salt

While cake is still hot drizzle over the top. Let the cake set in the pan until completely cool.

Banana - Nut Frosting

½ cup mashed bananas
1 teaspoon lemon juice
⅓ cup softened butter or oleo
1 16-ounce box plus 3 cups powdered sugar
3 tablespoons evaporated milk
1 cup toasted flake coconut
⅔ cup finely chopped pecans

Combine bananas and lemon juice. Set aside. In large bowl, beat butter until creamy. Add sugar, bananas, and milk. Beat until fluffy. You may have to add more milk to obtain desired consistency. Stir in coconut and pecans.

"Marvelous" Banana Cake

1 cup butter or oleo at room temperature
3 cups sugar
2 mashed bananas
4 beaten eggs
4 cups sifted all-purpose flour
2 teaspoons baking soda
1 cup buttermilk
1 teaspoon vanilla
2 tablespoons bourbon
1 cup chopped pecans

Cream butter and sugar until light and fluffy. Add bananas; mixing until smooth. Stir in beaten eggs. Sift together flour and baking soda. Add to banana mixture alternating with buttermilk, mixing well. Add vanilla, bourbon and pecans. Pour into 3 greased and floured 9-inch pans. Bake at 350° for 35 to 40 minutes or until cake tests done. Cool 10 minutes then remove from pans. Cool completely.

Alice Cauthorn
Comstock

Fresh Pear Cake

4 cups diced pears
1 cup chopped pecans
2 cups sugar
3 cups flour
½ teaspoon nutmeg
½ teaspoon cinnamon
½ teaspoon salt
2 teaspoons baking soda
2 well beaten eggs
¾ cup oil

Mix together pears, pecans and sugar; let stand an hour or until it makes its own juice. Sift dry ingredients. Add eggs and oil to pear mixture, then add the dry ingredients; mix by hand. Bake at 350° for 1 hour in one large bundt pan or two loaf pans.

Vallree Draper
Sonora

Chocolate – Banana Cake

2 cups sugar
1 cup shortening
2 well beaten eggs
2 large or 3 small bananas
½ cup cocoa
2½ cups flour
2 teaspoons baking soda
¼ teaspoon salt
½ cup buttermilk
1 cup boiling water

Cream together sugar, shortening, eggs, and bananas. Sift dry ingredients and add alternately to banana mixture with buttermilk. Add in boiling water. Mix well, batter will be very thin. Pour into 9x13 inch baking dish that has been greased and floured. Bake at 300°.

Carrie and Alice Karnes
Submitted by Glenda McMullan
Iraan

Chocolate Icing

1 cup sugar
¼ cup cocoa
¼ cup milk
½ stick butter
1 teaspoon vanilla

Combine sugar, cocoa, milk, and butter and bring to boil for 1 minute. Remove from heat; add vanilla. Beat until creamy. Pour over cake.

We grew up knowing what drought could do and we went through the flood of "54". Even with all the obstacles and adversities of ranch life, what a wonderful way to grow up. We had wonderful times to be thankful for! How grateful we are that our forefathers persevered. No wonder the people of our heritage are called the "Salt-of-the-earth" people.

This recipe is from a friend at Fort Davis when we taught there in the early 1950's. This is a very good cake to serve instead of fruit cake.

Lemon Nut Cake

1 pound butter
1 pound sugar
6 eggs
2 ounces lemon extract
1 pound flour
1 teaspoon baking powder
1 pound pecans
1 pound white raisins

Cream butter and sugar; add eggs and beat well; add lemon extract and blend. Sift together flour and baking powder; mix half flour mixture with raisins and pecans. Add other half dry mixture to liquid mixture; then add floured pecan and raisin mixture. Pour into a pan that has been greased and dusted with flour. Bake at 300° for about 1½ hours.

Doris Haby
Brackettville

Bacardi Rum Glaze
¼ pound butter
½ cup water
1 cup sugar
½ cup rum

Melt the butter in saucepan. Stir in water and sugar. Boil for 5 minutes while stirring constantly. Remove from heat and stir in rum. Pour over cake.

Bacardi Rum Cake

1 cup chopped nuts
1 18½-ounce package yellow cake mix
1 3¾-ounce vanilla instant pudding
4 eggs
½ cup cold water
½ cup oil
½ cup rum

Preheat oven to 325°. Grease and flour bundt pan. Sprinkle nuts on bottom. Mix ingredients and pour batter in pan. Bake for 1 hour. Cool and invert on serving plate. Prick top with toothpick and glaze.

Marka Mitchell
Sanderson

Cakes

White Fruit Cake

1 pound butter or 2 cups shortening
2¼ cups sugar
11 eggs
4 cups flour
1 teaspoon cream of tartar
½ teaspoon salt
½ teaspoon baking soda
¼ cup orange juice
1 grated lemon rind
1 quart broken pecans
1 cup moist coconut
1 pound moist white raisins
1 large can crushed pineapple, drained

Cream butter, sugar and add eggs one at a time. Mix some (portion) flour with raisins, pecans, and coconut. Add baking soda, salt, and cream of tartar to remaining flour; then add the rest. Bake in three loaf pans at 300° for approximately 1 hour.

Jeri Ann Johnson Willoughby
San Angelo

This White Fruit Cake recipe has been handed down through several generations. My grandmother, John Zack Millican Owen was named for a cousin to her mother, John Zack Means from Fort Davis. She was born on the 23rd of December and John Zack, who was there for Christmas, gave my great grandfather a $20.00 gold piece to name the new baby after him. The baby turned out to be a girl - none the less, she was named John Zack. My mother, Eleanor Owen Johnson, and I make at least one recipe every Christmas. This cake keeps well in the refrigerator or freezer. Makes excellent Christmas gifts. If you don't like dark fruit cake, you will love this!

Don't leave the gate open if you found it closed.

Frieda's Light Old Fashioned Fruit Cake

4 cups flour
½ teaspoon baking powder
1½ teaspoons salt
1½ teaspoons cinnamon
1½ teaspoons nutmeg
1 cup whole pecans
1¾ cups candied pineapple
1¾ cups candied cherries
1 cup golden raisins
1 cup butter
2¼ cups sugar
6 eggs (beat well after each)
3 tablespoons rum or brandy flavoring

Sift together first five ingredients three times. Mix all fruit and nuts in dry ingredients until well coated. Set aside. Cream butter and sugar until light and fluffy. Beat in the eggs one at a time beating well after each addition. Mix in rum or brandy flavoring. Combine with dry ingredients and nut mixture. Line baking pan with wax paper, grease the sides and bottom. Bake at 275° for 2¾ to 3 hours. Cool completely, then wrap tightly in foil and store in ziplock bag.

If desired, coat cooled cake with favorite rum or brandy before wrapping in foil.

Frieda Huff
Submitted by Laura Miller of San Antonio

Red Velvet Cake

½ cup shortening
1½ cups sugar
2 eggs
1 teaspoon vanilla
2 ounces red food coloring
2-3 tablespoons cocoa
1 scant teaspoon salt
2½ cups flour
1 cup buttermilk
1 teaspoon baking soda
1 tablespoon vinegar
1 teaspoon butter flavoring (optional)

Cream shortening, sugar, eggs, and vanilla. Make a paste of coloring and cocoa. Add to mixture. Add salt and flour with buttermilk, alternately. Add baking soda and vinegar - do not beat hard, just blend. Bake in two 8-inch pans (I use my 9-inch pans) at 350° for 30 minutes. Split layers with thread to make 4 layers.

Icing

1 8-ounce package cream cheese
1 box powdered sugar
1 stick butter
1 teaspoon vanilla
1 cup chopped pecans
¼ cup evaporated milk

Cream everything together and refrigerate to harden.

Totsy Hagelstein
Ozona

Icing Variation

1 cup milk
3 tablespoons flour
1 cup sugar
1⅔ sticks butter or margarine
1 teaspoon vanilla

Cook together the milk and flour, stirring constantly until thick. Cover, place in refrigerator until very cold. Cream sugar and butter until very smooth. Add vanilla to the flour mixture. Beat until smooth. For whiter icing, use shortening instead of butter (or half of each).

Lou Deaton and Miles Miller.

Living on the ranch sixteen miles from the nearest grocery store necessitated an extra supply of groceries in the pantry. Totsy's household duties, which had been complicated by Coleman lights and no electricity, became easier with a 32-volt light plant. And her "mix-master" helped with all the baking she loved to do. REA brought into her home luxuries like the electric churn, washing machine, electric iron, and carpet sweeper.

When icing cake keep putting your spatula under hot water to spread easier. You may want to make 1½ times the icing recipe.

This has always been Miles' special birthday cake.

To coat your cake pans: Stir together 1¼ cups shortening, ¼ cup salad oil, and ¼ cup flour. Store in an airtight container in the fridge until needed. Keeps beautifully. When ready to use, just coat the pans thoroughly with a pastry brush or your fingers.

Mama's Red Earth Cake

½ cup shortening
1½ cups sugar
2 eggs
2 cups minus 2 tablespoons flour
1 teaspoon baking soda
¼ teaspoon salt
3 tablespoons cocoa
1 teaspoon red food coloring
1 cup buttermilk
3 tablespoons coffee, or more to taste

Cream shortening and sugar; add eggs. Cream cocoa and coffee together, add coloring. Put baking soda and buttermilk together. Blend in with salt and flour. Bake at 350° until cake test done.

Icing
1 box powdered sugar
3 tablespoons cocoa
1 stick butter
1 teaspoon red coloring
2 tablespoons coffee

Blend ingredients well and spread on cake.

Vee Blankenship
Livingston
Submitted by great-granddaughter Laura Miller
of San Antonio

Cakes

Christmas Dutch Cakes

¼ **pound butter or oleo**
1½ **cups sugar**
2 **whole eggs**
6 **egg yolks**
½ **cup cocoa**
1 **cup Brer Rabbit molasses**
1 **teaspoon allspice**
1 **teaspoon nutmeg**
1 **teaspoon cinnamon**
2 **cups chopped pecans**
2 **packages chopped dates**
1 **teaspoon salt**
1 **teaspoon baking powder**
3½ **cups sifted flour**
½ **cup water**

Cream butter, sugar and eggs; add cocoa, molasses and spices. Beat well. Combine ½ cup of the 3½ cups flour with pecans and dates; add to mixture. Sift baking powder, salt and remaining flour; add to batter slowly with water. Batter will be stiff. Use an oblong pan or 2 square ones with 2-inch sides. Grease well - cut heavy brown paper to fit pan - grease and flour well. Bake in slow oven (250 to 300°) for about 1 hour.

When done, remove from pan; cut in 2-inch squares while still warm. When cool, pack in cookie tins with slices of bread to keep moist. Ice with white frosting using egg whites left from the 6 eggs. Ice on all sides and if you prefer dust with powdered sugar.

The dates can be optional; add 1 small package chopped candied pineapple; omit nutmeg; use shortening rather than butter; omit icing.

> *The Mitchell Family*
> *Marfa, Presidio County, Texas*
> *Josephine Mitchell*

W.F. Mitchell brought his family to this area in 1884. At first the men lived in a dugout at the Antelope Springs Ranch. In the fall of each year the women would collect ingredients for their Christmas Dutch Cakes. The original recipe called for a "cooking spoon" of lard but ¼ pound of butter tastes better to me! Raisins were substituted, too, as dates were often unavailable. After the cakes were made, usually in November, they were stored in stone crocks with apples and potatoes packed around them to keep them moist. They were iced as the women could spare the eggs. Today, there are as many variations as there are branches of the Mitchell family.

This was the cake my mother and grandmother usually made for birthdays and Christmas. They were teetotaling Methodist, so we had boiled custard instead of eggnog for Christmas.

One, Two, Three, Four Cake

1 cup butter or margarine
2 cups sugar
3 cups flour
4 large eggs
1 teaspoon salt
2½ teaspoons baking powder
1 cup milk
1 teaspoon vanilla

Cream sugar and butter (may use shortening) until smooth. Sift dry ingredients. Beat eggs separately and add to creamed butter and sugar. Add dry ingredients alternately with milk, mixing well after each addition. Add vanilla and beat until smooth. Pour into three greased cake pans. Bake at 350° for 20 minutes or until toothpick comes out clean. Turn out on racks to cool.

You may want to wax paper line your pans.

Fudge Icing
3 cups granulated sugar
½ cup cocoa
2 tablespoons white corn syrup
pinch of salt
1 cup whipping cream or half and half
1 stick butter or margarine
1 teaspoon vanilla extract

Mix sugar, cocoa, and corn syrup well. Add salt and cream. Cook, stirring constantly over low heat until sugar dissolves. Then cook at a high temperature until mixture comes to a full boil. Continue to cook over low heat stirring occasionally, until mixture forms a soft ball. Test in a cup of cool water or use candy thermometer. Add butter and vanilla. Beat until a smooth consistency to spread on layers.

If icing becomes too thick to spread, add a little cream. This frosting is best made when the weather is sunny.

Margaret Galbreath
Sonora

228

Angel Food Cake

12 egg whites
1½ teaspoons cream of tartar
1½ cups sugar, divided
1½ teaspoons vanilla
½ teaspoon almond extract
1 cup sifted cake flour
¼ teaspoon salt
fruit or frosting, optional

Beat egg whites with cream of tartar at high speed until foamy. Add ¾ cup sugar, 2 tablespoons at a time, beating constantly until sugar is dissolved and whites are glossy and stand in soft peaks. Beat in flavorings. Sift together flour, remaining sugar and salt. Sift about ½ cup of the flour mixture over whites and gently fold just until flour disappears. Repeat, folding in remaining flour mixture ½ cup at a time. Pour into ungreased 10x4-inch tube pan. Gently cut through batter with metal spatula. Bake in preheated 375° oven until top springs back when lightly touched with finger, about 30 to 40 minutes. Invert cake in pan on funnel or bottle neck. Cool completely, about 1½ hours. With narrow spatula or knife, loosen cake from pan and gently shake onto serving plate. Top with fruit or frost, if desired.

Rub just a bit of meringue between thumb and forefinger to feel if sugar has dissolved.

Chocolate variation: Omit almond extract and increase vanilla to 2 teaspoons. Reduce flour to ⅔ cup and sift in ⅓ cup unsweetened cocoa. Prepare batter and bake as above.

American Egg Board

I never saw my grandmother, Margaret Whittington Westbrook, cook anything but the taffy candy which, when I was a child, she would make for me. But she knew how to show the cook how to cook!

During World War II, the rationing of butter, fats and oil began on March 1, 1943. This cake became popular with the ranch women who had access to the products of a milk cow on the ranch. The recipe was given to me in 1946 by my mother-in-law, Mazie Buttrill Wittenburg, when I came to Edwards County as a bride.

Sponge Cake

3 eggs
1 cup sugar
3 tablespoons water
1 cup flour
1 tablespoon baking powder
½ teaspoon vanilla
pinch of salt

Beat eggs; add sugar, salt, vanilla, and water. Beat well. Mix flour and baking powder and fold into egg mixture. Bake in moderate oven.

Mocha Icing
2 rounded tablespoons butter
2 cups powdered sugar
pinch of salt
2 tablespoons strong coffee
2 tablespoons thick cream
2 squares of melted chocolate

Cream butter with sifted powdered sugar. Stir in salt, coffee, cream, and chocolate. Frost cake.

Jean Findlater Millspaugh (Mrs. Austin)
San Angelo

Sweet Cream Cake

1 cup heavy cream
2 beaten eggs
1 cup sugar
1 teaspoon flavoring
1½ cups flour
1½ teaspoons baking powder
½ teaspoon salt

Cream sugar, eggs, flavoring and cream together. Stir in dry ingredients. Pour into greased and floured layer pans and bake at 350° for 30 minutes. Bake in a loaf pan for about 45-50 minutes.

Ruth H. Wittenburg
Rocksprings

 *Cakes*

Never Fail Cream Cheese Pound Cake

1 8-ounce package softened cream cheese
3 sticks softened margarine or butter
3 cups sugar
6 eggs
3 cups flour
1 teaspoon vanilla or lemon flavoring

Cream cheese, margarine, and sugar until smooth. Add eggs and flour, starting and ending with flour. Add vanilla and pour into a greased and floured bundt or tube pan. Bake at 300° for about 2 hours. Cool in pan for 20 minutes.

Jane Ellis Wardlaw (Mrs. Warren)
San Angelo

Sour Cream Pound Cake

3 cups flour
¼ teaspoon baking soda
3 cups sugar
2 sticks butter
6 eggs
1 8-ounce carton sour cream
1 teaspoon vanilla extract
1 teaspoon lemon extract

Sift flour and measure; add soda to flour and sift again. Sift sugar into another bowl. Butter, eggs and sour cream should be at room temperature before mixing. Cream butter; slowly add sugar and cream well. Add eggs, two at a time and beat well. Add flour ½ cup at a time. Beat well after each addition. Add flavorings and beat. Pour batter into a well greased and floured 10-inch tube pan or two loaf pans and bake at 325° for 1 hour and 10 minutes or until cake tests done.

Martha Gries
Ozona

This cake's name says it all! It can't be messed up. I have even cooked it by mistake at 200° for 2 hours and then 300° for 1 hour. I am always asked, "it doesn't have any baking powder, did I forget?" No, it does not have baking powder. This also freezes well. Never visit anyone without taking something homemade, food is always appreciated.

This is an old family favorite, my mother's (Mrs. Elmo Arledge) recipe and her standby to please everyone for over 30 years. It still gets AAA+ from everyone I have ever seen eat it!

This cake is one of those wonderful childhood memories! It was wonderful when Mama made it, and my family has loved it too!

This is a good time to make Forgotten Cookies with the three egg whites left over.

Pound Cake

3½ sticks butter
4 cups sifted cake flour
8 eggs
2 cups sugar
⅛ teaspoon salt
1 teaspoon baking powder
1 teaspoon vanilla
1 teaspoon lemon extract
1 tablespoon bourbon

Cream butter, work in sifted flour until mixture is a fine mealy texture. Beat eggs until lemon colored, add sugar, then add to flour mixture. Add salt, baking powder, extracts, and bourbon. Beat 15 minutes on low or 5 minutes on high. Grease tube pan or bundt pan. Bake at 250° for 40 minutes, then at 325° for 40 minutes. When cool, cut cake in 3 layers, and fill with pineapple filling.

Pineapple Filling
1 cup sugar
1 tablespoon flour
¾ cup crushed pineapple
3 beaten egg yolks
1½ tablespoons lemon juice
1 tablespoon butter

Blend sugar with flour and combine with pineapple. Add egg yolks, lemon juice, and butter. Cook over low direct heat; stir constantly until thick and smooth - 20 minutes. Cool and spread on each layer of pound cake. You can also dribble on top of cake.

I cook this filling in the microwave, stirring every couple of minutes until thickened.

Mary John Espy Phinizy

Gail

 Cakes

Gladie's Pound Cake

3 cups flour
3 cups sugar
10 large eggs
1 pound butter at room temperature

Sift flour 4 times. Sift sugar 1 time. Beat eggs until light and fluffy; gradually add sugar. Mix flour into butter. Add butter mixture to egg mixture. Bake in a large tube pan at 350° for 1 hour.

Gladie McKnight Davis
submitted by daughter-in-law Kay Davis
Sterling City

Too Good Chocolate Cake

2 cups flour
2 cups sugar
2 sticks oleo
¼ cup cocoa
1 cup water
½ cup buttermilk
1 teaspoon baking soda
2 slightly beaten eggs
1 teaspoon vanilla

Mix flour and sugar together, set aside. Combine oleo, cocoa, and water; cook to beginning of boil. Add baking soda to buttermilk. Add all ingredients together. Pour in lightly greased 9x13-inch cake pan. Bake at 400° for 20 minutes. Make icing while cake is cooking.

Nancy Johnson
Sonora

Miss Gladie was well known for this large pound cake, as she always took it to church and school functions.

Eggs and butter are best if left overnight out of the refrigerator.

Too Good Chocolate Cake Icing
1 stick oleo
⅓ cup milk
1 cup chopped pecans
1 teaspoon vanilla
¼ cup cocoa
1 box powdered sugar

Melt oleo, milk and cocoa together, add chopped pecans, vanilla and stir in powdered sugar. Pour over hot cake. You can sift the powdered sugar to take out any lumps.

This has been Preccia's birthday cake for many years. It is wonderful!

This is an easy to make cake, delicious and not too sweet. The recipe has been handed down in the Rose Family.— Who was Alma Gluck?

Alma Gluck Cake

1 cup butter or oleo
1½ cups sugar
5 whole eggs
2 squares melted Baker's chocolate
1½ cups flour
2 teaspoons baking powder
¾ cup milk
little salt

Beat butter and sugar. Add eggs one at a time. Add flour, baking powder, salt, and milk. Bake in greased and floured 8- or 9-inch pans at 350° for 35 minutes.

Filling and Icing
⅓ cup butter
2 cups powdered sugar
¼ cup cocoa
1 teaspoon vanilla
cream or milk
chopped pecans

Combine butter and sugar; add cocoa and vanilla. Stir in enough cream to make icing easy to spread. Ice layers and top of cake, then sprinkle with pecans.

Mrs. Abb Rose
New Braunfels

German Chocolate Up-Side Down Cake

1 cup coconut
1 cup pecans, chopped
1 German chocolate cake mix
1 8-ounce package cream cheese, soften
1 stick of oleo, soften
1 box of powdered sugar

Butter the sides and bottom of a 13x9 inch pyrex pan, line the bottom with coconut and pecans. Mix the cake according to the directions on box. Pour over top of coconut and pecan mixture. Mix together cream cheese, oleo, and powdered sugar; spoon over cake. Bake 1 hour at 350°. Icing will sink to bottom of cake during baking.

Jean Rink
Lubbock

I have made this cake for my Bridge and Skip-Bow parties and everyone always wants the recipe. Easy and very good!

Black Russian Cake

1 package yellow cake mix
1 package instant chocolate pudding mix
1 cup oil
¾ cup water
¼ cup vodka
¼ cup Kahlúa
4 eggs

Put all ingredients in a large bowl of mixer, beat for 4 minutes until well blended. Pour into a greased and floured bundt pan. Bake at 350° for 50 to 60 minutes.

Glaze
½ cup sifted powered sugar
2 teaspoons cream or milk
2 teaspoons Kahlúa

Mix well together and drizzle over cake while still barely warm.

Dorothy Rink
Dallas

My daughter, Jennifer got this recipe from her grandmother when she was a little girl. Her first cake recipe. It is always delicious and you will enjoy it as much as we do.

235

Donna Kaye's Pie Crust

5 cups flour
2 cups shortening
1 egg
1 cup cold water

Cut the shortening into the flour with a pie cutter until mixed. Stir the egg into the water. Add the egg mixture to the flour and mix with hands until dough forms. It will be sticky at the beginning but as you work with it, it will all stay together. Then roll out and make your pie crust. Bake at 450° or until done. This makes enough for four pies. You can pinch off what you need for the pie and freeze the rest and thaw it out as you need it.

Living on the ranch not knowing who might drop by or when you might get to town next; I keep this pie crust made up and in the freezer all the time. It thaws out really quick for unexpected company.

Donna Kaye Herring
Ozona

Never Fail Water Whip Pie Crust

2 cups flour
1 teaspoon salt
⅔ cup shortening
1 tablespoon milk
¼ cup boiling water

Sift flour and salt. Stir together shortening, milk, and boiling water. Beat flour mixture into shortening mixture. Roll in a ball then sprinkle flour on board and roll out dough. Place in pie pan and bake.

Laura C. McMullan
Submitted by Glenda McMullan
Iraan

From windmill detail to the many hours spent pulling bitter weed, there was always plenty to keeps kids busy. But, for past-time, we swam in the stock tanks and hunted jack rabbits during the cool of the day. We were also avid deer hunters during hunting season and loved to go fishing when possible. We had a lot of neighborhood fish fries, and camp cooking at the hunting camps.

Pies & Cobblers

Sour Cream Pie

1 cup sugar
1 teaspoon flour
1 egg
1 cup sour cream
1 teaspoon vanilla
½ cup raisins

Mix sugar and flour, combine with sour cream, egg and vanilla. Cook in top of double boiler until thick, stirring constantly. Cool thoroughly, add raisins. Pour into unbaked pie shell and cover with top crust as for any fruit pie. For richer pie, another egg and more cream can be used. Bake at 325° until golden. Don't over bake!

Jan Van Shoubrouek
Ozona

Butterscotch Cream Pie

⅔ cup brown sugar
6 tablespoons flour
½ cup cold milk
1½ cups scalded milk
3 egg yolks
¼ teaspoon salt
2 tablespoons butter
1 teaspoon vanilla
1 9-inch baked pie shell

Mix sugar and flour; add cold milk and blend thoroughly. Stirring constantly, pour mixture into scalded milk set over hot water (double boiler pan). Stir and cook until thickened throughout. Cover and cook about 10 minutes. Stir 2 or 3 times to keep smooth. Blend a small quantity of the hot mixture with the beaten egg yolks. Combine with mixture in double boiler. Cook - stirring constantly 2 or 3 minutes. Remove from heat; add salt and butter. Cool slightly, add vanilla. Cool. Pour into cooled baked pie shell. Cover with meringue. Bake at 350° until browned; cool.

Melba York
Alto, New Mexico

My great-grandmother, Mrs. George S. Allison's, recipe has been in the family for generations. My grandmother, Mrs. Alfred Schwiening, and my mother, Mary Jones Wilson, fixed this pie for special holidays.

This was my cowboy's favorite pie that I made when Bob and I first started our ranch life right after World War II.

My mother told me to never handle my pie crust dough. It made it tough. You should always use a fork or blender. -1941

237

I have never cared for lemon pie but this is the exception. It gets rave reviews! This recipe came from my Aunt Annette Allen who got it from a friend in San Antonio.

Roll oranges or lemons until slightly soft before squeezing. You will get more juice easily.

Lemon Sour Cream Pie

1 cup sugar
3 tablespoons cornstarch
dash of salt
1 cup milk
3 eggs, separated
4 tablespoons butter
1 teaspoon grated lemon rind
¼ cup fresh squeezed lemon juice
1 cup sour cream
1 baked 9-inch pie shell
¼ teaspoon cream of tartar
½ teaspoon vanilla
6 tablespoons sugar

Combine sugar, cornstarch, and salt - stir thoroughly. Slowly stir in milk; cook and stir until mixture is boiling and thick. Blend small amount of hot mixture into slightly beaten egg yolks. Return to hot mixture cooking and stirring constantly for 2 minutes. Add butter, lemon rind, lemon juice, and stir. Cover and cool. Fold in sour cream. Spoon into cool baked pie shell.

Meringue: Beat 3 egg whites with cream of tartar and vanilla to soft peaks. Gradually add sugar, and beat to stiff peaks. Cover pie with meringue - sealing edges. Bake at 350° for 12 to 15 minutes or until golden. Cool before serving.

Randee Fagan
Del Rio

Lemon Meringue Pie

juice of 3 lemons
grated rind of 2 lemons
4 separated eggs
1 cup milk
1½ cups sugar
6 tablespoons cornstarch
¼ teaspoon salt
1 cup water
1 tablespoon butter
1 baked pie shell

This pie does not stick to the knife when cut and looks like a restaurant meringue.

This is my favorite pie. Nearly everyone asks for the recipe.

Mix lemon juice and grated rind. Blend egg yolks and milk in bowl. Mix sugar, cornstarch and salt in either a double boiler or a 2 quart microwave bowl and stir in milk slowly. Add water and lemon juice. This makes a tart pie and you might want to adjust lemon to your taste. If using double boiler, place over boiling water and stir constantly until smooth and thick. If using microwave, cook 2 minutes at a time and stir the first couple of times and then a minute. Even if it lumps a little, it stirs smooth. The microwave is much quicker, but needs watching. Cover with wax-paper and let it cool while making meringue.

Mile High Meringue
½ cup sugar
1 tablespoon cornstarch
½ cup water
4 egg whites
⅛ teaspoon salt
½ teaspoon vanilla

Combine 2 tablespoons sugar, cornstarch and water. Cook (microwave ½ minute at a time and stir) until thick and clear. Cool slightly. Beat egg whites, salt and vanilla, gradually adding remaining sugar until soft mounds form. Beat in cooled mixture slowly. Continue beating until soft peaks form. Too much beating causes mixture to become bumpy, still good but not as pretty. Pour cooled lemon filling into baked pie shell and pile meringue on top of filling. Bake at 350° for 12 to 15 minutes or until slightly browned.

Nancy Jones
Fort Stockton

Ora Malon's Caramel Pie

2 cups sugar (divided)
4 teaspoons flour
¼ teaspoon salt
3 cups milk
4 large eggs (separated)
2 tablespoons butter
1 teaspoon vanilla

Melt 1 cup sugar in skillet until caramel colored, set aside. Mix 1 cup sugar with flour and salt. Add milk slowly, stirring until smooth. Cook over low heat until it begins to boil, stirring constantly. Add caramelized sugar. Add one cup of hot mixture to slightly beaten egg yolks, then add back into mixture in saucepan. Continue cooking, stirring constantly, until thick. Remove from heat add butter and vanilla. Beat until smooth. Pour into two 9-inch baked pie shells. Make meringue from egg whites. Place on filling of pies. Bake 8 to 10 minutes at 400°.

Lou Deaton
Ozona

This simple to make pie is always wonderful! I use half and half for the rich milk.

Variations to Mrs. Espy's Pie

Chocolate Pie: Add 5 to 7 tablespoons cocoa to eggs and sugar.

Coconut Pie: Add box of coconut.

Lemon Pie: Use 1 to 1½ cups of warm water instead of milk. Flavor with juice and rind of one lemon.

Mrs. Espy's Cream Pie

6 eggs
¼ cup butter or oleo
1 cup rich milk or cream
2 cups sugar
3 tablespoons flour
vanilla to taste

Beat the egg yolks and 2 egg whites until light colored. Add sugar mixed with flour and softened butter, one at a time, beating vigorously. Add milk or cream and vanilla and put into uncooked pie shells. Bake at 450° for 10 minutes, then turn down the oven to 325° for 30 minutes, bake until pie is set or a knife comes out clean when inserted in the center. Use remaining egg whites for meringue or top with frozen whipped topping.

Tommy Espy Whitehead
Sonora

Chocolate Pie

4 tablespoons flour
¾ cup sugar
3 tablespoons cocoa
¼ teaspoon salt
1½ cups milk
2 egg yolks
1 tablespoon butter
1 teaspoon vanilla

Combine flour, sugar, cocoa and salt. Stir in milk, cook until thickness desired. Separate the eggs; stir some hot mixture into beaten egg yolks. Add to hot mixture and cook 2 minutes longer. Remove from heat, add butter and vanilla. Cool. Pour into baked shell, cover with meringue. Bake at 375° for 11 minutes.

Minnie G. Schmidt
Mason

This family recipe is over seventy-five years old—still my favorite chocolate pie!

Jeff Davis Pie

1 cup sugar
¼ teaspoon cloves
¼ teaspoon allspice
½ teaspoon cinnamon
4 eggs
1½ cups milk
¼ cup half and half
1 9-inch pie shell, uncooked

Mix sugar and spices thoroughly. Add remaining ingredients until it is a creamy consistency. Pour into pie shell, bake at 400° for 30 to 40 minutes, or until crust is brown and filling is set. Cover with foil if crust is browning too much.

Carmen Sutton
Ozona

This recipe came from Lela Bradford, grandmother of Jeff Sutton. Mrs. Bradford was married to Ray Bradford, a pioneer rancher in Menard County whose mother used the recipe in the 1860's. The recipe has been passed down through several generations.

This was my mom's basic pudding recipe and over the years I have made it many times and the response is always the same. They say it is the best pie they have ever had! It has fed many a hungry cowboy.

In raising your children, "Give in when it really doesn't matter and stand your ground when it really does."

Chocolate Pie

4 cups milk
3 cups sugar
8 heaping tablespoons flour or 4 heaping tablespoons cornstarch
2 heaping tablespoons Hershey's European Chocolate
4 egg yolks
1 teaspoon vanilla
3 heaping tablespoons margarine

Sift together dry ingredients; slowly add the milk stirring as you do this. Cook on medium heat until it comes to a boil. Beat egg yolks and add a little of the hot liquid; return to pan and cook a little longer, but not too long. Take the pan off; add the butter and the vanilla, beat by mixer or hand. This will take care of any lumps in the pudding mixture. Pour into baked pie crust and top with meringue. Bake at 450° until golden brown. Makes two 8-inch pies or one really big 9-inch pie.

You can use this for coconut cream, or banana pudding - just omit the chocolate.

The Hershey's European Chocolate can be bought at any grocery store and it is better than the old Hershey's cocoa.

Meringue
  4 egg whites
  ½ cup sugar

Beat the egg whites until stiff peaks form and then slowly add the sugar.

Use Donna Kayes' Pie Crust for your pie crust.

Donna Kaye Herring

Ozona

242

Miss Lilly's Chess Pie

½ cup butter
1½ cup sugar
1 tablespoon flour
1 tablespoon vanilla
¼ teaspoon salt
3 eggs
½ cup milk

Cream together butter and sugar. Add flour, vanilla, and salt. Add in the eggs, one at a time; add in milk. Pour into unbaked pie shell and bake at 350° for 40 minutes.

Molly Allison
San Angelo

This is the pie my father, Asa Jones, likes for a coffee break when he is working at the ranch west of Ft. Stockton. One of "Miss Lilly" Allison's most used recipes.

Lemon Chess Pie

4 eggs
2 cups sugar
¼ cup lemon juice
¼ cup butter
¼ cup milk
1 teaspoon flour
1 teaspoon cornmeal
4 tablespoons grated lemon rind

Beat the eggs; add the flour and sugar mixed with butter, rind, juice, and milk. Then add cornmeal. Pour into unbaked shell. Bake in hot oven, 450°, for 10 minutes then reduce heat to 275° for 1 hour.

Lucille McMillan
Sonora

My grandmother's tried and true recipe. Old and very good!

Buttermilk Pie

3 eggs
1½ cups sugar
1 teaspoon vanilla
¼ cup melted margarine or butter
3 heaping teaspoons flour
1 cup buttermilk

Cream eggs, sugar, vanilla and margarine. Add flour and mix well with wire whisk. Add buttermilk, mix well. Pour into a 9-inch unbaked pie crust. Bake at 350° for 45 to 50 minutes or until set, depending on the altitude.

Sally Espy
Ft. Davis

This recipe has been in the Espy family for more than 60 years.

Variation:
2 tablespoons flour
½ cup buttermilk
2 teaspoons vanilla

Sprinkle nutmeg on top.

Mrs. Jack Brown
Del Rio

We use this recipe a lot because it is so easy and a favorite of my mother's.

Variation:
½ stick melted butter
¼ teaspoon cinnamon

Jodie Finklea
Sonora

Buttermilk Pie is a West Texas favorite with many variations. Each variation is wonderful - try them all to find your favorite!

Mimi's Pecan Pie

1 unbaked pie crust
5 eggs
1 cup sugar
1½ cups corn syrup
½ teaspoon salt
1½ teaspoons vanilla
1½ cups chopped pecans
6 tablespoons melted butter
16 pecan halves
1 cup whipping cream

Prepare pie crust and line 9½-inch Pyrex pie plate. Beat eggs and sugar together. Add corn syrup, salt, vanilla, chopped pecans, butter and mix thoroughly. Pour into unbaked pie shell. Bake at 325° for 1 hour and 15 minutes or until filling is set. Garnish with pecans. Serve slightly warm or cold, topped with whipped cream.

Melissa Graham Douglass
Rocksprings

Always a family favorite, my grandmother, Mary Phillips Hough, passed it on to my mother, Elizabeth Ann Hough Graham, who passed it on to me. The three generations of us have all been ranching families. In fact, my mother, Elizabeth Ann Hough Graham, was "Miss Mohair of 1956."

Pecan Pie

1 stick oleo
½ cup sugar
3 eggs, beaten
¾ cup corn syrup (½ light-½ dark)
¼ teaspoon salt
1 teaspoon vanilla
1 cup pecans

Make your favorite pie crust and chill while you make the filling. Mix melted oleo, adding sugar, eggs, syrup, salt, and vanilla; fold in pecans. Bake at 350° for 40 to 45 minutes or until tested when a knife comes out clean.

Gladys Dearman
Monahans

I was 89 years old on July 1, and I have had this recipe for 70 years. I still fix this for my family on all holidays. It's a special recipe for my family and I would like to share it with you.

Fudge Pecan Pie

¼ cup melted oleo
3 tablespoons cocoa
¾ cup hot water
1½ cups sugar
½ cup flour
1 small can evaporated milk
½ cup crushed pecans

Mix flour, sugar, and cocoa. Add hot water, oleo and milk. Fold in pecans. Pour into pie shell. Bake at 350° for 50 minutes.

June Foster
Sterling City

German Sweet Chocolate Pie

1 bar German Sweet Chocolate
1 stick oleo
3 eggs
1 teaspoon vanilla
1 cup sugar
3 tablespoons flour
1 cup chopped pecans

Melt chocolate with oleo. Beat with spoon. Combine eggs, vanilla, sugar, flour and mix at high speed for 5 minutes. Fold in chocolate and pecans. Pour in oleo greased pie pan and cook at 325° for 35 to 40 minutes. Cool and top with whipped topping or whipped cream. This rich pie makes a crust on top. Quick and easy when you're in a hurry.

Sadie Puckitt
San Angelo

Pumpkin Pie

1 cup sugar
1 heaping tablespoon flour
2 tablespoons butter
1 teaspoon cinnamon
1 teaspoon nutmeg
pinch of salt
3 egg yolks
1 cup canned pumpkin
2 cups whole milk, warmed slightly
3 egg whites

Cream together sugar, flour, and butter. Add in order listed: cinnamon, nutmeg, salt, well beaten egg yolks, canned pumpkin, and milk. Last, fold in stiffly beaten egg whites. Cook in an unbaked pie shell at 400° for 10 minutes. Reduce heat to 300° and cook for about 35 minutes or until a silver knife blade comes out clean.

Claudia Abbey Ball
Hudspeth River Ranch

This recipe was my grandmother's, Mrs. Claude B. Hudspeth, who lived on this ranch when I was little. Claude Hudspeth was a Congressman from this district from 1917 to 1932 and Hudspeth county is named for him. We always have this pie on Thanksgiving.

Cranberry Nut Pie

½ cup cranberries
4 eggs
1⅓ cups sugar
¼ pound butter or oleo
1 cup broken pecans
1 teaspoon vanilla
½ teaspoon nutmeg
½ teaspoon cinnamon
⅓ cup orange juice
1 tablespoon lemon juice
2 tablespoons flour

Cut or finely grind the cranberries. Cream sugar and butter. Add well beaten eggs. Add orange juice, lemon juice, vanilla, nutmeg and cinnamon. Add flour to pecans and stir in batter. Cook in an unbaked crust at 400° for 5 minutes. Cool oven slightly and bake at 300° until firm. This may look curdled but it does not matter.

Mae Ward
Sonora

This is a wonderful Christmas recipe. It came to me from my mother's youngest sister, Mayce Marshall, from Del Rio.

Mincemeat Cream Pie

1¼ cups water
½ package mincemeat
3 egg yolks
1 cup sugar
¼ cup flour
½ stick oleo or butter

Bring water and mincemeat to a boil, beat the egg yolks, adding sugar, flour, butter, cook until thick. Pour into 9-inch pie crust. Cover with your favorite meringue and brown.

Jann Miller
Ozona

Mom's Favorite Apple Pie

1 double crust
6-7 cups fresh apples
¾ cup sugar
2 tablespoons flour
½ teaspoon ground cinnamon
¼ teaspoon nutmeg
1 tablespoon margarine

Preheat oven to 425°. Press bottom crust into pie tin and prick thoroughly with a fork. In a small bowl, mix sugar, flour, cinnamon, and nutmeg. Sprinkle this onto the sliced apples and with a folding motion, mix until the apples are coated. Place the apples inside the crust and dot the top with thin slices of margarine. Cover with the slit top crust and flute. Bake for 1 hour. Foil may be placed under the pie and around the edges of the crust, to prevent hot filling from bubbling over into the oven and to protect the crust from burning.

Fresh pears make a wonderful substitute for this pie, as long as they are the type from your own tree (not the type that turn to mush when they ripen.)

Laura Miller
San Antonio

Adding the juice of one lemon to apple pie makes a nice change.

Pies & Cobblers

Granny Allison's Osgood Pie

1½ cups nuts
1½ cups raisins
4 eggs
2 cups sugar
2 tablespoons vinegar
2 tablespoons butter
2 tablespoons milk
1 teaspoon cloves
1 teaspoon allspice
1 teaspoon nutmeg
1 teaspoon vanilla

Chop nuts and raisins. Beat eggs with sugar. Mix in other ingredients, including nuts and raisins. Pour into unbaked pie shell and bake at 375° for 10 minutes. Then at 325° for 30 minutes or until pie is firm. Serve with whipped cream.

Jan Jones Van Shoubrouek
Ozona

Love Pie

4 egg whites
1 teaspoon vinegar
1 cup sugar, white or brown
1 cup rolled cracker crumbs
½ teaspoon baking powder
1 cup chopped pecans
1 teaspoon vanilla

Beat egg whites with vinegar until stiff. Add sugar, cracker crumbs, baking powder, pecans, and vanilla. Grease a pie plate and bake at 350° for 30 minutes. Top with whipped cream.

Mrs. H.O. Word
Submitted by Ethel Miller
Ozona

This cherry pie recipe came to me from Mama Aycock in deep East Texas. I have used it for many years and is one of my favorites because it is delicious and a little unusual. It can be prepared way ahead of time (even a day or so before needed) and yet, when served, they seem to have been "just made." The crust stays fresh and crisp when you don't put the filling in until ready to serve. It does take a bit of time to shape the crust over the bottom of the muffin pans but leave them different and "scraggly." It accentuates the fact that they are really "home made" and in this day of "fast foods" that is refreshing.

Individual Cherry Pies

1 No. 2 can sour pitted cherries
1½ cups sugar
1 heaping tablespoon flour
2 eggs
red food coloring
butter the size of an egg
½ teaspoon vanilla

Mash cherries and beat them. Add to mixture of sugar, flour and eggs. Add butter and a few drops of red food coloring and cook until mixture begins to thicken. Store in refrigerator when cool. Add ½ teaspoon vanilla. Mix well and put into pastry shells just before serving. Top with whipped cream.

Pastry Shells
1 heaping cup flour
¼ teaspoon salt
¼ teaspoon sugar
3-4 tablespoons shortening

Combine flour, salt, and sugar. Work in shortening with a fork until it looks like meal. Add enough ice water in different spots gradually until right consistency. Shape on bottom of muffin pans and cook at 425° until done.

Clellia Harris
Austin

Green Grape Pie

1 beaten egg
1½ cups sugar
3 tablespoons flour
¼ teaspoon salt
1 cup heavy cream
½ teaspoon lemon juice
¼ teaspoon vanilla
2 cups green grapes
1 unbaked pie shell

Cream egg and sugar. Mix in flour, salt, cream, juice, vanilla, and grapes. Pour into unbaked pie shell. Add top crust or strips of lattice on top. Bake at 350° for 45 minutes or until done.

Betty Hill Nall
Junction

Glazed Strawberry Pie

1 quart strawberries
1 cup sugar
½ cup water
¼ cup cornstarch
¾ cup cold water
`/ teaspoon salt
1 tablespoon lemon juice
red food coloring

Wash and hull the strawberries. Bring water and sugar to a boil. Dissolve cornstarch in ¾ cup cold water. Add to syrup, stirring constantly. Cook 5 to 10 minutes until clear. Blend in salt, lemon juice and red coloring. Pour over strawberries and coat well. Cool and place in cooked pie shell. Cover with sweetened whipped cream.

Clara Maudell Drake (Mrs. Glen)
Corpus Christi

This recipe has been in my family for many, many years. You must have access to wild mustang grapes which are in abundance in the Junction area. The grapes should be about the size of an English pea or they will explode.

My grandmother, Mrs. E.G. Hill, advises when making Agarita Jelly, cook berries the same day as picked and don't allow juice to stand after it has been boiled or jelly will appear cloudy.

This recipe was given to me by my next door neighbor when Lisa, my daughter, was 3 years old in about 1951. I've used it ever since.

Mile High Strawberry Pie

1 10-ounce package frozen strawberries
1 cup sugar
2 egg whites
1½ tablespoons lemon juice
1 teaspoon strawberry flavoring (optional)
½ cup whipping cream
dash of salt
1 teaspoon vanilla

Place defrosted strawberries, sugar, egg whites, lemon juice, flavoring, and salt in a bowl and beat at medium speed for 15 minutes. Mixture will look like meringue. Whip cream and add vanilla. Fold into mixture. Pile lightly into crumb crust. Freeze for several hours and keep in freezer.

Margaret Drake Fowler
Ozona

Blueberry Pie

This is a quick dessert and a pretty presentation.

1 8-ounce package cream cheese
⅓ cup sugar
1½-2 cups bananas
1 can blueberry pie mix
1 carton frozen whipped topping

Beat cream cheese and sugar together. Spread in pie shell - you can use graham cracker crust or pastry, either works well. Slice the bananas and place on cream cheese. Spread blueberry mix, then top with whipped topping.

Alice Sisco
Water Valley

Angel Food Pie

4½ tablespoons cornstarch
¾ cup sugar
1½ cups boiling water
⅜ teaspoon salt
3 egg whites
3 tablespoons sugar
1½ teaspoons vanilla
1 cooked pastry shell
whipped cream
chopped pecans or grated chocolate

Mix cornstarch and sugar in heavy saucepan; gradually add boiling water, stirring constantly, and cook until thick and clear. Add salt to egg whites and beat until stiff. Add 3 tablespoons sugar and vanilla to whites, and beat until mixture is creamy. Pour hot cornstarch mixture slowly over whites, beating constantly, until well blended. Cool mixture slightly and pour into baked shell. Refrigerate. When pie is thoroughly chilled, top with whipped cream, and garnish with finely chopped pecans or grated chocolate.

Joy Carruthers
Sanderson

As a child, I always looked forward to Mother serving this pie to her bridge club when she was hostess - and always hoped for leftovers, of course! She doesn't recall the origin of the recipe, and though I search every new cookbook I can find, I have never seen it elsewhere.

God never closes the door without opening a window.

253

My grandmother, Nancy Ellen, from Slick, Oklahoma, has handed this recipe down through 3 generations.

Romana's Apricot Side Pies

16 ounces dried apricots
1 cup sugar
2 cups water

Boil dried apricots in water until tender, add sugar, then let cool. Mash or run through food processor.

Make your favorite pie crust or I use pre-made pie crust from the grocery store. Cut in to 4 pieces. Fill with ¼ cup apricot filling, dot with butter and a little sugar on top of apricots. Fold in half and seal edges with a fork. Bake at 350° for 10 minutes or light brown.

Sweet Sauce Topping
1½ cups sweet milk
¼ cup sugar
½ teaspoon nutmeg
½ teaspoon cinnamon
2 tablespoons cream of tartar

Bring the milk almost to a boil, add last 4 ingredients. Stir constantly with whisk until thick. Pour over hot pies.

Jonnie Hodges
Sonora

The men in my family are crazy about this quick and easy dessert!

Count to three before you speak: 1. Is it true? 2. Is it kind? 3. Is it necessary?

Tortilla Cobbler

1 dozen flour tortillas
2 cans pie filling (peach, apricot, etc.)
1 cup sugar
1 cup water
1 stick margarine

Spray large size baking dish with non-stick spray. Roll tortillas with filling inside and place in dish. Cook sugar, water and margarine until sugar is dissolved and pour over tortillas. Bake at 350° for 30 minutes.

Connie Parmer
Veribest

Fried Pies

Filling:
2 8-ounce packages dried apricots
water
2 cups sugar or to taste

In covered pan, cook fruit in water until tender. Blend in sugar and mash with potato masher. Cool.

Dried apples or peaches are also wonderful.

Pastry
3 cups flour
1 teaspoon salt
1 tablespoon sugar
1 cup shortening
9 tablespoons water

Mix flour, sugar, salt; cut in shortening. Make a well and add water. Mix with a fork to form a ball. Roll out to about ⅛-inch thick. Cut out circles using a dessert dish or saucer. Add a heaping tablespoon of the cooked fruit to each circle. Fold pastry over, moisten edges with milk or water, and crimp with fork or finger tip. Fry in a large skillet in oil or shortening until brown on both sides. Drain on paper towels and sprinkle with sugar.

Anita Allison

Clay is probably not as proud of me as Mother is for learning to make these pies. Once when I was making them, Clay was trying to steal one off the platter. I was still busy frying a pie and had two hot metal spatulas in my hands. When he grabbed, I swatted. I'm glad he can laugh about this story now - as he shows off the scar on his forearm. McNeil just never got caught! - Anita

Fried Pies are always a special treat. I remember my grandmother, Me-ma, making these pies for us at the ranch at Loma Alta when I was a little girl. I can still see her standing in front of the stove frying these pies and my brother, Martin, sneaking around the corner to make off with one almost as fast as she could cook them. I never could eat them as hot as he could! Now, it gives me great pleasure to see Anita do just as good a job on these as her great grandmother. And also to watch her brothers enjoy them as much as mine. — Mimi

This is plenty for eight. That is unless you have three hungry men who really like it! It is a little time consuming, but for my bunch it is worth it!

Sauce
1 pear
1 cup water
½ cup sugar
2 teaspoons cornstarch
¼ teaspoon nutmeg
3 tablespoons butter

While roll bakes, cut the peeled, cored pear in little cubes. Cook in water for 15 minutes. In a separate bowl combine sugar, cornstarch, and nutmeg. Stir into the cooked pears along with butter and continue cooking until sauce is clear and bubbly. Stir constantly. Serve the sauce warm over warm cobbler.

Pear Cobbler

Pastry
1½ cups sifted flour
½ teaspoon salt
¼ cup shortening
1 egg
3 tablespoons water

Make the pastry first. Sift flour and salt together in a bowl. Cut in shortening with pastry blender until mixture looks mealy. Beat egg and sugar together slightly and stir into the flour combination to form a soft ball of pastry. Preheat oven to 350°. Roll pastry on a floured board into a rectangle about 15x12 inches in size.

Filling
½ cup sugar
2 tablespoons flour
1 teaspoon nutmeg
4 cups thinly sliced pears (about 3 large)
3 tablespoons butter

Mix sugar, flour, and nutmeg together and sprinkle half the mixture over the pastry. Cover with peeled and thinly sliced pears. Scatter remaining sugar mixture over tip of pears and dot with butter. Roll pastry as you would a jelly roll and transfer to a large shallow baking pan. Bake 50 minutes in all, but after the first 30 minutes are up, brush the surface of the roll with some of the syrup that bakes out of the cobbler. This gives the top a golden shine.

Tot Holmsley
Ozona

Granny's Cobbler

1 large can peaches or fresh peaches
2 cups sugar
1 teaspoon vanilla
1 teaspoon butter
dash of cinnamon
flour

Use enough peaches to fill your crust. If using fresh peaches, peel and slice into pot. Cook the peaches with the ingredients listed using enough flour to thicken the mixture. Careful not to make it too thick.

Crust
2 cups flour
1 cup shortening
½ cup milk
1 teaspoon salt

Mix the above. Roll out between two floured sheets of wax paper to make handling it easy. Place half of the crust in a 9x13-inch dish. Add the peach mixture. Cover with remaining crust and dot the crust with butter and sugar. Bake this at 350° for about one hour or until lightly browned. This recipe comes from my mother's mom and is one of my favorites. We usually eat the whole cobbler in two days.

I don't have the exact measurements for this because Granny just does it.

Jess Black
Menard

My family has been ranching the same land in Llano county since 1880. The ranch, settled by my grandparents, has been recognized by the Texas Family Ranch Heritage group. After pursuing my college degree at Angelo State University, I plan to return and maintain this family tradition.

I have made this recipe since I was very young and have given it to friends who say they still make it. It is very good and easy and quick to make! It called for salt, but I never use it.

I used to make this for Jerry Johnson for his birthday, or when I needed a favor. It is his favorite.

Quick Peach Cobbler

½ cup flour
½ cup milk
1 cup sugar
1 teaspoon baking powder
1 large can sliced peaches

Mix batter and pour into buttered baking dish. Heat the peaches, juice and all in pan until starts to boil. Spoon the peaches over the batter and then slowly pour the juice over. Use about a tablespoon of butter to grease pan. A 11x7 inch Pyrex dish about 2 inches deep is the perfect size for this cobbler. Bake at 350° until brown. When done, a crust will appear on top. This is good topped with frozen whipped topping or ice cream.

Winnie Lynn Reiley Joseph
Sonora

Jerry's Cherry Cobbler

1 16-ounce can red tart or sour cherries
¾-1 cup sugar
2½ tablespoons flour
3-4 drops red food coloring

Drain cherry juice into measuring cup and add enough water to make 1 cup liquid. In saucepan stir sugar and flour. Slowly stir in cherry juice (no lumps) and the food coloring. Heat to a boil until liquid turns clear, add cherries and pour in 8-inch squared baking dish top with crust and bake at 400° for 30 to 45 minutes until bubbly and crust is golden brown.

Crust
1 cup biscuit mix
¼ cup margarine, melted
3 tablespoons boiling water

Mix the above ingredients together. Generously flour surface with biscuit mix and pat dough by hand into square. Cut into strips, criss-cross over cherries and sprinkle with sugar.

Nita Ware
El Paso

1775 Joe Froggers

1 cup butter
2 cups sugar
7 cups flour
1 tablespoon salt
1 tablespoon ginger
2 teaspoons cloves
2 teaspoons allspice
2 teaspoons nutmeg
2 teaspoons cinnamon
2 cups molasses
2 teaspoons baking soda
1 cup raisins
½ cup chopped pecans
⅓ cup dark rum
½ cup hot water

Cream butter and sugar. Sift flour, salt, and spices. Add slowly to butter mixture. Stir baking soda into molasses and add to mixture. Mix hot water with rum and add to mixture. Chill dough 2 hours. Preheat oven to 375°. Roll out dough ¼-inch thick. Cut into cookies. Bake at 350° on greased cookie sheet 8 to 10 minutes.

Leonard Naylor
Submitted by Linda Hayes
Ivanhoe

These cookies were made in the Navy 200 years ago because they keep so well.

These are a little trouble, but well worth it. They are nice to have on hand for a quick snack or strawberry shortcake.

These are the best sugar cookies in the world! They are one of my favorite food memories of growing up. Granma would always bring them to our family reunions and store them in a large glass jar. I remember they were big and soft and all of the cousins would fight for them. - Anita

Old Fashioned Vanilla Cookies

4 cups sifted flour
1 teaspoon baking soda
1 teaspoon salt
1 cup shortening
1 tablespoon vanilla
2 cups sugar
2 egg yolks
1 cup buttermilk
2 egg whites
vanilla sugar (see recipe)

Sift flour, baking soda, and salt together, set aside. Beat shortening with vanilla extract in a large bowl. Add sugar gradually creaming thoroughly. Beat in the egg yolks until mixture is light and fluffy. Alternately add dry ingredients in fourths and buttermilk in thirds to creamed mixture, beating only until blended after each addition . Using a clean beater, beat egg whites until stiff (not dry) peaks are formed. Fold into batter until blended. Drop about 2 tablespoons batter for each cookie onto greased baking sheets, spacing batter 3 inches apart. Using the back of a spoon, spread and shape to 2½-inch round, ½-inch high. Sprinkle generously with Vanilla Sugar. Bake at 375° about 15 minutes, or until browned around the edges. Immediately remove to wire racks and sprinkle with Vanilla Sugar. Makes about 2½ dozen cookies.

Vanilla Sugar: Pour 2 pounds sugar into a container having a tight-fitting cover. Split a vanilla bean in half lengthwise then cut into 1-inch pieces. Poke pieces down into the sugar at irregular intervals. Cover container tightly and store. The longer the sugar stands, the richer the vanilla flavor. Stir in additional sugar as sugar is used.

Sour milk may be used. Measure 1 tablespoon cider vinegar or lemon juice into a measuring cup for liquids and fill with milk to one-cup line; stir.

Mary Ellen McEntire
San Angelo

Cookies & Bars

Estella's Sugar Cookies

½ cup granulated sugar
½ cup powdered sugar
½ teaspoon cream of tartar
½ teaspoon baking soda
1 stick corn oil oleo
1 large egg
⅓ cup corn oil
1 teaspoon vanilla
2 cups plus 1 tablespoon sifted flour

Melt oleo and combine with vanilla, sugars, corn oil and egg. Combine flour, cream of tartar, baking soda; mix well and combine with sugar mixture. Place in refrigerator to set - overnight. Make teaspoon size balls from dough mixture. Place 2-inches apart on a greased cookie sheet. Dip buttered glass in granulated sugar and flatten. Bake at 375° for 10 minutes.

Doris Whitworth Kensing
Menard

My mother was still making these cookies when she was past ninety years and was so pleased she could bake them so quickly. Her cookie jar was usually full.
Save your pennies and watch your dollars grow.
- My Daddy's often repeated statement.

Norwegian Cookies

2 hard boiled egg yolks
2 raw egg yolks
1 cup sugar
1 cup butter
2½ cups flour

Cream the butter and sugar together. Grate the yolks of the hard boiled eggs and add to the above mixture. Beat the raw egg yolks well and mix into mixture. Add flour and mix. Pinch off a little dough, roll and shape into a crescent shape. Bake at 350° until starting to turn golden brown.

Judy Allison
San Angelo

Handed down from George's (Puddin) Aunt Minnie Dahl who married a Norwegian.

Families used to visit up and down the Pecos River frequently. Aunt Lee Dudley kept a full cookie jar. Grown-ups enjoyed dunking these cookies in coffee while youngsters enjoyed theirs with fresh cow's milk.

Aunt Lee's Sugar Cookies

4 cups sugar
1½ cups lard
4 cups flour
1 cup sour milk
4 eggs
½ teaspoon baking soda
2 teaspoons baking powder
2 teaspoons cinnamon
1 teaspoon vanilla

Mix altogether. Chill overnight in icebox. Roll out on floured board; cut and bake in moderate oven 350° until light golden color. For easy handling of dough, divide into thirds.

To make sour milk; Mix 1 cup sweet milk and 1 tablespoon vinegar or lemon juice and let stand for 5 minutes.

Alma Ingham Smart
Rocksprings

Mexican Wedding Cookies

1 cup margarine
5 tablespoons powdered sugar
2 teaspoons vanilla
2 cups flour
1½ cups chopped nuts

Mix ingredients together and roll into balls. Flatten onto an ungreased cookie sheet. Bake at 325° for 15 to 20 minutes or until light brown. Roll in powdered sugar.

Molly Allison
San Angelo

Ranger Cookies

1 cup butter flavored shortening
1 cup brown sugar
1 cup sugar
2 eggs
2 teaspoons baking soda
1 teaspoon baking powder
1 tablespoon vanilla
2 cups flour
2 cups oatmeal
1 cup coconut
1-2 cups pecan pieces
2 cups cornflakes

Cream shortening, sugars; add eggs and mix well. Add baking soda, baking powder and vanilla; then add flour, oatmeal, coconut and pecans. Add cornflakes last; stirring until just mixed (you don't want to smash em all.) Drop by teaspoonfuls onto ungreased cookie sheets; grease bottom of a glass, dip in sugar and "bop" each cookie flat with the sugar. Bake at 375° for 10 to 12 minutes.

Use a large bowl - this makes a lot of cookies! You may add chocolate chips or white baking chocolate chunks.

Marcella Anderson
Rocksprings

These cookies are a ranch cowboy's favorite. Who knows - maybe Texas Rangers used to haul them around in their saddlebags!

Write in your cookbooks! The date you used the recipe, who you cooked it for, or what was going on in your life that day. Someday this book will be a treasure to someone special. A news event is also fun to read and reflect on. Has anyone ever asked for this recipe and who did you give it to? Slip in a "chuckle" or "gem" you may have heard or read that day.

I was going to name these cookies "Big Brother's Favorite Cookies" because my brothers love them. Instead, I'm naming them after my cat Cinco. He sat with me as I typed in all the recipes for this book. But without the help of the cat, these cookies really are great- McNeil has me make them for him whenever I see him.

This recipe won 1st Place at the 4th of July Celebration in Ozona in 1993. Kids love them! I can't get my two kids, Koby and Payton, out of them.

Cinco's Peanut Butter-Chocolate Chip Cookies

1 cup shortening
2 teaspoons vanilla
1 cup sugar
1 cup firmly packed brown sugar
2 eggs
1 cup peanut butter
2 cups flour
2 teaspoons baking soda
½ teaspoon salt
1 12 ounce package chocolate chips

Beat together shortening and vanilla, add in sugar and brown sugar. Beat in eggs until fluffy. Blend in peanut butter. Stir in flour, baking soda, and salt. Add in chocolate chips. Shape into small balls; place on ungreased baking sheet. Flatten with a glass dipped in sugar. Bake at 350° for 8 minutes or until brown. Makes 7 dozen.

Anita Allison
San Angelo

Molasses Cookies

¾ cup shortening
1 cup sugar
¼ cup molasses
1 egg
2 teaspoons baking soda
2 cups flour
½ teaspoon cloves
½ teaspoon ginger
1 teaspoon cinnamon
½ teaspoon salt

Melt shortening. Add sugar, molasses, and egg; beat well. Sift dry ingredients together and combine with sugar mixture. Then chill for at least 1 hour. Form into 1-inch balls and roll in granulated sugar. Place on greased pan and bake at 375° for 8 to 10 minutes.

Peri Fenton
Ozona

Oatmeal and Chocolate Chip Cookies

1 cup butter, oleo or vegetable shortening
1 cup sugar
1 cup brown sugar
1 egg
1 teaspoon vanilla
1½ cups flour
1 teasp⌇⌇⌇ baking soda
1 teaspoon salt
3 cups oatmeal
1 cup chocolate chips
chopped nuts (optional)

Cream butter and sugars; add egg and vanilla. Add flour, salt, and baking soda. Stir in oatmeal and chocolate chips. Add nuts if desired. Drop teaspoon size onto cookie sheets and bake at 350° for 8 to 10 minutes.

Elaine Wardlaw
Del Rio

Brown Sugar Cookies

1 box brown sugar
1 cup butter
2 beaten eggs
1 teaspoon cream of tartar
1 teaspoon baking soda
3¾ cups flour
1 cup (or more) coarsely chopped pecans

Beat brown sugar and butter; add beaten eggs. Sift flour, cream of tartar and baking soda and add to mixture, mix well. Add chopped pecans. On wax paper, shape cookie dough into 1 or 2 rolls; 2 to 2¼ inches in diameter. Put in refrigerator until hard or until you are ready to slice and cook. Slice rather thick for chewy - thinner for crisp. Bake at 425° for a few minutes until slightly brown on edges.

Winifred Rose (Mrs. Pat Rose, Jr.)
Del Rio

This cookie recipe has been in the Pat Rose family for many years. All ages - from children, parents, grandparents, great-grandparents and friends - all have enjoyed this cookie. We like them chewy.

I wish I had a quarter for every batch of these cookies I have made! The trick is to not get too much grease in them - that's what makes them flat. I also think that using half shortening and half butter really makes a difference. If you don't have the butter flavored, plain will work just as well. My friend, Carmen Symes, claims these cookies are better if you use milk chocolate chips. We even had a cookie cook-off one time. I think the judges were tied in their vote. Maybe they just wanted to keep on sampling! You decide.

Everyone's Favorite Chocolate Chip Cookies

½ **cup butter**
½ **cup butter flavored shortening**
¾ **cup sugar**
¾ **cup firmly packed brown sugar**
2 **eggs**
2 **teaspoons vanilla**
1 **teaspoon baking soda**
1 **teaspoon salt**
2½ **cups flour**
1 **12-ounce package semi-sweet chocolate chips**
1 **cup pecans (optional)**

Soften butter to room temperature, blend in shortening. Mix in sugar and brown sugar, stirring until creamy. Add in eggs and vanilla. Stir in baking soda, salt, and flour. Stir in chocolate chips and pecans. Drop by rounded teaspoon onto ungreased baking sheet. Bake at 375° for 8 to 10 minutes or until golden brown. Leave cookies on the sheets to finish cooking, then remove to wire racks or cup towel. Makes about 5 dozen cookies if you don't eat all the dough!

Anita Allison
San Angelo

266

World's Best Oatmeal Cookies

1 cup butter or margarine
1 cup white sugar
1 cup brown sugar
1 cup salad oil
1 cup rolled oats
1 cup crushed cornflakes
1 cup chopped pecans
3½ cups flour
1 teaspoon salt
1 teaspoon baking soda
1 teaspoon vanilla

Cream butter with sugars. Add oil, then oats, cornflakes, and pecans. Mix well. Add remaining ingredients. Roll into walnut-sized balls and flatten with fork dipped in water. Bake on ungreased cookie sheet at 350° for about 12 minutes. Let cool slightly before removing. Makes about 12 dozen.

Eva M. Rink
San Angelo

These were judged The World's Best Oatmeal Cookies by the World's Best Grandchildren.

Granny's Peanut Butter Cookies

1 cup shortening
2 teaspoons vanilla
1 cup sugar
1 cup firmly packed brown sugar
2 eggs
1 cup peanut butter
3 cups flour
2 teaspoons baking powder
1 teaspoon salt

Blend vanilla into shortening. Mix in sugar and brown sugar. Blend in eggs, then peanut butter. Stir in dry ingredients. Roll dough into small balls and place on an ungreased cookie sheet. Mark cookies in a criss-cross using the back of a fork. Bake at 350° for 8-10 minutes or until brown.

Pearl Lee Shurley
Submitted by Anita Allison

Iced Chocolate Cookies

½ cup butter
1 beaten egg
½ teaspoon baking soda
¼ teaspoon cream of tartar
1 teaspoon vanilla
1 cup brown sugar
½ cup milk
1½ cups flour
2 squares chocolate, melted
1 cup chopped nuts

Cream butter and sugar, add egg and milk in which baking soda has been dissolved. Sift cream of tartar with flour and add to mixture, along with melted chocolate, vanilla, and nuts. Drop by teaspoonfuls onto baking sheet. Bake at 325° for 15 minutes. Makes 4 dozen.

Wendy Barrows
San Angelo

Iced Chocolate Cookie Icing
1 egg white
2 tablespoons water
1 teaspoon vanilla
2 squares of chocolate (melted)
1 pound powdered sugar

Add powdered sugar to slightly beaten egg white, melted chocolate, water, and vanilla until right consistency to spread. If it gets too thick add a few drops of water.

Butter Crisps

1½ cups powdered sugar
1¼ cups butter
1 beaten egg
1 tablespoon vanilla
3 cups sifted flour
pecans

Cream together powdered sugar and butter, add egg, vanilla and flour. Drop by teaspoon on ungreased sheet. Place ½ pecan on top of each cookie. Bake at 375° for 8 to 10 minutes. Makes 5 or 6 dozen.

Virginia McFarlane
Submitted by Eva McFarlane Rink

Fruit Cake Cookies

2 pounds candied cherries, chopped in small pieces
1½ pounds candied pineapple, chopped in small pieces
1 box white raisins
1 cup 100% whiskey
1½ cups sugar
4 eggs
3 cups flour
6 cups chopped pecans
1 stick oleo
3 tablespoons milk
1 teaspoon cinnamon
1 teaspoon nutmeg
1 teaspoon mace
3 teaspoons baking soda
¼ teaspoon salt
1 teaspoon vanilla

Dredge fruit with part of flour. Mix butter and sugar, add 1 egg at a time and beat. Add whiskey and milk. Mix and sift rest of flour and dry ingredients. Add fruit and pecans. Drop by teaspoonful on greased cookie sheet. Cook at 275° for 15 minutes or until done.

May be baked in small Christmas cupcake liners.

Emma Phillips Adams
Ozona

Buy the thin skinned oranges; they are generally the juiciest.

Apricot Jumbles

2 tablespoons melted butter
1½ cups chopped dried apricots
2 eggs
1 cup sugar
1 teaspoon vanilla
1 cup chopped pecans
1 cup graham cracker crumbs
1 cup coconut

Melt butter and add apricots; stir over low heat for a few minutes to soften. Beat the eggs, add sugar and beat thoroughly. Add sugar mixture to apricots and cook over low heat for 15 minutes, stirring constantly. Add vanilla, pecans, graham cracker crumbs and coconut. Mix completely and spoon onto waxed paper. These keep well in a can.

Venetta Smith
Sonora

Mama's Tea Cakes

This cookie was usually topped with a pecan half or sprinkled with sugar.

2 eggs
1½ cups sugar
1 cup butter
¼ cup buttermilk
3½ cups sifted flour
1 teaspoon baking powder
1 teaspoon baking soda
¼ teaspoon salt
1½ teaspoons vanilla

Sift dry ingredients four times. Cream butter and sugar. Add eggs, beat. Add buttermilk, beat. Add sifted flour mixture and beat until well blended. Chill 1 hour. Drop or roll and cut out. Cook on greased cookie sheet. Bake at 375° for 10 to 12 minutes.

Jennie Spiller McKnight
by Kay Davis
Sterling City

Jammies

2 cups sifted flour
3 teaspoons baking powder
1 teaspoon salt
⅓ cup shortening
¾ cup milk
3 tablespoons soft butter
1½ cups leftover jam, jelly, or preserves

Sift flour, salt and baking powder together. Cut shortening into flour until mixture resembles coarse meal. Add milk slowly and blend. Turn dough onto floured surface and knead lightly. Roll ½ inch thick and spread with softened butter and jam mixture. Roll like a jelly roll, cut into slices, and place in greased muffin tins. Bake at 400° for 12 to 15 minutes. Makes 12 to 16.

You can use a combination of 2 or 3 jellies and if you are in a hurry, Bisquick may be substituted for the dough.

Pansy Espy (Mrs. J.P.)
Fort Davis

When my ancestors came to the Davis Mountains in 1884, they made wild cherry jelly and algerita jelly until they could plant their fruit orchards and have their own fruit. This recipe, given to me by Mrs. J.W. Merrill, is a wonderful way to use bits of jams and jellies that are left in the refrigerator.

Rene's Cereal Snacks

4 tablespoons margarine
5 cups miniature marshmallows
6½ cups Graham Chex and Crispy Mini Grahams
4 Hershey Bars

Melt butter and marshmallows on low heat stirring constantly. Mix in cereal. Pour ½ mixture in greased 9x9 inch pan. Place Hershey's on top and then pour remaining mixture on top. Mash down to melt chocolate. Cool and cut into squares.

Rene Stewart
Sterling City
Submitted by Anna Balch

Rene's greatest treasures were her friends. She recently remarked "What would life be without your friends?" If you were Rene's friend you knew you were loved.

Every year during the San Angelo Stock Show and Rodeo, the women who set up the exhibits in the Creative Arts Department bring lunch. The salads, desserts and vegetables are voted on. This year (1995) my dessert won! It was everyone's favorite!

Three Layer Cookie

First Layer
½ **cup butter or margarine**
1 **square unsweetened chocolate**
¼ **cup sugar**
1 **teaspoon vanilla**
1 **beaten egg**
2 **cups crushed graham crackers**
½ **cup chopped nuts**
1 **cup flaked coconut**

Melt butter and chocolate in pan over low heat. Add sugar and vanilla and blend. Add beaten egg and cook for about 5 minutes or until egg is cooked. Add graham crackers, nuts and coconut. Press (firm) into 9x9-inch pan and chill for 15 minutes.

Second Layer
½ **cup butter or margarine**
2 **tablespoons instant vanilla pudding mix**
3 **tablespoons milk**
2 **cups powdered sugar**

Cream butter until fluffy. Add instant pudding mix, milk and powdered sugar. Beat until smooth and spread over first layer. Chill for 15 minutes.

Third Layer
4 **squares semi-sweet chocolate**
1 **tablespoon butter**

Melt chocolate squares with butter over low heat. Spread over second layer. Chill until firm and cut into small squares. These may be frozen.

Jeri Duncan
San Angelo

Caramel Cookies

¼ **stick butter**
2 cups packed brown sugar
2 well beaten eggs
1⅓ cups flour
2 teaspoons vanilla
2 cups chopped pecans

Mix in order given, beating well after each egg is added. Pour into greased and floured pan. Bake 350° for 20 to 30 minutes. Cut while warm.

Sherry Wipff
San Angelo

Brownies

½ **cup butter or margarine**
1 cup sugar
2 eggs
1 teaspoon vanilla
1½ squares unsweetened chocolate
½ **teaspoon salt**
⅔ **cup pecans**
1 cup cake flour
¼ **teaspoon baking powder**

Melt chocolate in warm oven and cool. Cream butter and sugar, sift salt, flour and baking powder together. Add chocolate to sugar mixture. Add flour mixture and eggs. Beat well. Add vanilla and pecans. Bake at 325° for about 35 minutes.

I always double this recipe and cook in a 13x9x2 inch pan.

Jo Valliant
San Angelo

This recipe has been in our family and passed down about 30 years.

My grandmother used to say "There is a lot of thread between the sheep and the shirt."

273

These brownies are a shearing time tradition at the Allison Ranch. If I don't take them, I have to make them when I get there. Some fight for the corner pieces, while others will take them all!

The Best Brownies

1 cup butter
4 1-ounce squares unsweetened chocolate
4 eggs
2 cups sugar
1 cup flour
2 teaspoons baking powder
2 teaspoons vanilla
1 cup chopped pecans

Melt together butter and chocolate in saucepan on stove top or glass bowl in microwave. Remove from heat. Stir in sugar, flour, baking powder, vanilla, and nuts. Add eggs; beat thoroughly. Spread in greased 16 to 18 inch long baking pan.

Bake in 350° oven for 30 minutes or until done. Cool in pan and dust with confectioners sugar and cut in squares.

Lori Woehl
Midland

Orange Slice Bars

2 cups flour
2½ cups brown sugar
¼ teaspoon salt
4 well beaten eggs
1 pound sliced oranges
1 cup chopped pecans

Mix dry ingredients; add to eggs and then add orange slices and pecans. Spread in 9x13 inch pan. Bake at 350° for 40 minutes. Cut into bars and roll in powdered sugar.

This is very easy and very good.

LaVerne Reeh

Doss

Spice Bars

1 cup sugar
¾ cup oil
¼ cup honey
1 egg
¼ teaspoon salt
1 teaspoon baking soda
1 teaspoon vanilla
2 cups flour
1 cup chopped nuts
1 teaspoon cinnamon

Mix first 6 ingredients well, then add the ones remaining. Bake at 350° for 15 minutes. Spread on glaze while still warm. Cut into squares.

Bernice Cottle
Rocksprings

Lemon Bars

4 eggs
2 cups sugar
1 teaspoon vanilla
1 cup melted butter
2 teaspoons lemon extract
1½ cups flour
1 teaspoon baking powder
½ cup chopped pecans

Beat eggs, sugar, vanilla, melted butter, and extract together. Add sifted flour and baking powder. Mix well. Fold in pecans. Bake in a 13x9x2 inch greased pan at 350° for 25 minutes. Ice brownies when cool. Makes 2 dozen.

Ora Rhae Word Whittenburg
Ft. Stockton
Submitted by Ethel Miller
Ozona

Spice Bar Glaze
1 cup powdered sugar
1 teaspoon water
2 tablespoons mayonnaise
1 teaspoon vanilla

Combine all ingredients and spread on while still warm.

My grannie said, "All cowgirls should know that the way to a cowboy's heart, is through his stomach."

Lemon Bar Icing
1½ cups powdered sugar
1 tablespoon butter
1 tablespoon lemon juice
2½ tablespoons water

Combine the first three ingredients. Add enough water to make frosting easy to spread.

My mother says, "I make these so much because when you were first married, Donald walked in while they were baking and made such a fuss over how good they smelled; and besides, it's another 'quick and easy.' "

Praline Brownies

¼ **cup butter**
1 **cup brown sugar**
1 **egg**
1 **teaspoon vanilla**
1 **cup flour**
1 **teaspoon baking powder**
½ **teaspoon salt**
½-1 **cup nuts (pecans)**

Melt butter in saucepan. Stir brown sugar until dissolved. Cool slightly. Beat in egg and vanilla. Sift flour, baking powder, and salt. Stir flour into mixture. Add nuts. Bake at 350° for about 30 minutes. Cut into bars.

Molly Allison
San Angelo

Frank's Favorite Raspberry Bars

½ **cup butter, softened**
½ **cup margarine, softened**
1 **cup sugar**
2 **egg yolks**
2 **cups flour**
1 **cup chopped walnuts**
½ **cup raspberry preserves**

Cream butter, margarine and sugar until light and fluffy. Add egg yolks; blend well. Add flour, mix thoroughly, stir in walnuts. Spread ⅓ of batter into greased 9 inch pan. Drop preserves by spoonfuls over batter and spread almost to edges. Completely cover preserves with remaining batter. Bake at 325° until golden brown about 50 minutes. Cool and cut into bars. Yields: 2 dozen

Icy Rink Donnelly
San Antonio

Clay's Flan

1 cup sugar
4 eggs
3 cups milk
½ teaspoon vanilla
dash salt

Caramelize ½ cup sugar. Divide the caramelized sugar into 8 custard cups and set aside. Beat together the remaining ½ cup sugar, eggs, milk, vanilla and salt. Divide into the custard cups. Place the custard cups in a baking pan to which water has been added and bake at 350° for about 30 minutes or until tested done. To test for doneness insert silver knife and if it comes out clean the custard is done. To serve, invert the custard cup into a bowl, lift custard cup off allowing the caramel sauce to flow over custard. Can also be cooked in one large bowl in the same manner.

To caramelize sugar melt the ½ cup sugar in a small iron skillet. You must stir constantly as it will burn quickly.

Clay Allison
Sheffield

Clay and his grandmother, Mary Ellen McEntire, worked up this recipe one weekend at the U Ranch so he could cook it for 4-H. We ate a lot of Flan that weekend but he got the recipe down and did win a blue ribbon. Papa Mac (George McEntire) loved Flan and he was the perfect one to have around to eat all of Clay's practice batches.

This is lighter and more flavorful than usual. It came from "A Taste of the World" Cleveland Council on World Affairs in 1964.

Brown Betty Pudding

6 tart cooking apples, peeled, ⅛ inch slices
½ cup water
½ cup orange juice
¼ cup sugar
½ teaspoon nutmeg
16 graham crackers, rolled fine into crumbs
½ cup sugar
1 teaspoon grated orange peel
¼ chopped almonds
2 tablespoons butter

Place together in a saucepan, the sliced apples, water and orange juice and cook until slightly tender. Add sugar and nutmeg. Pour into a shallow baking dish. Mix cracker crumbs with sugar, orange peel and nuts. Sprinkle on top of apples and dot all over with butter. Bake at 375° for 20 to 30 minutes, until top is crusty. Serve warm with cream, a light wine sauce, or custard sauce.

It is much better if you use cinnamon and sugar graham crackers.

Mrs. Ford Boulware
San Angelo

Cottage Pudding

1 cup sugar
½ cup oleo
1 egg
1½ cups flour
2 teaspoons baking powder
¼ teaspoon salt
1 teaspoon vanilla

Cream sugar, oleo, and egg. Sift and add flour and baking powder. Add salt and vanilla. Pour in a long 9x13 inch pan and sprinkle sugar on top before baking. Serve cake cut in squares with sauce.

Peggie McMullan
Iraan

Sauce
1 cup sugar
3 tablespoons flour
⅛ teaspoon salt
2 cups cold water
1 teaspoon vanilla
2 tablespoons oleo

Sift together sugar, flour, and salt. Add to water. Boil until sauce thickens; add vanilla and oleo.

Texas Aggie Banana Pudding

2 cans evaporated milk
1 cup sugar
3 egg yolks
1 teaspoon vanilla
1-2 tablespoons cornstarch
1-3 tablespoons water
1 box vanilla wafers
4-5 ripe bananas
3 egg whites

In a large saucepan over medium-low heat combine evaporated milk, sugar, egg yolks (reserve whites for meringue) and vanilla. Stir constantly at slow rate with wire whisk. Do not allow mixture to become frothy, mix slow.) Stir until custard thickens - may use cornstarch mixed with water to help thicken. This will take about 20 minutes to thicken.

In a large deep dish casserole place 1 layer of vanilla wafers, then place a layer of cut bananas. Alternate with another layer of wafers, then bananas - until all gone. Pour custard over layers, letting it run throughout layers. Whip egg whites with hand mixer. Once peaks form add a little sugar. Cover the top of pudding with meringue and place in 350° oven for 10 minutes or until golden.

Vanessa Kickhoefer
Honolulu, Hawaii

This recipe for old fashioned pudding has been handed down through three generations. You will never go back to instant pudding again!
Vanessa is one of my dear friends from Texas A&M who now lives in Hawaii. She use to come over to our house and make this pudding for my brother, Clay, and me. I'm sure we didn't study much after eating the whole dish of this! - Anita

This recipe originally came to me from Bulah Baggett Pace, long deceased, but a wonderful friend from West Texas.

We have made this recipe for as long as I can remember. Since Clellia and my mother, Mary Ellen McEntire, have been friends since college days, they must have gotten it from the same place. My mother made it often, as I have for my kids growing up. It is always a treat for when they are sick or had a tooth pulled and need "soft foods." - Mimi

Individual Lemon Cups

¼ cup flour
1 cup sugar
2 tablespoons melted butter
⅛ teaspoon salt
5 tablespoons lemon juice
1 grated lemon rind
1½ cups milk
3 egg yolks
3 egg whites

Mix together flour, sugar, butter, and salt. Add lemon juice and grated rind. Slowly add scalded milk to egg yolks and pour into first mixture, mixing well. Beat egg whites until stiff and fold into mixture. Put in greased custard cups and set in a pan of hot water and bake at 325° for 45 minutes. Loosen around edge of custard cup and turn upside-down onto serving saucer. Spoon out all of custard.

Top with whipped cream and a maraschino cherry if desired. These dessert cups can be refrigerated while in the cups and prepared and served at a later time.

Clellia Harris
Austin

Bread Pudding

1 cup sugar
2 eggs
1 stick of butter
1 teaspoon nutmeg
1 teaspoon vanilla
¼ teaspoon salt
2 cups milk
4 slices cubed bread

Mix sugar, eggs, butter, nutmeg, vanilla and salt. Add milk to this. Pour over bread cubes. Press down any bread out of mixture. Bake at 400° until brown.

Kathleen Moore
Sonora

Old Fashioned Boiled Custard

6 cups milk
8 eggs
pinch of salt
nutmeg
sugar
vanilla
pieces of thick orange peel

Scald milk (do not boil.) Beat the eggs separately. The yellows should be thick and lemon colored, and the whites beaten stiff but not dry. Add the yellow eggs first then fold in the whites. Cook slowly, stirring constantly until the mixture coats the spoon. Remove from heat and add sugar, nutmeg, and vanilla to taste. Pour over orange peel. Serve hot or chilled. May top with whipped cream.

Be especially careful not to allow to boil, as it will form a scum if you do.

Margaret Galbreath
Sonora

Boiled Custard

2 quarts scalded milk
¾ cup sugar
¼ cup flour
3 beaten egg yolks
8 marshmallows
3 egg whites
1 teaspoon vanilla

Mix sugar, flour, and egg yolks. Pour in scalded milk. Cook until the mixture coats the spoon. Add the marshmallows. Stir until they melt. Fold in the egg whites and vanilla.

Lisa Herring
Sterling City

My grandmother, Fay Modina Foster Hildebrand was born in Sterling County in 1893. She was a small feisty woman who did not like to cook but she had some specialties. Boiled Custard was one of them. Grandmother made if for her grandchildren when they were sick. She served it in a large goblet. Often we would tell Grandmother we were sick so that she would make Boiled Custard.

My grandmother ran a boarding house in Blewett - Texas's largest asphalt mines - located about 18 miles west of Uvalde off highway 90. This was during the depression and Big Mama knew how to feed 10 to 15 men on very little. She was a marvelous cook and could fix leftovers so you couldn't recognize them the next day. The men use to laugh and say "If we don't eat it all today, boys, Myrtle will fool us tomorrow" and she would. I spent many happy days with her as she was alone and I was her only grandchild at that time. This recipe was hers.

To prevent milk from sticking to pan when scalding - heat the pan first.

Raisin Pudding

Part I
- **¾ cup white sugar**
- **1 cup flour**
- **2 teaspoons baking powder**
- **1 cup sweet milk**
- **1 cup raisins**
- **1 teaspoon vanilla**

Mix the above ingredients together and put in greased pan.

Part II
- **1 cup brown sugar**
- **3 teaspoons butter**
- **2½ cups boiling water**
- **pinch of salt**

Mix and pour onto Part I. Bake at 350° until crust is brown. May be baked in a 8x8 square pan or a 7x13 pan. The more shallow the pan the more crust there is.

Betty J. Harrell
Dryden

Peppermint Ice Cream

For a refreshing change, use Nancy's Homemade Vanilla Ice Cream recipe and make great peppermint or chocolate chip mint ice cream. Add one small package peppermints that has been crushed. The best way to do this is to put the peppermint in a plastic sack, cover it with several sheets of newspaper and hit it with a hammer. I have also put it under the wheel of a car and run over it. Anything to get it crushed!

Chocolate Chip Mint: Add 2 teaspoons peppermint extract and 1 small package chocolate chips that have been grated. I use the food processor for this job.

Mimi Allison

Fresh Coconut Ice Cream

1 quart plus 3 cups whole milk
1 quart heavy cream
12 egg yolks
2 cups honey
4 teaspoons vanilla
2 teaspoons coconut extract
1 cup shredded fresh coconut

Scald milk. In separate bowl, beat egg yolks until light. Fold in 3 cups hot milk stirring constantly. Add hot milk, add honey, cook at moderate heat until it starts thickening. Cool. Fold in cream, flavors, and coconut. Chill, then freeze.

Mrs. Sid Harkins
Sanderson

My friend, Charles Curry, gave me this recipe.

Mexican Ice Cream

¼ cup sugar
2 teaspoons cornstarch
2 eggs
2 cups milk
1 cup heavy cream
½ teaspoon vanilla
½ cup halved maraschino cherries
2 tablespoons maraschino syrup
½ cup caramelized sugar
⅔ cup chopped pecans

In heavy saucepan blend the sugar and cornstarch. Add the eggs and beat to blend well. Stir in the milk until smooth. Stir and cook over medium heat until thick and smooth. Remove from heat, cool a little, add the cream and vanilla and cool thoroughly. Freeze in an ice cream maker according to the manufacturer's directions. When partially frozen, fold in the cherries, syrup, caramelized sugar bits, and pecans; freeze.

Nancy Johnson
Sonora

To make caramelized sugar: in a heavy saucepan heat ½ cup sugar with 2 tablespoons water until the sugar melts and turns caramel in color. Pour at once onto a greased cookie sheet and let cool for 10 minutes. Pry off and break into small pieces. The caramelized sugar, pecans, and maraschino cherries make this a festive and fun ice cream.

My family loves this and they always want "Granny" to make it for their company and their parties.

Granny made this for our "You Might Be a Redneck If…" rodeo party this year - it was gone before anything else! Later that night, I discovered that her grandson, Greg, had hidden his own stash in the cabinet. Which turned out fine because we ate it during clean-up. - Anita

This is also a favorite - I have filled "hundreds" of tins with these and my toffee to have ready for whoever stops by to see me!

English Toffee

1 cup sugar
1 cup butter
3 tablespoons water
1 tablespoon white corn syrup
pecans
1 6-ounce package milk chocolate chips

Butter a 9x13-inch pan. Crush pecans to cover the bottom of pan. Pour chocolate chips over pecans. Bake at 250° just to soften the chips. Cook sugar, butter, corn syrup, and water in saucepan to "hard crack" on candy thermometer. Pour this mixture over warm chips. Cool in refrigerator. Crack into small pieces.

Don't substitute margarine for the butter! It has to be the REAL thing!

Cecile McDonald
Sterling City

Millionaires

1 1-pound package caramels
2-3 tablespoons milk
1 7-ounce Hershey bar
3-4 cups pecan halves
¼ pound block of paraffin

Melt the caramels with milk over low heat. Stir in pecans and drop by teaspoonfuls on waxed paper. Cool. Melt the Hershey bar and paraffin in double boiler. Dip candy in this mixture with a spoon. Return to waxed paper to firm. Makes about 3 dozen.

Cecile McDonald
Sterling City

Candy

Grandma's Candy

1 cup sugar
⅔ cup sweet milk
½ cup molasses
2 heaping tablespoons butter
pinch of baking soda
2 cups pecans

A heavy cast iron skillet is best to cook candy. Combine sugar, milk, molasses, and butter. Cook, stirring constantly, until candy is brittle when dropped in cold water. Remove from heat, add baking soda and stir. Add pecans. Pour onto greased pan and allow to cool. To serve: warm the bottom of the greased pan to loosen candy. Break into small pieces.

Frances (Frannie) Kellis Davis
Submitted by Margarie Davis
Sterling City

Chewey Pralines

2 cups sugar
2 cups white corn syrup
1 pound butter (not oleo)
2 cups whipping cream (not whipped)
2 teaspoons vanilla
7 cups chopped pecans

Over medium-low heat, cook together sugar and corn syrup until thermometer reaches 250°. Remove from heat and add the butter. It will melt fast. Then add the whip cream slowly. Return to heat and cook to 242° stirring constantly. Remove from heat and add vanilla and pecans. By the time you mix the pecans in, it will be ready to spoon out on foil. Not, repeat, not, wax paper.

Savannah Mayfield
San Angelo

Lower oven temperature 25° for Pyrex dishes.

This recipe is fool proof! The Mexican Vanilla and the salted wax paper make these pralines taste a little different.

Pralines

1 stick margarine
1 box brown sugar
1 cup milk
3-4 cups pecans
2 teaspoons Mexican Vanilla
1 cup powdered sugar

Combine first four ingredients and cook over medium heat to the soft ball stage. Stir occasionally. Remove from heat; add vanilla and sugar. Mix by hand. Spray nonstick spray on wax paper, lightly salt the paper, and spoon mixture on paper.

Tulisha Wardlaw
Brackettville

Pecan Pralines

2 cups white sugar
¼ cup brown sugar
¼ teaspoon baking soda
1 tablespoon white corn syrup
1 cup canned milk
¼ teaspoon salt
⅓ stick butter or margarine
1 teaspoon vanilla
2 cups pecan halves

Combine sugars, baking soda, corn syrup, milk and salt. Cook to soft ball stage stirring constantly. Remove from heat and add butter and vanilla; beat until it begins to thicken. Add pecans and drop by teaspoonfuls onto waxed paper.

Mattie D. Word Gallenkamp
Longview
Submitted by Ethel Miller

Candy

Date Loaf

2½ cups sugar
1 cup milk
1 8-ounce package pitted dates, cut
1 cup finely chopped pecans

Boil sugar with milk. When cooked well enough to form soft ball in water, pour dates into it. Boil, stirring constantly until dates are dissolved. Remove from heat, add pecans and beat until cool. Rinse a dish towel (not terry cloth) in a bowl of cold water and wring out well. Pour candy onto cloth in a long row. When it starts to thicken; wrap. When cold, cut in slices.

Mrs. George Joseph
Sonora

It is easy to cut up the dates with kitchen shears. You can chop the pecans in a zip-lock bag with a knife handle.

Peanut Brittle

1 cup sugar
1 cup light corn syrup
2 cups salted Spanish peanuts
1 teaspoon baking soda
pinch of salt
1 teaspoon vanilla
2-3 tablespoons butter

Bring sugar and corn syrup to a boil and add the peanuts. Stir constantly and cook until mixture turns light brown in color (very important). Remove mixture from heat and add the baking soda, vanilla and salt. Pour mixture thinly onto foil and let cool. Break up into bite sized pieces.

Preccia Miller
Dallas

Cinnamon Hard Candy

3¾ cups sugar
1½ cups light corn syrup
1 cup water
¼-1 teaspoon flavoring (cinnamon oil)

Mix first three ingredients in a large saucepan. Stir over medium heat until sugar dissolves. Boil, without stirring, until temperature reaches 310°F or until drops of syrup from hard brittle threads in cold water. Remove from heat. After boiling has ceased, stir in flavoring and coloring (red). Pour onto lightly greased cookie sheet. Cool; break into pieces.

Preccia Miller
Dallas

Brown Sugar Candy

2 cups sugar
1 cup brown sugar
½ cup white syrup
1 cup cream
1½ cups pecans
1 teaspoon vanilla
1 teaspoon butter

Boil cream, sugar and syrup to soft ball stage. Beat until creamy, add nuts, vanilla and 1 teaspoon butter. Pour into pan and let cool, cut into squares.

Virginia McFarlane
Submitted by Eva McFarlane Rink
San Angelo

Candy

Goop

Use dried fruit.
- **8 ounces peaches**
- **12 ounces raisins**
- **24 ounces prunes, pitted**
- **8 ounces apples**
- **6 ounces apricots**
- **7 ounces coconut**
- **16 ounces dates**
- **12 ounces mixed nuts**
- **12 ounces peanut butter**
- **12 ounces honey**
- **12 ounces wheat germ**
- **powdered milk (up to a cup or to taste)**
- **Vitamin C powder (optional)**
- **2 cups corn oil**

Grind the ingredients in the food processor, a little at a time. Then mix it in a large mixing bowl, use only enough to mold mixture keep its shape - it's easy to get too much oil. Line a jelly roll pan with wax paper and mold the mixture into the pan. Let it dry. Cut into squares and package in plastic bags.

Donald Allison
San Angelo

Donald obtained this recipe from Phillip Robbins, a Ft. Stockton rancher. This is good to take on long rides, camping trips, etc. While Donald was making this "health food", I think he gained 20 pounds. He assures me that he could survive a long time with this packed in his survival pack.

Quick Cookies

- **1 package cinnamon graham crackers**
- **1 cup butter**
- **1 cup brown sugar**
- **1½ cups chopped pecans**

Arrange a single layer of graham crackers to cover the bottom of jelly roll pan. Bring the butter, brown sugar, and pecans to a boil. Cook and stir until butter and brown sugar come together. Spread mixture over graham crackers and bake at 350° for 10 minutes. After cooling cut into squares.

Mimi Allison
San Angelo

Mama D makes these with chocolate chips. Of course, Anita says they are better that way. Mama D was Anita's Tri-Delta house mom at Texas A&M.

These are so good and so quick. It is so easy to always have the ingredients on hand for when you need something in a hurry.

The Best Apple Pie

1 quart fresh Jonathan apples
juice of 1 orange (about 3 tablespoons)
1 teaspoon lemon rind
2 tablespoons flour
1 cup sugar
1 teaspoon nutmeg
1 teaspoon cinnamon
2 tablespoons butter
¼ cup condensed milk
2 tablespoons butter

Combine apples, orange juice and lemon rind and place in unbaked pie crust. Combine flour, sugar, nutmeg, and cinnamon and sprinkle over apple mixture. Dab 2 tablespoons butter evenly over apple and spice mixture. Cover with top crust. Melt 2 tablespoons butter and allow to cool. Combine with condensed milk and brush over top crust. Sprinkle lightly with sugar and cinnamon if desired. Bake at 350° for 35 to 45 minutes or until golden brown. Let sit for 30 minutes.

Stephanie Elliot
San Angelo

Our Favorite Recipe

This is named for our wonderful cat, Liberty, because she has watched us type and/or edit almost every recipe that has gone into this cookbook. I am sure we could not have gotten it all done without her being right there. Anita has had to take many breaks just to make over the cat! Enjoy your Liberty Pie!

Liberty Pie

1 9- to 10-inch pie crust
sliced cooked turkey
½-1 cup each broccoli,
cauliflower, celery,
carrots, onion, and/or
mushrooms
1 cup shredded mozzarella
cheese

2 medium tomatoes
1 sliced green bell pepper
seasoned salt
chopped fresh or dry basil
leaves

Bake the pie crust until crispy but not yet brown. Slice or chop whatever vegetables you choose to have in your pie and gently steam them. Place turkey slices in bottom of crust. Next add whatever mix of vegetables you like. Sprinkle seasoned salt over all. Sprinkle on shredded mozzarella; place thin pepper and tomato slices over cheese and add fresh chopped basil over the top. If you wish you can add 4 American cheese slices to top. Bake at 325° until cheese is melted.

Be careful and don't get the dish overly full.

Cactus jelly has always been a favorite with my family. The flavor is delicate and delicious. It is a beautiful red jelly and, along with the green mint jelly, makes wonderful Christmas gifts. When you go out to gather your ripe red tunas, be sure to wear heavy leather boots (you have to watch out for rattlers), leather gloves and use long kitchen tongs to pluck the tunas off the prickly pear. You will want to gather several buckets and cook down all the juice at one time. I have done this and frozen the juice to make my jelly later. Although I am more likely to get it done if I do it all at once.

Jalea de Nopal (Cactus Jelly)

50 tunas (cactus fruit)
2 quarts juice
½ cup lemon juice
3 boxes Sure-Jell
5 pounds sugar

Scrub or burn thorns off tunas. Slice, skin and all, into a large pot and cover with water. Simmer until tender (about 30 minutes). Strain juice through cloth which has been placed in a colander. Bring juice and Sure-Jell to a good boil. Add sugar and lemon juice and continue to boil for 5 minutes stirring constantly. Skim off foam. Pour jelly into hot sterilized jam jars and seal with lids.

Mimi Allison

Mint Jelly

3 cups fresh firmly packed mint
6½ cups water
2 boxes powdered pectin
8 cups sugar
green food coloring

Pick and wash fresh mint. Heat to a boil with water; remove from heat, cover and allow to steep for about 10 minutes. Strain; measure 6 cups mint infusion. Add a few drops (20-25) green food coloring. Add pectin; bring to a boil. Add sugar and bring to a hard rolling boil. Boil for 1 minute, stirring constantly. Remove from heat and skim off foam with metal spoon. Pour at once into hot sterilized jars and seal with jar lids. Yield: 12 to 13 half pint jars.

Mimi Allison

Cranberry Jelly

4 12-ounce package of berries
½ cup water
4½ cups sugar
1 packet Certo

Place berries in water, cook until berries split open. Put through sieve to remove skins and seeds. Add sugar and cook 3 minutes. Add Certo, then pour into clear glasses and seal. Yield: 5 pints.

Jack Shurley
San Angelo

Strawberry Preserves

1 cup strawberries (don't heap)
1 cup sugar

Wash strawberries then pick them. Put sugar and berries in pan and let set until melted some. Cook as low as possible until sugar is melted. Then cook on high 8 to 10 minutes. Stir some to keep them from sticking. Pour in dish, cover and let set over night. Put in jars next morning.

Never cook more that 2 or 3 crops at one time.

Kay Wall Bates
San Angelo

This recipe is from my mother, Catherine Funk Wall, which was from her mother, Ella Sterrett Funk, early settler with her husband, Joe Funk. This is copied the way I found it written in Mother's hand writing, i.e. "set" rather than "sit".

This was my Aunt's recipe and has been proven to never turn to sugar. The best!

Fig Preserves

1 quart figs
1 quart sugar
1 lemon
1 cup water

Pick figs before fully ripe, peel and measure. Pour sugar into large saucepan, add water, bring to a good boil, then drop in figs and thinly sliced lemon. Cook until clear. Set off fire; cover and let set until the next day. Place on fire, cook about 10 to 15 minutes, remove from fire, cover and let set until third morning. Place on fire and bring to a good boil, pour into hot sterilized jars and seal.

Lou Deaton
Ozona

My Aunt in Palestine gave me this recipe, she had a good friend who made it for years to sell - for that reason would not share the recipe. It is very good and also pretty.

Peach Marmalade

18 peaches
5 medium oranges
sugar

Grind up oranges and peelings together, using coarse blade of chopper. If you have no chopper, slice oranges and peelings with very sharp knife. Measure above fruits after it has been mixed and add: 1½ times as much sugar as fruit. Cook until it cuts from spoon like jelly. Just before done add: 1 cup chopped red cherries. Pour up into glasses and seal with paraffin.

Frances Armstrong
Abilene

Spiced Watermelon Pickles

5 cups sugar
2 cups vinegar
1 tablespoon allspice
2 cups water
1 tablespoon whole cloves
4 sticks cinnamon
1 tablespoon lime to each quart
watermelon rind

Soak rind overnight in water and lime. Rinse next morning and boil in clear water until tender. Weigh 2 pounds of rind. Make syrup of sugar, vinegar, and water; boil for 5 minutes. Add rind and bring to boiling point. (Add green or red food coloring now, if desired.) Remove from stove and let stand overnight. Tie spices in a cloth bag and add the next morning; boil until rind is transparent and syrup is clear and thick. Cook and pack in sterilized jars. When packed add 2 whole cloves and 2 sticks cinnamon in jars to make them look pretty.

Virginia McFarlane
submitted by: Eva M. Rink

This recipe is really a very good one that my mother would make during the summer and would save them for Thanksgiving and Christmas. They really dress up a special dinner. She would divide the rinds up and have, half green and half red. Very pretty!

Yellow Squash Pickles

8 cups yellow squash
2 medium onions
1 cup cider vinegar
1¾ cups sugar
2 cups diced bell pepper
½ teaspoon mustard seed
½ teaspoon celery seed

Slice squash and onions; sprinkle 1 tablespoon salt on slices, set for one hour, don't wash. Combine vinegar, sugar, bell pepper, mustard seed, and celery seed; bring to boil. Add squash and onions, boil again 3 minutes. Spoon into pint or quart jars. Seal.

Carolyn S. Wilson
Ozona

This recipe came from Patsy Bulverde to Shirley Mitchell and then to Mary F. Harkins. These pickles are the best I've ever tasted.

Crispy Sweet Pickles

1 gallon jar whole sour pickles
5 pounds sugar (use whole sack)
1 teaspoon alum
1 small bottle Tabasco sauce
8-10 cloves of garlic, sliced thin

Mix alum and sugar together, drain pickles in colander. Slice and drain again. In gallon jar layer sugar, ½ to full bottle of Tabasco sauce, garlic, and pickles. Repeat each layer: sugar, Tabasco sauce, garlic, and pickles, until all ingredients are used. Tighten lid and turn jar over each morning and night for 5 days.

I keep my jar in refrigerator. You can put finished pickles in jars to give someone.

Mrs. Sid Harkins
Sanderson

Bread and Butter Pickles

4-5 quarts sliced cucumbers
6 medium onions
garlic salt
⅓ cup table salt
crushed ice

Slice cucumbers and onions. Sprinkle with garlic salt and table salt. Cover with crushed ice and let stand for 3 hours.

Mix together:
   3 cups cider vinegar
   5 cups sugar
   1½ teaspoons celery seed
   2 tablespoons mustard seed

Bring all this to a boil. Add cucumber and onion mixture—DO NOT LET PICKLES AND ONIONS BOIL; just get good and hot. Put in sterilized jars and seal.

Jean Owens
Iraan

This pickle recipe came from my mother-in-law, Laura Owens. The whole family loves them and she would usually give us 2 or 3 jars at Christmas time.

Sweet -n- Hot Sauce

3 quarts diced fresh tomatoes, skinned, or 12 ounces canned tomatoes
3 large bell peppers, chopped
3 large onions, chopped
7-8 jalapeños, fresh
2 quarts sugar

Mix the above ingredients together, cook on medium heat until thick, stirring occasionally. Pour into sterilized jars and seal.

This makes a great gift. Serve over cream cheese.

Nancy Johnson
Sonora

Pickled Jalapeño Peppers

2 bay leaves
2 cloves garlic
1 bunch jalapeño peppers
1 quart white vinegar
¼ cup salt
2 tablespoons sugar
1½ cups water
1 tablespoon celery seed
1 tablespoon mustard seed

Put bay leaves and garlic into a sterilized quart jar. Cut fresh peppers in halves; clean out all seeds. Wash the peppers well and pack tightly in jar. Boil the vinegar, salt, sugar, water, and seeds together until salt dissolves. Pour over peppers in jar and seal.

Use rubber gloves to handle hot peppers! They can really burn the skin.

Joy Carruthers
Sanderson

This recipe was handed from friend to friend, so I don't know its true origin. These are usually not too hot for anyone, since the seeds and white membrane are cut from peppers. You'll be sharing the recipe with others!

R.C.'s Jalapeño Pickles

1-2 pounds jalapeños
½ tap water per jar
½ vinegar per jar
1 teaspoon salt per jar

Use rubber gloves. Cut jalapeños in half and then lengthwise, clean out seed, wash well. Put into pint jars with salt, tap water, and vinegar. Soak seals to jars in hot water. Seal jars tightly and date 21 days ahead. DO NOT OPEN UNTIL THAT DATE. They will be mild and crisp and anyone can eat them.

Ronald Pennington
Farmington, New Mexico

Mother's Chow-Chow

1 head cabbage
1 gallon pears (or green tomatoes)
½ cup salt
5 sweet peppers
2 or more hot peppers
12 medium onions
1 stalk celery - optional
1 bunch carrots
3 pints vinegar
4 cups sugar
2 teaspoons turmeric
2 teaspoons allspice
1-2 teaspoons cinnamon
2 teaspoons dry mustard

Chop cabbage and pears. Add salt and let stand for 20 minutes; then drain. Grind sweet and hot peppers. Mix all ingredients together and let stand about 1 hour. Cook about 15 minutes and put into sterilized jars and seal.

Alta M. Dutton
Rocksprings

Old Fashion Chow-Chow

1 gallon green tomatoes
1 gallon cabbage
1 quart onions
2-3 pods of green hot peppers
4 tablespoons dry mustard
2 tablespoons ginger
1 tablespoon cloves
1 tablespoon mace
1 tablespoon cinnamon
1 ounce celery seed
6 cups sugar
1 quart vinegar or enough to cover mixture

Chop the tomatoes, cabbage, onions, and peppers. Combine with remaining ingredients. Boil 30 minutes. Put in jars and seal.

Mrs. Otis (Ora) Deal
Eldorado

Very good with red beans. This recipe was given to me by my mother, the late Mrs. R.W. Grimsley of Abilene, Texas, more than 60 years ago.

Green Tomato Relish

1 gallon chunked green tomatoes
4 cups chunked onions
1 cup chopped jalapeños
4 cups vinegar
2 cups sugar
¼ cup salt

Add salt to chunked tomatoes and let stand while preparing the other ingredients. Drain off all salty water. Add the rest of the ingredients to the green tomatoes. Place in a large pot and slowly bring to a boil. Shut off heat and put into hot pint jars quickly and seal. This can be processed in boiling water canner for 10 minutes. Yields: 7-8 pints.

Mary Jane Esser Morrison
Esser Ranch at Kendalia
"A Century Ranch"

Mrs. Arthur (Mary) Esser of Esser Ranch that has been operated by the family for over 100 years and was inducted into the Texas Department of Agriculture's Family Land Heritage Program in Austin, Texas, January 1994.

This recipe was one I created when pears were so plentiful and I wanted something different that our family and friends would enjoy. So over the years I have given this to many friends!

Mary Jane's Pear Relish

8-9 cups hard pears, chopped
4 cups onions, chopped
2½ cups red and green peppers, chopped
4 cups sugar
1 tablespoon dry mustard
1 tablespoon turmeric
4½ tablespoons salt
1 tablespoon celery salt
1 teaspoon ginger
1 teaspoon garlic salt
4 cups vinegar

Chop pears, onions, and green peppers in a food processor or coarsely grind. If red peppers aren't available use a jar of pimentos to get the red color in the relish. Add the remaining ingredients. Cook about 35 minutes and seal hot.

Chopped hot peppers can be used according to taste. This can also be processed in hot water canner for 10 minutes for pints.

Mary Jane Esser Morrison
Esser Ranch at Kendalia
"A Century Ranch"

Index

GAME

M

Index

312

R

Index

Bluebonnet Trail Cookbook
PO Box 62532
San Angelo, Texas 76906

Please send _____ copies   @ $ 17.95 each _____

Postage and handling   @ $3.00 each _____

Texas residents add sale tax   @ $1.39 each _____

                                       Total _____

Name _____

Address _____

City _____ State _____ Zip_____

Make checks payable to *Bluebonnet Trail Cookbook*

- -

Bluebonnet Trail Cookbook
PO Box 62532
San Angelo, Texas 76906

Please send _____ copies   @ $ 17.95 each _____

Postage and handling   @ $3.00 each _____

Texas residents add sale tax   @ $1.39 each _____

                                       Total _____

Name _____

Address _____

City _____ State _____ Zip_____

Make checks payable to *Bluebonnet Trail Cookbook*

- -

Bluebonnet Trail Cookbook
PO Box 62532
San Angelo, Texas 76906

Please send _____ copies   @ $ 17.95 each _____

Postage and handling   @ $3.00 each _____

Texas residents add sale tax   @ $1.39 each _____

                                       Total _____

Name _____

Address _____

City _____ State _____ Zip_____

Make checks payable to *Bluebonnet Trail Cookbook*